Global
Sourcing
Strategy

GLOBAL SOURCING STRATEGY

R&D, Manufacturing, and Marketing Interfaces

MASAAKI KOTABE

QUORUM BOOKS

New York • Westport, Connecticut • London

Library of Congress Cataloging-in-Publication Data

Kotabe, Masaaki.
    Global sourcing strategy : R&D, manufacturing, and marketing
interfaces / Masaaki Kotabe.
        p.   cm.
    Includes bibliographical references and index.
    ISBN 0–89930–667–5 (alk. paper)
    1. International business enterprises—Management.   2. Export
processing zones.   3. Offshore assembly industry.   I. Title.
HD62.4.K68   1992
658'.049—dc20   91–47074

British Library Cataloguing in Publication Data is available.

Library of Congress Catalog Card Number: 91–47074
ISBN: 0–89930–667–5

First published in 1992

Quorum Books, One Madison Avenue, New York, NY 10010
An imprint of Greenwood Publishing Group, Inc.

Printed in the United States of America

∞™

The paper used in this book complies with the
Permanent Paper Standard issued by the National
Information Standards Organization (Z39.48–1984).

10 9 8 7 6 5 4 3 2 1

Contents

Tables and Figures   vii

Preface   xi

Acknowledgments and Credits   xv

Chapter 1.   Global Sourcing Strategy: An Overview   1

PART I: The Case of European and Japanese Multinational Firms   23

Chapter 2.   Sourcing Strategies and Market Performance   25

Chapter 3.   Product and Process Innovations   63

Chapter 4.   Corporate Product Policy   91

Chapter 5.   Marketing Strategy   117

Chapter 6.   New Product Development: The Japanese Model   135

PART II: The Case of U.S. Multinational Firms   151

Chapter 7.   Hollowing-Out   153

Chapter 8.   Offshore Sourcing and Innovativeness   183

Chapter 9.   New Trends   203

Bibliography   215

Index   231

Tables and Figures

TABLES

2–1 Taxonomy of Global Sourcing Strategies   34

2–2 Nationality of the Parent Headquarters of Participating Firms   37

2–3 Industry Classification of Participating Firms   38

2–4 Analysis-of-Covariance Results for the Product's Market
     Performance   45

2–5 Takeshita Kogyo's Business Transactions in 1986 Inside and
     Outside the Maekawa Keiretsu   54

3–1 A Framework for the Development of a Taxonomy of
     Innovation-Sourcing Linkages   74

3–2 Measurement   76

3–3 Correlation Matrix of Variables   79

3–4 Regression Analysis for Market Performance, without an
     Interaction Term   80

3–5 Regression Analysis for Market Performance, with an
     Interaction Term   82

4–1 Measurement   102

4–2 Multiple Regression Analysis for Product and Process
     Innovations   106

5–1 Comparison of the Means   125

5–2 Customer Satisfaction, Market Selection, and Nationality of
     the Firm   126

5–3 Analysis-of-Covariance Results for Market Performance   128

6–1 Incrementalist versus Giant Leap View of New Product
     Development   140

7–1 Concordance between United States Enterprise Standard
     Industrial Classification (ESIC) and United Nations
     International Standard Industrial Classification (ISIC)   162

7–2 Correlation Coefficients between Hollowness of U.S. Firms
     and Their Domestic Employment Relative to Global
     Employment, 1977 and 1982   168

7–3 Correlation Coefficients for the Changes from 1977 to 1982 in
     Hollowness of U.S. Firms and in Their Domestic
     Employment Relative to Global Employment   169

7–4 Absolute Domestic Employment by U.S. Parent Firms   169

7–5 Change in the Effect of Three Strategic Thrusts on the U.S.
     Multinationals' Global Market Share Relative to World
     Production, 1977–85   174

7–6 The Relationship among Changes in Export Orientation,
     Home Market Orientation, Multinationality, and Global
     Market Share, 1977–85   177

8–1 Concordance between Tariff Schedules of the United States
     Classification (TSUS) and Standard Industrial Classification
     (SIC)   189

8–2 The Variables   190

8–3 Data Sources of Items Used for Development of the Variables   191

8–4 Correlation Matrix of the Variables   193

8–5 Multiple Regression Analysis for Innovation Propensity   194

FIGURES

1–1 Interfaces among R&D, Manufacturing, and Marketing   5

1–2 International Trade Flows   8

2–1 Conceptual Model of Global Sourcing Strategy   26

2–2 Multiple Sourcing of Products by European Firms   40

2–3 Multiple Sourcing of Products by Japanese Firms   41

2–4 Frequency of Major Sourcing Strategies for European Firms   42

2–5 Frequency of Major Sourcing Strategies for Japanese Firms   43

3–1 NEC Strategic Horizon   72

3–2 Interactive Nature of Product and Process Innovations for
     Market Performance   83

4–1 Determinants of Innovative Behavior and Market
     Performance in Global Competition   92

5–1 Cumulative Foreign Direct Investment Positions in the United
     States   118

6–1 Sources of the Competitive Strengths of Japanese Firms   136
6–2 Sequence of Industrial Development   139
7–1 Expected Relationships among the Variables Linking
     Hollowness of U.S. Firms and Their Global Competitiveness   160
7–2 Observed Relationships among the Variables Linking
     Hollowness of U.S. Firms and Their Global Competitiveness
     for 1977 and 1982   165
8–1 Trends of Total U.S. Imports and Imports under 9802.00.60
     and 9802.00.80, 1970–88   185

Preface

This book addresses what I call a "boundary issue" of multinational business management. When I studied international economics as an undergraduate some 20 years ago, I was fascinated by the flow of a wide variety of products, components, and raw materials around the world. International trade economists are interested in finding what factors determine such trade flows. Wrongly or correctly, balance of trade is often considered to represent the economic strengths of a trading nation. However, nations do not engage in trade; individual firms do. In other words, real players of trade are not in the equation of international trade economists. Ever since my enlightenment with this reality, I have wanted to study the flow of products and components *as managed by multinational firms* around the world.

Multinational firms' management of the flow of products and components transcends the bilateral concept of trade statistics. Let us take a look at a hypothetical German firm exporting finished products to the United States. To the executives of this firm, this export transaction may be nothing more than a last phase of the firm's value-adding activities they have managed. Indeed, this German company procures certain components from Britain and Japan, other components from the United States, and also from itself in Germany, and assembles a finished product in its Dusseldorf plant for export to the United States. A British supplier of critical components is a joint venture majority-owned by the German company, while a Japanese supplier has a licensing agreement with this German company that provides most of technical know-how. A U.S. supplier is in fact a subsidiary of the German company. In other words, this particular export transaction by a German firm for the U.S. market involves a joint venture, a licensing agreement, subsidiary operation, local assembly, and R&D—*all managed* directly or indirectly by the German company.

Unfortunately, much of academic research has focused on each of these value-adding activities *as if* they could be investigated independently. Obviously, they are not independent of each other, and cannot be. These value-adding activities should be examined as holistically as possible, by linking the boundaries of various functional areas. For lack of a better descriptive term, I call this boundary issue "global sourcing."

Multinational firms have been pursuing integrated sourcing to a greater extent than ever before because such an operation permits them to exploit not only their competitive advantages but also the comparative advantages of various countries in which they operate more efficiently than would otherwise be possible. The configuration and coordination necessary for a successful sourcing strategy have of late received an increasing amount of research attention. However, there has been little empirical research investigating sourcing coordination issues centering on management of innovative activities in product and manufacturing process development on a global basis.

Throughout this book, sourcing strategy is defined to indicate a strategic arrangement in which to coordinate innovative activities and sourcing of components supplied for production and marketing. Furthermore, the book attempts to show that successful management of these value-adding activities will jointly determine corporate performance.

My research has focused on the *performance implications* of multinational firms' management of sourcing strategies and innovative activities on a global basis. In this book, I emphasize global sourcing strategies of European and Japanese multinational firms for two major reasons. First, now that European and Japanese multinational firms are advancing more methodically than, and increasingly at the expense of, U.S. multinational firms around the world, it is worthy of learning more about these foreign multinational firms' corporate strategies. Second, there exist many aggregate studies of U.S. multinational firms' sourcing strategies (except for performance implications). It is expected that much can be learned about U.S. multinational firms' performance from the European and Japanese experiences. In order to complement the findings from European and Japanese firms, similar performance implications will also be demonstrated with available data on U.S. multinational firms.

Based on these research findings, I will also offer my own conjectures on likely future developments for global sourcing strategy and their ramifications for product design, new product development, manufacturing, and marketing on a global basis. As such, the book will offer normative suggestions (with implications on what *should* be done) to the executives of multinational firms, irrespective of nationality. At the same time, efficient management of global operations has become an increasingly important research issue among academics.

Given the somewhat macroscopic nature of my research in this area, this book is written for corporate strategic planners and academics who wish to see "big pictures" of global sourcing management. Purchasing and sourcing managers who are making day-to-day decisions on the front line will also find this book thoughtful as it permits them to see the forest instead of trees of global sourcing.

Acknowledgments and Credits

This book would not have ever materialized without guidance, assistance, and encouragement of many of my mentors, research associates, and students. My first thanks go to John Fayerweather, professor emeritus at New York University, whose book had implanted in me a small seed of interest in global sourcing almost 20 years ago and who has given me a strong encouragement for this project. Robert T. Green of the University of Texas at Austin has provided useful comments, institutional support, and encouragement throughout the project. David A. Ricks, immediate past editor of the *Journal of International Business Studies* and vice-president at Thunderbird, has strongly supported the importance of "boundary" issues that I have been working on. Paul M. Swamidass of the University of Missouri-Columbia has given me a structured picture of what are essentially messy realities of global sourcing. John A. Bermingham, executive vice-president of Sony Corporation of America, has provided invaluable insight into the "workings" of global sourcing and innovative activities for which Sony is well known.

I would like to give my special thanks to Glenn S. Omura of Michigan State University, Michael R. Czinkota of Georgetown University, and Sam C. Okoroafo of the University of Toledo, all of whom have worked with me and given me a refreshing perspective on product development and marketing strategy reflected in this book. My students—Preet S. Aulakh, Aldor R. Lanctot, Prakash Mohan, Scott Swan (all at the University of Texas at Austin), Thomas R. Turcan (London Business School), and Janet Y. Murray (University of Missouri-Columbia)—have challenged my thinking and critically reviewed various parts of my manuscript. Their comments and enthusiasm were truly valuable.

I also owe a great debt to my acquisitions editor, Thomas Gannon of Quorum Books. Tom showed great interest in some of my earlier work and called on me several times to persuade me to write this book. Without his insistence and encouragement, I would not have engaged in this project. Katie Chase, my project editor, superbly handled the copyediting and production details. It is truly a pleasure to work with them.

Finally, I would like to thank my wife, Kay, and our children, Akie, Euka, and Hiro, for their cheerful encouragement and many warm smiles, which kept me energized throughout the project.

This book amalgamates my own thought and various findings reported in my earlier work. For each chapter, significant changes were made from the original articles. I acknowledge permission from the publishers to use in this book various parts of my articles published earlier. The chapters are based, and expanded, on my earlier work, as follows:

Chapter 2: Masaaki Kotabe and Glenn S. Omura, "Sourcing Strategies of European and Japanese Multinationals: A Comparison," *Journal of International Business Studies,* 20 (Spring 1989), 113–130, with permission from the Academy of International Business.

Chapter 3: Masaaki Kotabe and Janet Y. Murray, "Linking Product and Process Innovations and Modes of International Sourcing in Global Competition: A Case of Foreign Multinational Firms," *Journal of International Business Studies,* 21 (Third Quarter 1990), 383–408, with permission from the Academy of International Business.

Chapter 4: Masaaki Kotabe, "Corporate Product Policy and Innovative Behavior of European and Japanese Multinational Firms: An Empirical Investigation," with permission from the *Journal of Marketing,* 54 (April 1990), 19–33, published by the American Marketing Association, Chicago, IL 60606.

Chapter 5: Masaaki Kotabe and Sam C. Okoroafo, "A Comparative Study of European and Japanese Multinational Firms' Marketing Strategies and Performance in the United States," *Management International Review,* no. 4 (1990), 353–370, with permission from Gabler Publishers, Wiesbaden, Germany.

Chapter 6: Michael R. Czinkota and Masaaki Kotabe, "Product Development the Japanese Way," reprinted from the November/December 1990 *Journal of Business Strategy,* 31–36. Copyright © by Warren, Gorham & Lamont, Inc., 210 South Street, Boston, MA 02111. All Rights Reserved.

Chapter 7: Masaaki Kotabe, " 'Hollowing-Out' of U.S. Multinationals and Their Global Competitiveness: An Intrafirm Perspective," with permission from the publisher of *Journal of Business Research,* 19, 1–15. Copyright August, 1989 by Elsevier Science Publishing Co., Inc., New York; and Masaaki Kotabe, "Assessing the Shift in Global Market Share of U.S. Multinationals," *International Marketing Review,* 6, no. 5, (1989),

20–35, with permission from MCB University Press Limited, Bradford, England.

Chapter 8: Masaaki Kotabe, "The Relationship between Offshore Sourcing and Innovativeness of U.S. Multinational Firms: An Empirical Investigation," *Journal of International Business Studies,* 21 (Fourth Quarter 1990), 623–638, with permission from the Academy of International Business.

Chapter 1

Global Sourcing Strategy: An Overview

During the last decade or so, international business has experienced a major metamorphosis of an irreversible kind. Gone are the days when international business meant the one-way expansion of U.S. firms to the rest of the world. Also gone are the days when European and Japanese firms simply exported to, or manufactured in, the United States. Today, executives of the same firms have come to accept a new reality of global competition and global competitors. An increasing number of firms from around the world, particularly from the United States, Western Europe, and Japan, are competing head-on for a global dominance. Global competition no longer permits the firms a polycentric, country-by-country approach to international business. Simply, they do not have the luxury of time to do that.

International business is a fascinating phenomenon. It has existed since civilization was recorded, "extending back beyond the Phoenicians," claimed Fayerweather (1969). In the current sense of a large number of firms with interrelated production and sales operations located around the world, it is a relatively recent phenomenon that emerged with U.S. multinational firms in the 1950s and 1960s, and with European and Japanese firms in the 1970s and 1980s. The emergence of competitive European and Japanese multinational firms has brought forth the notion of global competition with a touch of extra urgency and significance.

As a result, a more general approach to understanding global competition has become urgently needed in recent years. One promising conceptual development is the value chain concept. Porter (1986), among others, has introduced the value chain concept for students of international business to understand what it takes to manage the interrelated value-adding activities of a corporation on a global basis. Value-adding activities include materials procurement, technology development and engineering (R&D), manufacturing, marketing, finance, personnel management, and so on. Thus, a global strategy is one in which a firm seeks to gain competitive advantage on a global basis through either an optimal arrangement of value-adding activities, coordinating among those dispersed value-adding activities, or both.

For the purpose of operationalizing a set of variables that are innately complex, we take the view that R&D, manufacturing, and marketing constitute the core of a manufacturing business as primary value-adding activities in the value chain and are lubricated by logistical management of those activities. The other activities are considered to be supportive of the primary activities in global strategy development. Management of the value chain or, more appropriately, management of the interactions of these primary activities serves as an overriding research subject for empirical investigations throughout the book.

While national boundaries have begun losing their significance both as a psychological and a physical barrier to international business, the diversity of local environments still plays an important role—not as a facilitator but rather as an inhibitor of optimal global strategy development. Now the question is to what extent successful multinational firms can circumvent the impact of local environmental diversity.

Indeed, we still debate the very issue raised more than 20 years ago: counteracting forces of "unification versus fragmentation" in developing operational strategies along the value chain. As early as 1969, Fayerweather wrote emphatically:

> What fundamental effects does [the existence of many national borders] have on the strategy of the multinational firm? Although many effects can be itemized, one central theme recurs, that is, their tendency to push the firm toward adaptation to the diversity of local environments which leads toward fragmentation of operations. But there is a natural tendency in a single firm toward integration and uniformity which is basically at odds with fragmentation. Thus the central issue is the conflict between unification and fragmentation— a close-knit operational strategy with similar foreign units versus a loosely related, highly variegated family of activities (pp. 133–134).

The same counteracting forces have since been revisited in such terms as "standardization versus adaptation," "globalization versus localization," more recently "global integration versus local responsiveness," and so on. Terms have changed but the quintessence of the strategic dilemma that multinational firms face today has not changed and will probably remain unchanged for years to come.

One thing that has changed, however, is the *ability* and *willingness* of these firms to integrate various activities along the value chain on a global basis in an attempt either to circumvent or to nullify the impact of differences in local markets to the extent possible. It may be more correct to say that these firms have been increasingly compelled to take a global view of their businesses, due primarily to increased competition, particularly among the Triad regions of the world: the United States, the European Community, and Japan. "If you don't do it, somebody else soon will to your disadvantage" epitomizes a contemporary view of competitive urgency shared by an increasing number of executives of multinational firms, irrespective of nationality.

The lack of competitive urgency can indeed be a problem. In his *Business Not As Usual,* for instance, Mitroff (1987) was very critical about the lack of this competitive urgency in the U.S. automobile industry in the 1970s and 1980s. He argued that the automobile industry minimized the need for constant innovation and its adoption into the working design of cars until it was forced on it by foreign competition. Not surprisingly, the result was an extreme isolation from the rest of the world—"a tunnel vision of the worst kind" (p. 84). This is not an isolated incident, however. Mitroff's indictment arguably applies to other industries, such as machine tools and electronics, in the United States.

In contrast, the last 20 years have seen a tremendous growth and expansion of European and Japanese multinational firms encroaching on the competitive strengths of U.S. multinational firms in almost all the markets around the world. While U.S. multinational firms have subsidiaries all over the world, they have been somewhat reluctant to develop an integrated and well coordinated global strategy that successful European and Japanese multinational firms have managed to establish. At the core of an integrated global strategy lies the firms' ability to coordinate manufacturing activities with R&D, engineering, and marketing along the value chain on a global basis. Indeed, European and Japanese multinational firms have heavily invested in, and improved upon, their strengths in manufacturing that many U.S. multinational firms have ignored. As a result, U.S. firms tend to have an ill-coordinated manufacturing strategy that results in a poor match between their manufacturing system capabilities and markets.

This functional mismatch can be traced to U.S. management's strategic emphasis having drifted away from manufacturing to marketing and to finance over the years (Buffa 1984). U.S. management's attention was focused on marketing in the 1960s, followed by a preoccupation with finance in the 1970s, culminating in the merger and acquisition craze of the 1980s—aptly called "paper entrepreneurship" (Reich 1983).

As a result, manufacturing management gradually lost its influence in the business organization. Production managers' decision-making authority was reduced such that R&D personnel prepared specifications with which production complied and marketing imposed its own delivery, inventory, and quality conditions, but not productivity considerations. In a sense, production managers gradually took on the role of outside suppliers within their own firms. Production managers' reduced influence in the organization led to a belief that manufacturing functions could be transferred easily to independent operators and subcontractors, depending upon the cost differential between in-house and contracted-out production. Thus, in order to lower production costs under competitive pressure, U.S. multinational firms turned increasingly to *outsourcing* of components and finished products from newly industrialized countries such as South Korea, Taiwan, Singapore, Hong Kong, Brazil, and Mexico, among others. Akio Morita, a cofounder of Sony, a highly innovative Japanese electronics company, chided such U.S. multinational firms as "hollow corporations" that simply put their well-known brand names on foreign-made products and sell them as if the products were their own (*Business Week* 1986).

However, we should not rush to a hasty conclusion that outsourcing certain components and/or finished products from foreign countries will diminish a firm's competitiveness. Many multinational firms with plants in various parts of the world are exploiting not only their own competitive advantages (e.g., R&D, manufacturing, and marketing skills) but also the locational advantages (e.g., inexpensive labor cost, certain skills, mineral resources, government subsidy, and tax advantages) of various countries. Thus, it is also plausible to argue that these multinational firms are in a more advantageous competitive position than are domestic-bound firms.

Then isn't the "hollowing-out" phenomenon indicative of a superior management of both corporate and locational resources on a global basis? What is wrong, if at all, with Caterpillar Tractor Company procuring more than 15 percent of components for its tractors from foreign suppliers? How about Honeywell marketing in the United States the products manufactured in its European plants? As implied at the outset of this chapter, answers to these questions seem to hinge on a firm's ability and willingness to integrate and coordinate various activities along the value chain.

As illustrated in Figure 1–1, a conceptual framework of what I call "interface" management of R&D, manufacturing, and marketing emphasizes the linkages among them in the value chain. Undoubtedly, these value-adding activities should be examined as holistically as possible, by linking the boundaries of these primary activities. For the encompassing nature of this investigation, I call this boundary issue "global sourcing." As Robinson (1987) succinctly summarized, five continuous and interactive steps involved in developing such a global sourcing strategy along the value chain are to:

Figure 1–1
Interfaces among R&D, Manufacturing, and Marketing

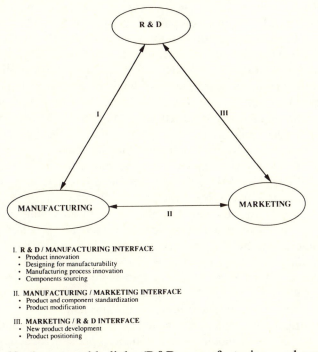

I. **R & D / MANUFACTURING INTERFACE**
 • Product innovation
 • Designing for manufacturability
 • Manufacturing process innovation
 • Components sourcing

II. **MANUFACTURING / MARKETING INTERFACE**
 • Product and component standardization
 • Product modification

III. **MARKETING / R & D INTERFACE**
 • New product development
 • Product positioning

1. Identify the separable links (R&D, manufacturing, and marketing) in the firm's value chain.

2. In the context of those links, determine the location of the firm's competitive advantages, considering both economies of scale and scope.

3. Ascertain the level of transaction costs between links in the value chain, both internal and external, and selecting the lowest cost mode.

4. Determine the comparative advantages of countries (including the firm's home country) relative to each link in the value chain and to the relevant transaction costs.

5. Develop adequate flexibility in corporate decision making and organizational design so as to permit the firm to respond to changes in both its competitive advantages and the comparative advantages of countries.

A treatise developed in this book differs from others in two crucial respects. First, much of the existing academic research has focused on each of these value-adding activities *as if* they were independent. Therefore, studies of R&D conclude that strong R&D capability is crucial for competitive viability. Likewise, studies of manufacturing suggest that manufacturing efficiency is essential for corporate performance. Independently, the marketing orientation for product development to meet the variegated needs of customers has been shown to have a positive impact on performance. If these independent findings are of a summative nature, then resultant managerial implications would be mercurial and untenable. In reality, there exist recurring conflicts in the tug-of-war of differing objectives among R&D, manufacturing, and marketing. It is known that excessive product modification and proliferation for the sake of satisfying the ever-different customer needs will forsake manufacturing efficiency and have negative cost consequences, barring a perfectly flexible computer-aided design (CAD) and computer-aided manufacturing (CAM) facility. Contrarily, excessive product standardization for the sake of lowering manufacturing costs will also be likely to result in unsatisfied customers. Similarly, innovative product designs and features as desired by customers may indeed be a technological feat but might not be conducive to manufacturing. Product design for manufacturability has therefore become a very important strategic issue today. It is not known, however, where a line should be drawn to exploit R&D, manufacturing, and marketing to the extent synergistically possible.

Second, the book emphasizes the logistics of components and products in the economics of global production, as opposed to behavioral and psychological determinants of "interface" management. It is held that the physical flow of components and products manifests a success or failure in management of the interfaces among R&D, manufacturing, and marketing. In other words, where and how these are performed on a global basis is considered to determine a multinational firm's market performance.

Therefore, global sourcing strategy can be defined broadly as

> management of the interfaces among R&D, manufacturing, and marketing on a global basis and of logistics identifying which production units will serve which particular markets and how components will be supplied for production, such that the firm can exploit both its own competitive advantages and the comparative advantages of various countries.

The overriding hypothesis throughout the book is that successful management of the interfaces or interactions of these three activities determines a firm's competitive strengths and consequently its market performance. In order to investigate this hypothesis, empirical studies conducted from various angles are reported in the book.

EXTENT AND COMPLEXITY OF
MULTINATIONAL OPERATION

Undoubtedly, multinational firms not only facilitate the flow of capital among various countries through direct investment abroad, but also significantly contribute to the world trade flow of goods and services as well. As shown in Figure 1-2, the total volume of international trade among the Triad regions alone increased more than tenfold in 20 years to $462 billion in 1990 from $44.4 billion in 1970 (in nominal terms), or approximately by 3.5 times in real terms (based on the GNP deflator during the same period).

Two notable changes have occurred in international trade. First, the last 20 years have observed a secular decline in the proportion of trade between the European Community and North America in the Triad regions, and conversely an increase in trade between the European Community and Japan. It strongly indicates that European countries and Japan have found each other as increasingly important markets above and beyond their traditional markets of North America. Second, newly industrialized countries (NICs) in Asia, including South Korea, Taiwan, Hong Kong, and Singapore, have dramatically increased their trading position vis-a-vis the rest of the world. Not only have these NICs become the ever-prosperous marketplaces, but more significantly they have become very important manufacturing locations for many multinational firms.

Unfortunately, trade statistics do not reveal anything more than the amount of bilateral trade flows between countries. It is false to assume that trade is always a business transaction between independent buyers and sellers across national boundaries. It is equally false to assume that a country's trade deficit in a certain *industry* equates with the decline in the competitiveness of *firms* in that industry.

There is ample evidence that portrays the extent and complexity of international trade managed by multinational firms. In a survey of 329 of the world's largest industrial firms, Dunning and Pearse (1981) revealed the extensive scope of operations by mature multinational firms. The average overseas market sourcing ratio (i.e., sales of overseas affiliates divided by sales of overseas affiliates plus parent company exports) was found to be as large as 68.1 percent. The sales of overseas affiliates in local markets do not usually register as exports as they are local sales that take place within a national boundary. This extensive market penetration via exports and local production by the world's largest multinational firms is what Barnet and Muller (1974) most appropriately called "global reach."

Today, much of international trade is indeed *managed* by multinational firms. Thus, trade does take place between a parent company and its subsidiaries abroad, and also between foreign subsidiaries across national

Figure 1–2
International Trade Flows ($ billion)

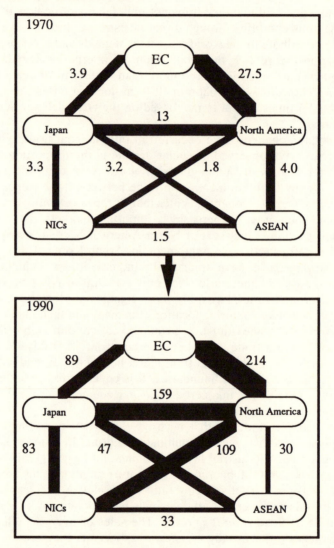

Note: North America: the United States, Canada
EC: Britain, Germany, France, Italy, the Netherlands, Belgium, Luxembourg, Denmark, Ireland, Spain, Portugal, Greece
ASEAN: Indonesia, Malaysia, the Phillipines, Thailand
NICs: South Korea, Taiwan, Hong Kong, Singapore

Sources: International Monetary Fund, *Direction of Trade Statistics*, various issues; trade statistics from each country.

boundaries. This is often referred to as "intra-firm" trade. Intra-firm trade makes trade statistics more complex to interpret, since part of the international flow of products and components is taking place between affiliated companies within the same multinational corporate system that transcends national boundaries. The latest survey by United Nations Center on Transnational Corporations (1988) reports data on intra-firm trade for the United States, Japan, and Britain. For the United States, about 30 percent of U.S. exports is attributed to U.S. parent firms transferring products and components to their affiliates overseas, and about 40 percent of U.S. imports is accounted for by foreign affiliates exporting to their U.S. parent firms. For both Japan and Britain, intra-firm transactions account for approximately 30 percent of their total trade flows (exports and imports combined), respectively.

Another study of 76 U.S. manufacturing multinational firms revealed that the composition of U.S. parent companies' imports from their overseas affiliates was as follows: finished goods 20–25 percent, components 65–70 percent, and raw materials 10 percent (Business International 1982). From the sourcing perspective, it appears that U.S. manufacturing firms were investing abroad in order to establish less expensive sources of supply of components and finished products for sale in the United States. As a result, North American bilateral trade with NICs has increased sixtyfold to $109 billion in 1990 from a meager $1.8 billion in 1970, of which the United States accounts for more than 90 percent. As mentioned earlier, this phenomenon is commonly known as "offshore" sourcing or "hollowing-out."

The offshore sourcing by U.S. firms for the U.S. market has been encouraged further by the U.S. tariff provisions for products imported under tariff items 9802.00.60 and 9802.00.80 of the U.S. Harmonized Tariff Schedule (formerly known as 806.30 and 807.00 of the Tariff Schedules of the United States until 1989). These tariff provisions permit the duty-free reentry to the United States of U.S.-made components sent abroad for further processing or assembly. During 1985–88, U.S. imports under 9802 provisions increased by 142 percent to $74 billion, at a faster pace than total U.S. imports, which rose by 27 percent to $437 billion.

The countries in the European Community and Japan also have similar tariff arrangements, although somewhat more restrictive in effect than the U.S. tariff provisions (Grunwald and Flamm 1985). It is recognized that sourcing patterns by European and Japanese firms are significantly different from those made by U.S. firms. Generally, European firms do relatively little foreign production for reimport to the home market, while Japanese firms manufacture components and products abroad, especially in Southeast Asia, primarily for export to countries other than Japan.

Evidence clearly suggests the complex nature of trade and foreign production managed by multinational firms in global competition. Therefore, the development of "global" sourcing and marketing strategies across different foreign markets has become a central issue for many multinational firms. In the past, a polycentric approach by which to organize operations on a country-by-country basis was the primary *modus operandi* by many multinationals. But today there is a growing realization of the advantages to be acquired by coordinating and integrating operations across national boundaries.

Much of the empirical work on sourcing strategy published so far has been aggregative in nature, usually focusing on intra-firm trade involving parent companies and/or parent countries (usually the United States). Generally, it has been examined under the general rubric of the international product cycle model, which is primarily an explanation of the evolution of sourcing strategy of a multinational manufacturing firm over time and space at the industry level. However, there has been little empirical investigation at the individual firm level of factors influencing sourcing policy. Despite such a limitation, the model provides conceptually rich insights into the dynamics of global sourcing strategy, and will be explained in the next section. This book attempts to fill the void by investigating global sourcing strategy at the firm level.

INTERNATIONAL PRODUCT CYCLE

Vernon (1966, 1974, 1979) is chiefly responsible for the development of the international product cycle thesis. The international product cycle model is not a monolithic theory that has weathered the change in the competitive climate over the past 25 years since its conception. It is instructive to present how the model has evolved with respect to its perspectives on global sourcing strategy. The model had been modified three times due to changes in the climate of the times. Vernon's viewpoints are reviewed here for illustrative purposes.

Principally, the international product cycle model provides a compelling description of dynamic patterns of international trade of manufactured products and direct investment as a product advances through its life cycle. The model is successful in allowing for the phenomenon of overseas direct investment in relation to international trade, stressing successive stages of product standardization (i.e., technology diffusion) through *time* and *space*. The model incorporates into a dynamic framework the timing of innovation, the effects of scale economies, and the roles of ignorance and uncertainty in influencing trade patterns. Changes in inputs and product characteristics toward standardization over time would determine the most economic production location at any particular phase of the product's life.

In its original form, the international product cycle model suggests three product stages: new product, maturing product, and standardized product

(Vernon 1966). The input requirements change over the life cycle of a new product. At the new product stage, highly skilled labor or entrepreneurial skills are required for the development and improvement of the product. Because of the temporary monopoly position that the new product enjoys, the innovating firm extends its geographical horizon by exporting it to the countries that are or are becoming similar in income levels and demand characteristics to the innovating country. As the product moves toward maturity, marketing efforts at product differentiation and capital outlays for mass production become dominant. The development of local competitors overseas may form a threat to the innovator, which will create an incentive for the innovator's foreign direct investment in order to maintain the status quo of its competitive position abroad. Finally, at the standardized product stage, the technology stabilizes and the product enjoys general consumer acceptance. This leads to mass production which largely requires raw materials, capital, and unskilled labor. As the product matures and becomes standardized, comparative advantage tends to shift from an advanced country relatively abundant in skilled labor to a developing country abundant in unskilled and inexpensive labor.

Vernon (1966) explained why the United States had a comparative advantage based on technology and innovation in the early stages of the product cycle. First, the United States had a high per-capita income by international standard—a fact that created a unique consumption pattern and a favorable market for new products. Second, the development of new products required much skilled labor, which was relatively abundant in the United States. Third, because of the U.S. high labor costs and the alleged tendency of innovations to be labor-saving in nature, there was a greater incentive for innovation in the United States. Finally, the large and high-income U.S. market made it possible for the U.S. firm to reap economies of scale associated with the development and marketing of new products.

In speculating on the last stage of the product cycle model in which the developing countries start exporting the mature products, Vernon (1966) alluded to the possibility of a multinational firm engaging in a mass production in these developing countries with unskilled and inexpensive labor of "standardized high-volume components." He did not, however, elaborate on intra-firm trade by multinational firms. Despite the model's contribution in linking international trade with direct investment abroad, it still failed to explain the interdependence among affiliates of the multinational firm.

In light of a dramatic rise in the 1970s in European and Japanese foreign direct investment, Vernon (1974) revised his views on the international product cycle model. Conceding that innovations of different sorts will originate from different countries (i.e., the United States, European countries, and Japan—all advanced industrialized countries), he noted that the innovations of European and Japanese firms have tended to place greater emphasis on land- and material-saving objectives, compared with those of U.S. firms, which have traditionally been labor-saving in nature.

The revised model consists of three stages: innovation, maturity, and senescence in oligopolistic competition. In this revised model, Vernon emphasizes the oligopolistic competition rather than the product per se, but the essence of the revised model is very much like that of the original model, except for (1) allowing innovations of a different nature to originate from different countries subject to their respective environmental conditions, and (2) recognizing the importance of global sourcing strategy under certain circumstances.

To the extent the national environments differ, U.S.-based multinational firms will tend to generate and develop innovations with special sensitivity to the conditions of the U.S. market, European-based firms with sensitivity to European conditions, and Japanese firms to Japanese conditions. Hence, the U.S. firms tend to specialize in innovations that are responsive to high incomes and high labor costs; the Europeans in innovations that are land- and material-saving; the Japanese in innovations that are material- and space-saving.

The innovating firm reaps monopoly profits and faces inelastic demand for its new product. The new product is initially exported from the home country, rather than manufactured by the innovating firm's foreign subsidiary located in foreign markets, for the following reasons: (1) since the firm's principal market tends to be at home, it may prefer a home location to minimize transport costs; (2) product specifications and production techniques for new products are typically in a state of flux; and (3) the inelasticity in the demand for new products makes the innovator relatively indifferent to production costs. It is a decline in the innovator's control over the technology of the product or production process, a standardization of the product and the process, and an increase in the demand elasticity for the product that will eventually lead the innovating firm to establish production facilities overseas.

Once innovational leads are eroded, the basis for the competitive advantage of the multinational firm shifts from product innovation to the barriers to entry generated by scale in production, transportation, and marketing. The overriding concern at this stage becomes the stable oligopolistic conditions achieved through pricing conventions (e.g, basepoint pricing and other coordinated pricing strategies), and hostages and alliances (e.g., concentration of production in the main marketing areas of rival firms, partnerships in joint ventures, and "follow-the-leader" overseas investment).

Finally, when the technology and consumer tastes become widely known and standardized, straightforward classical considerations of costs and prices become increasingly important. In some instances, the multinational firms may further try to differentiate their products to prolong their life. In some other cases, products may become "commodities" as in the case of computer silicon chips. The senescent oligopolies will evolve into competitive industries as innovation, product differentiation, and other barriers are gradually eroded.

At this senescent oligopolistic competition, Vernon similarly alluded to the importance of global sourcing strategy. However, the difficulty of his argument was that global sourcing would not become part of the multinational firm's corporate strategy until its innovational lead that created entry barriers to competition had been eroded.

Recognizing the change in the competitive climate in the 1970s, Vernon (1979) finally came to recognize the importance of global sourcing strategy, as follows:

> It is no longer easy to assume that innovating firms are uninformed about conditions in foreign markets, whether in other advanced countries or in the developing world. Nor can it be assumed that US firms are exposed to a very different home environment from European and Japanese firms; although the gap between most of the developing countries and the advanced industrialized countries palpably remains, the differences among the advanced industrialized countries are reduced to trivial dimensions (pp. 260–261).

Vernon anticipates that, seeking to exploit global scale economies, multinational firms are likely to establish various component plants in both advanced industrialized countries and developing countries, and to crosshaul between plants for the assembly of final products. Vernon recognizes that this pattern is at variance with the international product cycle model. As an explanation of international business behavior, the international product cycle model has limited explanatory power. It does describe the initial international expansion of many firms, but the mature multinational firms of today have succeeded in developing a number of other strategies for surviving in overseas sourcing and marketing.

LIMITATIONS OF THE INTERNATIONAL PRODUCT CYCLE MODEL

Although the international product cycle model has descriptive value, many authors have been critical of its explanatory power. Some key deficiencies relate to the model's failure to explain the operational interdependence among affiliates of a multinational firm. First, since the pace of new product introduction abroad has accelerated along with the shortening of innovational lead time (Davidson and Harrigan 1977), the migration of competitive advantage from the original innovator to follower firms is not just a function of changing factor costs and demand patterns, as predicated in the model. Indeed, it is rather the innovator's slow response to emerging competitive threats around the world that will cut short its competitive advantage over competition. If the innovator fails to maintain the original advantage by, among other acts, pursuing a global strategy aimed at dominating a set of product-market segments, the follower firms can gain the advantage at the expense of the innovator (Rapp 1973). This suggests that the identification and successful implementation of appropriate sourcing strategies by follower firms can overcome the preemptive move by the innovator.

Second, knowledge of the international product cycle model or its characteristic evolutionary pattern can lead international managers to alter predicted outcomes. The generation of MBA-trained businesspeople weaned on the international product cycle model have learned to anticipate, accelerate, and outsmart the expected course of production development through time and place (Giddy 1978). Indeed, shrewd competitors can "ride an international product cycle upstream" (Tsurumi 1984).

Third, the international product cycle model does not view the multinational firm as a proactive player, with simultaneous goals of establishing a global sourcing system, serving multiple global markets, and proactively driving the manufacturing and marketing experience curves (Leroy 1976; Porter 1986). Reactive motives are a response to a threat such as fear of losing a market or being "forced to invest to maintain a market," while proactive motives are a response to a favorable actual or potential market. As indicated earlier, Vernon (1979) was also aware of the feasibility of such exploitation of global scale economies by integrating R&D, manufacturing, and marketing operations on a global basis.

Despite these limitations, the international product cycle model was an innovative theory combining in a dynamic framework the competitive advantages of firms (e.g., technology, scale economies, and product differentiation) and comparative advantages of countries (e.g., labor cost, productivity, and transportation cost). Since it is beyond the scope of this book to survey new theoretical developments in the 1980s, it suffices to say that a new stream of theoretical developments (i.e., internalization theory, eclectic approach to international production, and transactions cost analysis) have evolved around these two advantages that primarily determine where the value-adding activities should be located across national boundaries and in what functional activities a firm should concentrate its resources (e.g., Kogut 1985; Dunning 1988).

Yet there appear to be as many views of these theoretical developments as there are authors. As such, research in global sourcing strategy is still in conceptual and theoretical flux. Added to it is the dearth of empirical information at the firm level, thereby making it difficult to provide managerially relevant and useful implications to globe-trotting executives of multinational firms. These realities indicate the necessity of empirically studying how and what sourcing strategies will lead to successful market performance.

Thus, this study is not intended to develop a theory of global sourcing strategy, but rather to provide empirical findings that will assist multinational executives in developing appropriate sourcing plans. In this perspective, the studies in the following chapters are more or less exploratory. This book is intended to examine existing ideas about relationships among concepts and perhaps to discover new hypotheses about these relationships in global sourcing strategy. Studies of this type not only are valuable as a means of testing hypotheses, but also present an opportunity for possible detection of new concepts and/or relationships (Zaltman, Pinson, and Angelmar 1973). It is also my hope that the book will be one step forward in laying out an empirical foundation as well as a direction for further theoretical development.

ORGANIZATION OF THE BOOK

This book is made up of eight more chapters, and is structured sequentially along the stream of my research on market performance implications of global sourcing strategy. As such, every succeeding chapter builds on the preceding chapters. Each chapter raises research questions and attempts to answer them with empirical data wherever applicable. The answers to these questions further raise a next series of questions that will be the subjects of a subsequent chapter. Although the chapters are related to each other, they are also written in a self-contained manner. Findings of the preceding chapters are briefly explained in a subsequent chapter to clarify the logical linkages between the two. For those who are not familiar with the issue of global sourcing strategy, it is strongly recommended that they read the book chapter by chapter. For those who are familiar, any chapter of their choice may be read independently of others without losing sight of the issue under investigation.

The book is divided into two parts. In Part I, Chapters 2 through 6 are devoted to understanding the performance implications of European and Japanese multinational firms' sourcing strategies and related management issues that facilitate development of their sourcing strategies. The study is based on survey data obtained from European and Japanese multinational firms listed in the *Fortune International 500 Directory*. Industries represented in the study are electronics, transportation equipment, scientific and photographic equipment, motor vehicles and parts, aerospace, computers and office equipment, and industrial and farm equipment. A common characteristic of these industries is that a manufactured final product is made up of easily identifiable and separable components. Manufacturing operations involving a significant change in the structure of components used, such as in chemical processing, are excluded because of the inherent difficulty in defining what constitutes components.

In Part II, Chapters 7 and 8 examine whether managerial implications gleaned from the experiences of European and Japanese firms will apply to U.S. multinational firms. For this phase of the study, the U.S. Department of Commerce's benchmark survey data base was used. Since reporting in the survey of all business transactions is mandatory under the International Investment Survey Act of 1976, the benchmark survey data well represent the transactions of U.S. multinational firms around the world. Although the European and Japanese data and the U.S. data are not directly comparable, similar findings warrant generalizability of the performance implications of various sourcing strategies. Finally, future research directions are explored in Chapter 9, based on the findings made in the preceding chapters.

SUMMARY OF THE BOOK

Part I: The Case of European and Japanese Multinational Firms

In Chapter 2, we develop a taxonomy of sourcing strategies employed by European and Japanese firms in serving the U.S. market. Such a systematic classification of sourcing strategies is useful, especially in an exploratory stage of research. Sixty-four different sourcing patterns are identified. It is found that Japanese firms tend to procure a higher proportion of major components from within their corporate systems than do European firms. However, this seemingly innocuous difference in components sourcing style is also found to have strong performance implications. The product's market performance is not at all related to its product life cycle stage or production location, but is positively related to the firm's capability to source major components internally and negatively related to the extent of product adaptation. These findings amply suggest the importance of product development, manufacturing ability, and components sourcing activities.

Then we address the above issues in Chapter 3. The purpose of this chapter is twofold. First, a taxonomy of sourcing strategies is revised to resolve some of the conceptual ambiguities and pave the way for further empirical investigation into the linkages among product development, manufacturing, and sourcing activities, or what I call "innovation-sourcing linkages." Second, based on a few variables identified in the revised taxonomy, performance implications of various innovation-sourcing linkages are explored. Findings suggest that product innovative activities and manufacturing innovative activities interact in an interesting way. Emphasis on either product innovations or manufacturing process innovations does not seem to be sufficient. However, if firms were to emphasize either one, they would be better off with product innovations than with manufacturing process innovations. Undoubtedly, a high level of product innovation, when backed simultaneously by a high level of manufacturing process innovation, unleashes by far the strongest competitive advantage. The firm's ability to procure major components internally appears to help improve its market performance independently of product and process innovative activities.

Chapter 4 casts light on the role of corporate product policy, which seems to have strong bearing on product and process innovative activities and sourcing strategies. It is clear from Chapters 2 and 3 that European and Japanese multinational firms that stress the strategic importance of both product and process innovations simultaneously are found to enjoy a higher level of market performance in the U.S. market than other firms. Also from a marketing perspective, it has become increasingly important for those firms to capitalize proactively on expanding commonalities across national boundaries rather than to focus on the differences of customers based on nationalities. Such a proactive approach to marketing on a global basis motivates standardization or harmonization of product designs. Product design standardization further permits standardization of components in the product. Yet, with such "standardized" products, different product positioning may still permit product differentiation in different segments of the market.

Subsequently, the roles of marketing strategy are explored in Chapter 5. European and Japanese multinational firms appear to have different marketing styles. Indeed, differences in marketing strategy, rather than nationality, account for market performance differences between European and Japanese firms. European firms emphasize short-term profitability and development of products to satisfy needs not met by their existing product line, while Japanese firms stress sales volume and successive improvement of existing products to better satisfy the same customer needs. However, these differences appear to have no bearing on performance differences between European and Japanese firms. Rather, regardless of nationality, firms that emphasize the strategic importance of future market growth and product standardization register a higher level of market performance than those that do not.

Chapter 6 focuses on the Japanese model of new product development as it is responsible for a phenomenal success of many Japanese firms. This chapter illustrates proactive product standardization as a precursor to the successful implementation of strategies involving innovation and sourcing activities on a global scale. As shown in Chapter 5, Japanese firms emphasize "incremental" improvement of existing products as their competitive strength. From a technological perspective, they adopt emerging technologies first in existing products to satisfy customer needs better than their competitors. This affords an opportunity to gain experience, debug technological glitches, reduce costs, boost performance, and develop designs to accommodate the products for customer use around the world. Ample examples are presented.

It is clear by now that the following four strategic thrusts have accorded market success to foreign multinational firms, particularly to the Japanese:

1. Proactive product standardization

2. Simultaneous emphasis on both product and manufacturing innovative activities

3. Integrated sourcing of major components

4. Marketing in all Triad regions of the world for growth.

Part II: The Case of U.S. Multinational Firms

In Chapters 7 and 8, we set out to examine the innovation-sourcing linkages of U.S. multinational firms operating globally. The primary objective of these chapters is to investigate whether similar strategic thrusts can be observed in successful U.S. multinational firms. Those U.S. multinational firms with extensive sourcing practices around the world have been criticized in the United States as pursuing "an economics of instant gratification, an abdication of responsibility to future (American) investors, workers, and consumers" (*Business Week,* 1986) at the cost of their long-term manufacturing and innovative abilities. Indeed, U.S. firms either have shifted their production to other countries (mostly, newly industrialized countries in Asia) or have come to buy components and assembled products from countries that can make quality products at low prices.

Now the question is: Is it indicative of a symptom of declining competitiveness of U.S. firms or rather their proactive global strategy to exploit their competitive and comparative advantages of various production locations around the world? In Chapter 7, we find a positive relationship between the "hollowness" of U.S. multinational firms and their market performance, measured by their global market share. It appears that U.S. parent firms "internally" export an increasing amount of high-tech equipment to support their foreign affiliates' R&D activities, which subsequently are geared not only toward increasing local sales but also toward exports to other markets including the United States. Increased employment of R&D-related people further suggests U.S. parent firms' strategic shift toward high-technology businesses at home, with manufacturing bases around the world to exploit comparative advantages of foreign production locations. This finding is consistent with the ability to procure key components internally being an important determinant of European and Japanese firms' market performance.

U.S. multinational firms' global market share may be indicative of their current competitive strength, but does not necessarily imply their future growth and profit potential. Therefore, Chapter 8 explores U.S. firms' future competitive viability as measured by their innovative capability. Based on various sources of data, the extent of offshore sourcing between the parent and their affiliates abroad—a measure of hollowness—is found to be positively related to U.S. firms' innovation propensity. Such a positive relationship does not necessarily imply that offshore sourcing directly improves the firm's innovative ability. However, there is also little reason to believe that U.S. firms' strategic mobility by way of offshore sourcing thwarts their competitiveness into the future.

Rather, it suggests that since the firms' innovative ability is a prerequisite for their sustained competitiveness in an increasingly competitive world, their offshore sourcing strategy indicates their proactive strategic readiness to exploit comparative advantages in various locations along with their corporate resources on a global scale. Although causal linkages are not clear at the current stage of knowledge on this issue, these findings suggest that U.S. multinational firms with a higher level of integration and coordination of production and marketing on a consolidated basis tend to retain innovative ability more efficiently and effectively than would otherwise be the case.

These findings with U.S. multinational firms are not inconsistent with those observed in European and Japanese counterparts. In recent years, strategic alliances have been increasingly used by many firms to seek market opportunities around the world, particularly in the Triad regions. With such reservations in mind, in Chapter 9 we explore the emerging issues of strategic alliances from a global sourcing perspective. Again, long-term performance implications are sought for those strategic alliances. It is conjectured that firms that enter into a strategic alliance to complement their product technology with the manufacturing and marketing competences of their partner are likely to lose their competitive advantage to the partner in the long run. The chapter points out industrial design as an increasingly important source of competitive advantage for years to come.

Much more research should be conducted before any definitive conclusions may be drawn. It is hoped that the stream of research presented in this book, albeit incomplete, provides normative implications to business planners and executives of multinational firms and also theory development and research directions to global sourcing researchers.

REFERENCES

Barnet, Richard J. and R. E. Muller (1974). *Global Reach: The Power of the Multinational Corporations*. New York: Simon and Schuster.

Buffa, Elwood S. (1984). "Making American Manufacturing Competitive." *California Management Review*, 26 (Spring), 29–46.

Business International (1982). *The Effects of U.S. Corporate Foreign Investment 1970–1980*. New York: Business International Corporation, May.

Business Week (1986). "Special Report: The Hollow Corporation," March 3, 56–59.

Davidson, William H. and Richard Harrigan (1977). "Key Decisions in International Marketing: Introducing New Products Abroad." *Columbia Journal of World Business*, 12 (Winter), 15–23.

Dunning, John H. (1988). "The Eclectic Paradigm of International Production: A Restatement and Some Possible Extensions." *Journal of International Business Studies*, 19 (Spring), 1–31.

Dunning, John H. and R. D. Pearse (1981). *The World's Largest Industrial Enterprises*. New York: St. Martin's Press.

Fayerweather, John (1969). *International Business Management: A Conceptual Framework*. New York: McGraw-Hill.

Giddy, Ian H. (1978). "The Demise of the Product Cycle Model in International Business Theory." *Columbia Journal of World Business*, 13 (Spring), 90–97.

Grunwald, Joseph and Kenneth Flamm (1985). *The Global Factory: Foreign Assembly in International Trade*. Washington, DC: The Brookings Institution.

Kogut, Bruce (1985). "Designing Global Strategies: Comparative and Competitive Value-Added Chains." *Sloan Management Review*, 26 (Summer), 15–28.

Leroy, Georges (1976). *Multinational Product Strategy: A Taxonomy for Analysis of Worldwide Product Innovation and Diffusion*. New York: Praeger.

Mitroff, Ian I. (1987). *Business Not As Usual: Rethinking Our Individual, Corporate, and Industrial Strategies for Global Competition*. San Francisco: Jossey-Bass.

Porter, Michael E. (1986). *Competition in Global Industries*. Boston: Harvard Business School Press.

Rapp, William V. (1973). "Strategy Formulation and International Competition." *Columbia Journal of World Business*, 8 (Summer), 98–112.

Reich, Robert (1983). *The Next American Frontier*. New York: Times Books.

Robinson, Richard D., ed. (1987). *Direct Foreign Investment: Costs and Benefits*. New York: Praeger.

Tsurumi, Yoshi (1984). *Multinational Management*. 2nd ed. Cambridge, MA: Ballinger.

United Nations Center on Transnational Corporations (1988). *Transnational Corporations in World Development: Trends and Perspectives*. New York: United Nations.

Vernon, Raymond (1966). "International Investment and International Trade in the Product Cycle." *Quarterly Journal of Economics*, 80 (May), 190–207.

——— (1974). "The Location of Economic Activity." *Economic Analysis and the Multinational Enterprise*, John H. Dunning, ed. London: George Allen and Unwin, 89–114.

——— (1979). "The Product Cycle Hypothesis in a New International Environment." *Oxford Bulletin of Economics and Statistics,* 41 (November), 255–
267.
Zaltman, Gerald, Christian R.A. Pinson, and Reinhard Angelmar (1973). *Metatheory and Consumer Research.* New York: Holt, Rinehart, and Winston.

Part I

The Case of European and Japanese Multinational Firms

Chapter 2

Sourcing Strategies and Market Performance

It is argued that in an era of global competition, well-managed companies emphasize globally standardized products that are advanced, functional, reliable, and low-priced in lieu of market customized products (Levitt 1983; Ohmae 1985). However, global standardization of products should not be equated to marketing of identical products all over the world. Rather it means multinational firms' continual efforts to streamline and standardize the core components of a product in such a way that only minor changes in the product will permit successful product differentiation. The marketing standardization issue will be explored further in Chapter 4.

The efficacy of the globalization argument has attracted heated debate, but little empirical research on the relationship between the product's degree of global standardization and its market performance has been conducted in spite of its managerial importance. Normative implications about the benefits of such a global strategy will be discussed in this chapter.

A major issue in developing a strategy to support a globally standardized product is closely related to how components for that product will be sourced. Sourcing strategy generally refers to identifying which production units will serve which particular markets and how components will be supplied for production (Davidson 1982). In the past, a polycentric approach by which to organize operations on a country-by-country basis was the *modus operandi* for many multinational firms. In such a polycentric approach, multinational firms established full-fledged manufacturing subsidiaries in all major markets. Central control and coordination were kept to a minimum. The result was an inevitable and inefficient

Figure 2–1
Conceptual Model of Global Sourcing Strategy

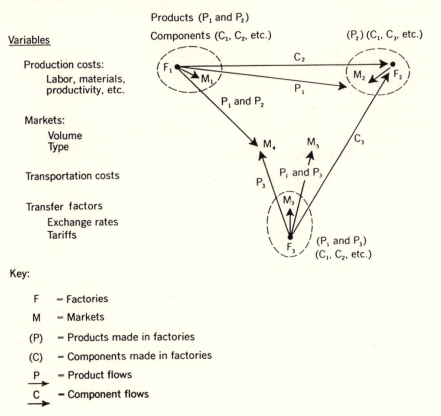

Source: John Fayerweather, *International Business Management: A Conceptual Framework*. New York: McGraw-Hill, 1969, p. 142. Used with the author's permission.

proliferation in the firms' product mix. Unfortunately, this approach was not necessarily conducive to exploiting economies of scale on a global basis due to the duplicative nature of manufacturing facilities around the world.

As early as 1969, Fayerweather described a conceptual model of global sourcing planning involving the dynamic relationships among factories, markets, products, components, and complex logistical flows connecting all these elements (as shown in Figure 2–1). He argued that since there were various categories of resources (i.e., natural resources, labor, capital, and technological and managerial skills) and a multitude of subcategories thereof, each with its own pattern of international differences, a strategic corporate planner equipped with a computer could work out a very complex sourcing scheme to achieve optimum economic results of unified global sourcing.

Indeed, it was a bold, and somewhat of a futuristic, proposition then. Little research ensued, however. Such complex logistical considerations were rarely needed in the 1960s and 1970s. The traditional treatise of exporting, licensing, and foreign direct investment was sufficient enough to understand the advantages and disadvantages of alternative modes of entry into foreign markets. (For an excellent treatise of various entry strategies, see Root 1987.)

Currently, the extensive geographical expansion of multinational firms (see, for example, United Nations Center on Transnational Corporations 1988) has led to a growing realization of the potential competitive advantages gained by coordinating and integrating operations across national boundaries (Kogut 1985; Porter 1986; Bartlett and Ghoshal 1989). Consequently, the development of global marketing in synchronization with cross national sourcing strategies has become a major concern for an increasing number of multinational firms. However, sourcing strategies are multidimensional and include such factors as production locations, phases of production, internal versus external components sourcing (i.e., make or buy decisions), and internal versus external assembly (i.e., decision-making regarding in-house assembly or contracting out).

IBM and Digital Equipment have historically produced almost all their own components in-house. On the other hand, many other computer makers use off-the-shelf components and procure them from independent suppliers of components. For example, Amstrad (Alan Michael Sugar Trading), an enormously successful British maker and vendor of word processors and IBM-compatible personal computers in Europe, keeps costs down by farming out most manufacturing to a network of Asian subcontractors. It is also argued, however, that the reliance on other manufacturing sources for components and subassemblies could eventually make computer makers vulnerable as too much of the corporate infrastructure necessary for continued innovations has moved offshore and to independent suppliers abroad (Schlender 1990).

So far, our understanding of the competitive benefit of various sourcing strategies has been anecdotal at best, and consequently is in a state of confusion. Thus, we are in desperate need of a systematic, yet parsimonious and logical, means of capturing the complex nature of sourcing strategies in the hope that it will assist executives of multinational firms in identifying alternative sourcing strategies across national boundaries and their performance implications. Also, such a sourcing taxonomy promises to provide a conceptual foundation for future research in this area.

PURPOSE AND SCOPE OF THE CHAPTER

Given the growing importance of global marketing in conjunction with global sourcing strategies, this chapter focuses on the following two research issues: (1) What are the configurations or basic types of sourcing strategies used by Western European and Japanese multinational firms serving the U.S. market? and (2) Does their market performance vary by the degree of global product standardization and type of sourcing strategy employed? The chapter emphasizes the intra-firm aspects of multinational firms' sourcing strategy. Also, only Western European (European, hereafter) and Japanese multinational firms marketing products in the United States are investigated. Hence, the analysis is limited to an examination of the international movement of components and products within the foreign multinational firms that serve the U.S. market.

CONCEPTUAL ORIGINS

Multinational firms were particularly an American phenomenon in the 1960s. It is in this period that studies on international business caught on and many of the conceptual frameworks and theories we know today were generated. As French journalist J-J. Servan-Schreiber (1968) vividly described in the 1960s, the awesome strengths of U.S. multinational firms were so overwhelming that Europeans were seriously afraid of an American dominance of European markets. However, the decades of the 1970s and 1980s found increasing numbers of multinational firms originating from European countries and Japan, in effect virtually rendering the European fear of the American dominance obsolete.

Now, U.S. multinational firms are faced with competition from European and Japanese multinational firms not only in the U.S. domestic market, but also in foreign markets including European and Japanese markets. The emergence of European and Japanese multinational firms has created a new competitive environment on a global scale. This new competition mandates the globalization of corporate strategy (Ohmae 1985; Porter 1986; Bartlett and Ghoshal 1989).

As demonstrated in Chapter 1, evidence abounds that multinational firms not only facilitate the flow of capital among nations through direct investment abroad, but significantly contribute to the world trade flow of goods and services as well. More significantly, these firms increasingly engage in international sourcing of major components and products *within* their corporate systems on an intra-firm basis, rather than *from* independent suppliers in different countries (Business International 1982; United Nations Center on Transnational Corporations 1988). The intra-firm sourcing of major components seems to be a strategic response to cope with global competition: the methods that multinational firms employ to source their major components and products are potentially important bases for competitive advantage (Moxon 1974; Edwards 1984; Porter 1986).

A frequently used framework to describe cross-national business practices related to sourcing strategies is the international product cycle model. This model and the critical discussion on its explanatory merit are valuable contributions to the conceptual foundations of the study in this chapter. The model has provided a compelling description of dynamic patterns of international trade of manufactured products and direct investment as a product advances through its life cycle (Vernon 1966, 1974, 1979). According to the model, changes in inputs and product characteristics toward standardization *over time* determine an optimal production location at any particular phase of the product's life cycle.

As explained in Chapter 1, however, three major limitations of the international product cycle model have to be borne in mind when assessing the performance implications of various sourcing strategies:

1. Increased pace of new product introduction and reduction in innovational lead time, which deprive firms of the age-old polycentric approach to global markets,

2. Predictable sourcing development during the product cycle, which permits a shrewd firm to outmaneuver competition, and

3. More active management of locational and corporate resources on a global basis, which gives a firm a preemptive first mover advantage over competition.

One successful example of such globally oriented strategy is Sony, which developed transistorized solid-state color TVs in Japan in the 1960s and marketed them initially in the United States before they were introduced in the rest of the world, including the Japanese market. Mass marketing initially in the United States and then throughout the world in a short time period had given this Japanese company a first-mover advantage as well as economies of scale advantages.

In contrast, EMI provides a historic case example of the failure to take advantage of global opportunities that existed. This British company developed and began marketing CAT (computerized axial tomography) scanners in 1972, for which its inventors, Godfrey Houndsfield and Allan Cormack, won a Nobel Prize. Despite an enormous demand for CAT scanners in the United States, the largest market for state-of-the-art medical equipment, EMI failed to export them to the United States immediately and in sufficient numbers. Instead, the British company slowly, and probably belatedly, began exporting them to the United States in the mid-1970s, as if to follow the evolutionary pattern suggested by the international product cycle model. Some years later, the British company established a production facility in the United States, only to be slowed down by technical problems. By then, EMI was already facing stiff competition from global electronics giants including Philips, Siemens, General Electric, and Toshiba. Indeed, it was General Electric that in a short period of time blanketed the U.S. market and subsequently the rest of the world with its own version of CAT scanners that were technologically inferior to the British model (Dell'Osso 1990).

In both cases, technology diffused quickly. Today, quick technological diffusion has virtually become a matter of fact. Without established sourcing plans, distribution, and service networks, it is extremely difficult to exploit both emerging technology and potential markets around the world simultaneously. General Electric's swift global reach could not have been possible without its ability to procure crucial components internally and on a global basis.

Despite the growing importance of global competitive strategies and, in particular, global sourcing, there is a dearth of empirical research on this topic. The sourcing patterns that deviate from the international product cycle model are especially interesting, not because they contradict the model, but rather because they demonstrate proactive strategizing as opposed to incremental, evolutionary thinking (Ohmae 1985). The increasing competitive intensity of the major global markets makes it imperative for analysts to provide international marketing managers with research-driven guidance on successful sourcing strategies with an empirically derived explanation.

TYPES OF SOURCING STRATEGIES

A taxonomy of sourcing strategies is used to identify systematically the whole gamut of alternative sourcing strategies, including and expanding on the locational implications of the international product cycle model. The term "sourcing" has been used in a number of different contexts by different writers. Although a semantic battle exists regarding the use of the term and the domain of the concept, this book adopts the following operational definition as it is suitably encompassing:

> Sourcing strategy includes a number of basic choices firms make in deciding how to serve foreign markets. Once choice relates to the use of imports, assembly or production within the country to serve a foreign market. Another decision involves the use of internal or external supplies of components or finished goods. An even more fundamental issue is the definition to manage sourcing activities on a market-by-market basis or from a centralized system perspective (Davidson 1982, p. 177).

Therefore sourcing is used to describe management by multinational firms of the flow of components and finished products in serving foreign markets. Components are defined here as intermediate products that require further processing or assembly into finished products, and therefore exclude raw materials.

Similarly, there is an unsettling argument on the definition of "international," "multinational," "transnational," "global," and the like, used in the international business literature. Suffice it to say that in general "international" indicates "between nations," whereas "multinational" connotes "among a number of nations." "Transnational" refers to "across national boundaries," and "global," to "worldwide." This book adopts the term "global" in order to allow "global" sourcing strategy to capture all possible sourcing patterns. Therefore, some global sourcing strategies may be "international" and others "multinational" in nature.

As this chapter focuses on the flow of components and finished products in serving foreign markets by multinational firms, global sourcing strategy is seen composed of four major dimensions for decision making: (1) production locations, (2) phases of production, (3) internal/external components sourcing, and (4) internal/external assembly or processing. The operationalization of these dimensions will be explained next.

Production Locations

Following the convention of the international trade literature, production locations are classified into four regional groups. Products, including components, can be made in a "home" country or region (i.e., Western Europe for European multinational firms and Japan for Japanese multinational firms), in a "market" country (i.e., the United States), or in some other "third-party" country. "Third-party" refers to any location other than a "home" country and a "market" country. "Third-party" countries will be further divided into "developed third-party" (e.g., Australia and Canada) and "developing third-party" countries (e.g., Taiwan and Brazil). This subclassification is useful such that "developed third-party" countries tend to be capital-abundant, while "developing third-party" countries tend to be labor-abundant. Different resource endowments are known to affect the international trade structure among countries.

Phases of Production

The production process is divided into intermediate products (components) and final processing or assembly. A manufactured final product is composed of components that have gone through final processing or assembly. Final processing may be a more appropriate term for operations involving a significant change in the structure of components used, such as in chemical processing, although this kind of industry was not included in this research, for reasons discussed later. On the other hand, final assembly may be more apt to describe operations involving a building-up of components, such as in automobile assembling. For the sake of simplicity, the terms "components" and "final assembly" will be used here-after.

Internal/External Components Sourcing

The third dimension of the concept of global sourcing strategy is a make-or-buy decision with respect to components. A clarification has to be made, however, regarding internal versus external sourcing. If a components transaction is of an intra-firm kind, it can be deemed internal sourcing. Transactions between a parent company and its wholly owned subsidiaries are clearly intra-firm. Transactions between the parent company and its majority-owned affiliates are also fairly clearly of an intra-firm kind. Either way, it is suggestive of a high level of administrative control of the affiliates by the parent company.

However, the degrees of intra-firmness become uncertain in the case of the company's transactions with 50/50 or minority-participated joint ventures abroad, with local firms under a management contract or licensing agreement, or even with local firms that have long-standing mutually trustworthy customer relationships. Therefore, some arbitrariness is bound to be necessary for the operational definition of internal or external sourcing. One commonly used criterion is that the relationship is internal if an affiliate is majority-owned; otherwise, external. This common definition is adopted throughout the study.

Internal/External Assembly

The last dimension has to do with who performs the assembly of components into final products. The same dichotomy is employed here as in the internal versus external sourcing decision. The internal assembly refers to the assembly performed by an internal member of the multinational firm, whereas the external assembly refers to the assembly by a firm external to the multinational firm. As in the case of the internal/external sourcing, the intra-firmness of the assembly is a matter of degree, and is subject to the same question as to what constitutes internal members. Therefore, for the sake of consistency, the same operational definition is used for the dichotomization of internal and external members.

The taxonomy encompasses four fundamental decisions related to sourcing strategies: (1) production locations, (2) phases of production, (3) internal/external components sourcing, and (4) internal/external assembly. To facilitate identification of all possible alternative sourcing strategies, the dimensions and the levels of each dimension are converted to simple notations as follows:

$$C_{ij}A_{kl}$$

where C = Components sourcing,

A = Final assembly,

i = 1,2,3,4: Location in which a majority of components is sourced (i.e., home country, market country [United States], third-party developed countries, and third-party developing countries, respectively),

j = 1,2: Whether or not a majority of components is produced by the internal members (majority- to wholly owned affiliates and the parent firm itself) of the multinational firm,

k = 1,2,3,4: Location in which a finished product is assembled, and

l = 1,2: Whether or not a finished product is assembled by the internal members of the multinational firm.

The taxonomy of sourcing strategies is presented in Table 2–1. We can identify 64 alternative sourcing strategies. For example, $C_{11}A_{11}$ refers to a foreign multinational firm directly exporting to the United States a product manufactured by the parent firm with its own components. Similarly, $C_{21}A_{21}$ represents a pure case of local manufacture in the United States by a foreign multinational firm procuring its components needs from within for final assembly. On the other hand, $C_{11}A_{22}$ symbolizes a licensing agreement that a foreign multinational firm entered into with a U.S. company, in which the foreign company provides its components to the licensee in the United States for local production. $C_{22}A_{31}$ is a complicated sourcing strategy in which a majority of components sourced from outside the multinational corporate system in the United States has been shipped to its own offshore production facility in a developed third-party country (such as Canada) for final assembly into a product for eventual sales back in the United States. $C_{42}A_{41}$ represents exports of finished products by a foreign multinational firm operating out of a developing country such as Malaysia with a majority of components procured from independent local suppliers. And so on. As shown in Table 2–1, sourcing ratios can also be computed to supplement the significance of domestic, market, and third-party country sourcing patterns.

Sourcing strategy measurement at the product level is significant for the following two reasons. First, while relatively aggregate intra-firm trade data (such as the trade statistics published by the U.S. Department of Commerce) are useful as a general guide to the extent and nature of intra-firm trade, there has been no substitute for micro-level studies of sourcing practices within particular firms (Buckley 1979; Helleiner 1981). Second,

Table 2–1
Taxonomy of Global Sourcing Strategies

PHASES OF PRODUCTION / LOCATION	COMPONENTS SOURCING		FINAL ASSEMBLY	
HOME	INTERNAL	C_{11}	INTERNAL	A_{11}
	EXTERNAL	C_{12}	EXTERNAL	A_{12}
MARKET	INTERNAL	C_{21}	INTERNAL	A_{21}
	EXTERNAL	C_{22}	EXTERNAL	A_{22}
DEVELOPED THIRD	INTERNAL	C_{31}	INTERNAL	A_{31}
	EXTERNAL	C_{32}	EXTERNAL	A_{32}
DEVELOPING THIRD	INTERNAL	C_{41}	INTERNAL	A_{41}
	EXTERNAL	C_{42}	EXTERNAL	A_{42}

NOTE: More precise measurements are introduced so as to supplement the significance of domestic, market, and third-party country sourcing patterns. The following notations are used for this purpose, with subscripts 1 and 2 for internal and external sourcing, respectively:

$w = w_1 + w_2$ = percentage of the value of the components sourced domestically,

$x = x_1 + x_2$ = percentage of the value of the components sourced in a foreign market country,

$y = y_1 + y_2$ = percentage of the value of the components sourced in a developed third-party country, and

$z = z_1 + z_2$ = percentage of the value of the components sourced in a developing third-party country,

where $w + x + y + z = 100$ percent,

$w_1 + x_1 + y_1 + z_1$ = total percentage of the value of the components sourced internally, and

$w_2 + x_2 + y_2 + z_2$ = total percentage of the value of the components sourced externally

the taxonomy deals with sourcing practices in a four-country framework involving a home country, a foreign market country, a developed third-party country, and a developing third party country. The latter two sourcing locations are clearly growing in use and must be measured. The taxonomy used here adds much more to realism. Available intra-firm trade statistics deal only with trade in the traditional "between-two-countries" framework. One such example is trade statistics on U.S. imports from U.S. majority-owned foreign affiliates.

THE SAMPLE

A sample of subsidiaries of European and Japanese multinational firms operating in the United States was used in this study for several reasons. First, initial correspondence with executives/directors in charge of corporate strategic planning at the headquarters of seven foreign multinational firms (four European and three Japanese) had indicated that chief executive officers (CEOs) of their U.S. subsidiaries were fully knowledgeable of and responsible for executing their parent firms' sourcing and product policies. Second, the United States, representing some 35 percent of the Triad regions' total production and consumption, is a pivotal market for many European and Japanese multinational firms (OECD 1985). This suggests how important the roles of U.S. subsidiaries are to these foreign multinational firms. Third, and of utmost importance, recent research studies indicate an increasing trend toward global rationalization strategies among European and Japanese multinational firms (e.g., Yoshino 1976; Franko 1978; Negandhi and Welge 1984; Kotler, Fahey, and Jatusripitak 1985).

The sample is limited to the firms whose major lines of business belong to selected industrial categories used in the *Fortune International 500 Directory* (electronics, transportation equipment, scientific and photographic equipment, motor vehicles and parts, aerospace, computers and office equipment, and industrial and farm equipment). A common characteristic of these industries is that a manufactured final product is made up of easily identifiable and separable components. Manufacturing operations involving a significant change in the structure of components used, such as in chemical processing, are excluded because of the inherent difficulty in defining what constitutes components as well as product and process innovations (which will be used in later chapters).

A total of 250 foreign subsidiaries (175 European and 75 Japanese) were randomly identified from the *International Directory of Corporate Affiliations* (1985). This directory is very extensive, with a listing of over 27,500 European and Japanese firms. It includes the names of parent firms and their affiliates, their approximate annual sales, size of employment, and SIC (Standard Industrial Classification) lines of business they are in (classified by SIC code).

During the winter of 1987, a personal letter and a questionnaire were sent to the CEO of each subsidiary, who were requested to identify one of their firms' major products that had been introduced in the United States within the past ten years, regardless of the origin of the product, and subsequently to respond to the questionnaire for this product or product line. After two waves of follow-ups, 75 responses were received. Four of these returns were later deemed unusable, resulting in 71 usable returns (43 European and 28 Japanese) with the effective response rate of 28.4 percent. Earlier respondents were compared with later respondents on several descriptive variables, including nationality, annual sales volume, corporate product policy, and type of product. As there were no significant differences observed, it is encouraging to note that nonresponse would not likely bias findings of this study (Armstrong and Overton 1977).

Profile of the Respondents

Over 80 percent of the respondents were in the cadre of top management (i.e., presidents, vice presidents, and directors), while the rest were functional managers (i.e., marketing, production, finance, etc.), thereby assuring the credibility of information provided. To see if the job position of the respondents had any impact on the way they responded to the questionnaire, they were classified by job position (top management, functional manager, or director of corporate planning). The variables in this study were then compared by job position. As no significant differences were observed, the respondents' job position would not bias the findings of this study.

As shown in Table 2–2, the level of involvement in U.S. operations by foreign multinational firms in the sample (measured by the number of manufacturing subsidiaries in the United States) generally matched the actual distribution of foreign multinational firms operating in the United States. Table 2–3 shows the industries represented by the sample. This further provides some assurance that a nonresponse bias is not a major problem in the sample. About 60 percent of the firms were of European origin, the rest being from Japan. British and West German firms together represented about a half of the European sample, followed by Swedish and Swiss firms, which constituted an additional quarter.

Product categories (industries) represented in the sample also closely matched the industrial distribution of European and Japanese multinational firms in the *Fortune International 500 Directory* (*Fortune* 1986a). Europeans are particularly involved in the industrial and farm equipment industry, whereas Japanese are highly involved in the electronics industry. Products are classified as either consumer durable products or industrial durable products. Some 74 percent of the European durable products are for industrial use, in contrast with 33 percent of the Japanese durable products. It is also noted that three-quarters of the products represented in the sample are marketed in all three Triad regions. Those that are not, are marketed in both the United States and the home region of the parent

Table 2–2
Nationality of the Parent Headquarters of Participating Firms

COUNTRY	SAMPLE[1]		ACTUAL DISTRIBUTION
	n	%	%
EUROPEAN	43	60.6	61.7
Belgium	1	1.4	1.6
Denmark	1	1.4	0.5
Finland	3	4.2	1.8
France[2]	1 1/2	2.1	9.4
Italy	1	1.4	2.6
Netherlands	0	0.0	2.6
Sweden	5	7.0	5.2
Switzerland	6	8.5	3.4
United Kingdom[2]	9 1/2	13.4	20.5
West Germany	11	15.5	13.9
Not specified	4	5.6	-
JAPANESE	28	39.4	38.3
TOTAL	71	100.0	100.0

[1]Individual numbers may not sum to the subtotals shown due to the rounding.
[2]One respondent reported a dual nationality.

firms. These statistics typify the commonly recognized business orientations by European and Japanese multinational firms.

The Variables

The following variables are used to capture the major dimensions of various sourcing strategies and their performance implications:

1. The Product's Market Performance (PERFORM): The product's relative market share and pretax profitability in the United States were measured on a 5-point scale. Similar to the PIMS (Profit Impact of Marketing Strategy) findings (Buzzell, Gale, and Sultan 1975), these two variables were significantly correlated ($r = .38$, $p < .001$). Hence, they were added together to create a composite measure of PERFORM.

2. Extent of Internal Major Components Sourcing (INTSORC): INTSORC[1] refers to the market value of major components in the product procured internally, or the total value of components less

Table 2-3
Industry Classification of Participating Firms

Industry	European			Japanese			Total		
	Sample n	%	Actual Distribution %	Sample n	%	Actual Distribution %	Sample n	%	Actual Distribution %
Metal Products	5	11.6	12.8	1	3.6	3.8	6	8.5	10.7
Electronics	5	11.6	23.1	18	64.3	43.4	23	32.4	26.7
Transportation Equipment	3	7.0	6.4	0	0.0	7.5	3	4.2	4.6
Motor Vehicles & Parts	1	2.3	21.8	1	3.6	7.5	2	2.8	26.0
Aerospace	1	2.3	7.7	0	0.0	0.0	1	1.4	3.8
Scientific & Photo Equipment	3	7.0	2.6	0	0.0	3.8	3	4.2	2.3
Computers & Office Equipment	5	11.6	9.0	5	17.9	26.4	10	14.1	9.2
Industrial & Farm Equipment	12	27.9	17.9	1	3.6	7.5	13	18.3	16.8
Not Specified	8	18.6	-	2	7.1	-	10	14.1	-
TOTAL	43	100.0	100.0	28	100.0	100.0	71	100.0	100.0

Note: Individual percentage figures may not sum to 100 due to rounding.

the value of standardized components. The percentage of the standardized components in the product was estimated by asking respondents a hypothetical question: "Ignoring transportation costs, approximately what percent of the total value of components in the product could be sourced from local firms in newly industrializing countries such as Taiwan, South Korea, and Brazil, without technical assistance from your firm?"

3. Internal Assembly (INTASBL): A dichotomous variable (Yes = 1, and No = 0) representing whether, in the assembly or final processing location indicated as the major one in a mix of multiple sourcing strategies, more than 50 percent of the U.S. sales volume of the product was assembled or finally processed by their parent firm or other internal members of the parent system.

4. Assembly Location (ASBLLOC): The major location in which the product was assembled or finally processed. Based on a four-

location framework, the first assembly location is the home location. For the European firms, the home location consists of their home country and other countries in the European Community. For the Japanese firms, it is Japan. The second assembly location is the United States as a foreign market to the European and Japanese multinational firms. The third assembly location is another developed country or countries. For the European firms, it is non-EC countries including Japan and excluding the United States. For the Japanese firms, it is any developed country including West European countries and excluding the United States. Finally, the fourth assembly location is the developing country or countries.

5. Size of the Multinational Firm (SIZE): It was measured by 1985 consolidated global sales volume of the multinational firm on a four-point scale, representing the *Fortune International 500*'s largest 100, second largest 100, third largest 100, and so on.

6. International Product Cycle Stage (PLC): The life cycle stage of the product is identified on a four-point scale question: new stage, growth stage, maturity stage, and decline stage in worldwide trade.

7. Level of Product Adaptation (ADAPT): The level of product adaptation is measured on a four-point scale, ranging from "not at all" to "substantially," in a question, "For the U.S. market, has this product been modified . . . ?"

8. Nationality of the Multinational Firm (NATION): The nationality of multinational firms is identified either as European (0) or as Japanese (1).

9. Type of the Product (TYPE): The type of the product is identified either as consumer durable (0) or as industrial durable (1). As there were five cases in which the same products were marketed both as industrial and as consumer durable products, they were classified as one of the two product types on the basis of the difference in sales volume between the two.

RESULTS

Types of Sourcing Strategies

Multinational firms frequently use a mix of sourcing strategies simultaneously when marketing a product in foreign markets, and Grosse (1985) offers theoretical underpinnings for multiple sourcing strategy. To gain some realistic insight into multiple sourcing strategy, respondents were initially asked which sourcing strategies were used to market the product in the United States, and how much of the sales volume was attributable to each sourcing strategy. Subsequently, they were asked to complete

Figure 2–2
Multiple Sourcing of Products by European Firms (N = 43)

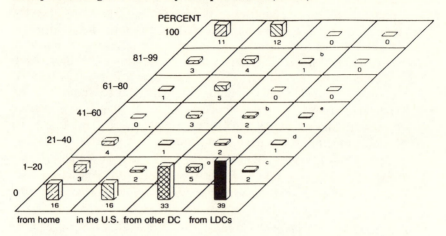

Notes: The cell number represent the frequency.

a. Includes two cases from Japan and one case from Canada

b. Other European countries

c. Brazil and unspecified LDC

d. Unspecified LDC

e. Puerto Rico (treated as LDC)

the remainder of the questionnaire while focusing on what they considered their major sourcing strategy. Figures 2–2 and 2–3 show the extent of multiple sourcing strategies being used by European and Japanese multinational firms, respectively.

Only 42 (59 percent) of the 71 respondents report a single sourcing strategy. For these 42 respondents, the product marketed in the United States is either exported from home to, or manufactured in, the United States. The remaining 29 respondents (41 percent) of the sample use a mix of two or more different sourcing strategies simultaneously for the U.S. market. Figures 2–2 and 2–3 also confirm that Japanese firms are more oriented toward exporting, while European firms tend toward local manufacture in the United States. No particular difference in sourcing practices was observed between marketers of consumer versus industrial durable products.

Because of both their geographic proximity and the impending European Integration by the end of 1992, it is not surprising to find that some European firms export the products manufactured in other European countries outside of their home countries. However, this strategy is not used in any significant way. Among the non-European developed coun-

Figure 2–3
Multiple Sourcing of Products by Japanese Firms (N = 28)

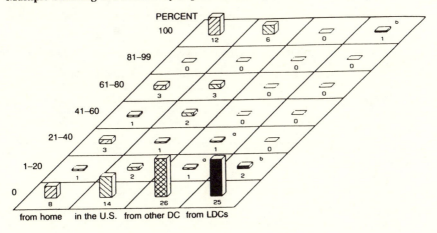

Notes: The cell number represents the frequency.

a. European country

b. Asian countries

tries (DCs), Japan and Canada are product sourcing sites for some European firms.

The reverse appears to be the case with Japanese firms. Two Japanese firms export their products to the United States from their European facilities. There are just a few cases in which the product is shipped from developing countries (LDCs), such as Brazil and Taiwan. Generally, in this sample of firms, product sourcing from developing countries is not a frequently selected alternative in global sourcing strategies.

For the sourcing strategies identified by respondents as *major*, the taxonomy of sourcing strategies allows measurement of the significance of components sourcing and product assembly on a global scale. Figures 2–2 and 2–3 show the final assembly locations from which the product is shipped to the U.S. market. Figures 2–4 and 2–5, on the other hand, reveal for a major sourcing strategy how components are produced and moved for manufacture of a product for sale in the United States. Although the taxonomy identifies 64 possible sourcing patterns, 13 different major sourcing patterns are reported in the European sample and 10 different major patterns in the Japanese sample. Although the remainder of this study focuses on what the respondents consider as major, the importance of other sourcing strategies in a multiple strategy mix should not be negated.

Several points are clear. First, assembly locations are generally major

Figure 2–4
Frequency of Major Sourcing Strategies for European Firms (N = 43)

Components Sourcing (C_{ij})		Home Internal	Home External	United States Internal	United States External	Other DC s Internal	Other DC s External	LDC s Internal	LDC s External
Home	Internal	9		2	1			1	
	External	7							
U.S.	Internal			2					
	External			8	7				1
Other DC s	Internal					2			
	External					1	1		
LDC s	Internal								
	External			1					

Header spanning: ASSEMBLY LOCATION (A_{kl})

Average Sourcing Patterns

$C_{11}A_{11}$ (w=74, x=16, y= 8, z= 1; INTERNAL COMPONENTS SOURCING=60%)
$C_{11}A_{21}$ (w=60, x=40, y= 0, z= 0; INTERNAL COMPONENTS SOURCING=72%)
$C_{11}A_{22}$ (w=90, x= 0, y=10, z= 0; INTERNAL COMPONENTS SOURCING=58%)
$C_{11}A_{41}$ (w=50, x=50, y= 0, z= 0; INTERNAL COMPONENTS SOURCING=60%)
$C_{12}A_{11}$ (w=81, x= 5, y=14; z= 0; INTERNAL COMPONENTS SOURCING=30%)
$C_{21}A_{21}$ (w=10, x=80, y=10, z= 0; INTERNAL COMPONENTS SOURCING=68%)
$C_{22}A_{21}$ (w=13, x=77, y= 6, z= 4; INTERNAL COMPONENTS SOURCING=43%)
$C_{22}A_{22}$ (w= 3, x=94, y= 3, z= 0; INTERNAL COMPONENTS SOURCING=15%)
$C_{22}A_{42}$ (w= 0, x= 0, y=40, z=60; INTERNAL COMPONENTS SOURCING= 5%)
$C_{31}A_{31}$ (w=10, x= 5, y=85, z= 0; INTERNAL COMPONENTS SOURCING=65%)
$C_{32}A_{31}$ (w= 0, x= 0, y=70, z=30; INTERNAL COMPONENTS SOURCING=13%)
$C_{32}C_{32}$ (w=10, x=30, y=60, z= 0; INTERNAL COMPONENTS SOURCING=21%)
$C_{42}A_{21}$ (w= 0, x=25, y= 0, z=75; INTERNAL COMPONENTS SOURCING=12%)

MEAN (w=39, x=42, y=14, z= 5; INTERNAL COMPONENTS SOURCING=41%)

components sourcing locations also, as indicated by a left-to-right diagonal distribution of sourcing patterns. These are primarily explained by the traditional paradigms of exporting ($C_{11}A_{11}$, $C_{12}A_{11}$, $C_{31}A_{31}$, $C_{32}A_{31}$, and $C_{42}A_{41}$), minority joint venture, subcontracting, or licensing ($C_{32}A_{32}$), and local manufacture by way of foreign direct investment ($C_{21}A_{21}$ and $C_{22}A_{21}$).

Figure 2–5
Frequency of Major Sourcing Strategies for Japanese Firms (N = 28)

Components Sourcing (C_{ij})		ASSEMBLY LOCATION (A_{kl})							
		Home		United States		Other DC s		LDC s	
		Internal	External	Internal	External	Internal	External	Internal	External
Home	Internal	14		4	1				
	External	1		1	1				
U.S.	Internal			1					
	External			3	1				
Other DC s	Internal								
	External								
LDC s	Internal								
	External							1	

<u>Average Sourcing Patterns</u>

$C_{11}A_{11}$ (w= 96, x= 1, y= 0, z= 3; INTERNAL COMPONENTS SOURCING=71%)
$C_{11}A_{21}$ (w= 64, x=36, y= 0, z= 0; INTERNAL COMPONENTS SOURCING=64%)
$C_{11}A_{22}$ (w= 50, x=30, y=20, z= 0; INTERNAL COMPONENTS SOURCING=59%)
$C_{12}A_{11}$ (w=100, x= 0, y= 0, z= 0; INTERNAL COMPONENTS SOURCING=38%)
$C_{12}A_{21}$ (w= 50, x=50, y= 0; z= 0; INTERNAL COMPONENTS SOURCING=25%)
$C_{12}A_{22}$ (w=100, x= 0, y= 0, z= 0; INTERNAL COMPONENTS SOURCING=13%)
$C_{21}A_{21}$ (w= 40, x=60, y= 0, z= 0; INTERNAL COMPONENTS SOURCING= n.a.)
$C_{22}A_{21}$ (w= 17, x=68, y= 3, z= 8; INTERNAL COMPONENTS SOURCING=32%)
$C_{22}A_{22}$ (w= 8, x=90, y= 2, z= 0; INTERNAL COMPONENTS SOURCING=12%)
$C_{42}A_{41}$ (w= 20, x=20, y= 0, z=60; INTERNAL COMPONENTS SOURCING=14%)

MEAN   (w=72, x=21, y= 2, z= 5; INTERNAL COMPONENTS SOURCING=56%)

Sourcing patterns off this diagonal are somewhat more complicated and offer interesting examples of complex global sourcing strategies in increasing use. For example, $C_{11}A_{21}$ involves a local manufacture of a product by a subsidiary in the United States with a majority of components produced and shipped to the subsidiary by its parent firm in a foreign country. $C_{42}A_{21}$ indicates a local manufacture of a product by a subsidiary in the United States with a majority of components produced and shipped to the subsidiary by unaffiliated or minority-owned firms in developing countries.

Second, in the case of local manufacture in the United States, Japanese firms are more likely to source major components from their home country than European firms. However, Japanese firms' dependence on their home sources appears to be declining as a result of the gradual transition of their strategy from export orientation to direct investment orientation and also as a means of coping with, and appeasing, the U.S. frustration over its massive trade imbalances between the two nations. It is documented elsewhere that Japanese firms' higher import propensity for components is not due to their national bias but to the relative inexperience of Japanese firms in foreign countries (Graham and Krugman 1989). It may also to some extent reflect Japanese reluctance to use U.S.-made components sourced locally from independent suppliers due to their unsatisfactory quality (*Fortune* 1986b).

Third, analysis of the origins of components (w, x, y, and z in Figures 2–4 and 2–5) reveals additional insight into sourcing strategy employed by European and Japanese multinational firms. Components can be sourced from various locations. One such example is a Japanese case of manufacture in the United States ($C_{22}A_{21}$), where a majority (68 percent) of the components was sourced in the United States while 17 percent originated from Japan, 7 percent from European countries, and 8 percent from developing countries. Even in the case of typical European direct exports ($C_{11}A_{11}$), components are sourced from all over the world, with about three-quarters of components sourced in their home countries, 16 percent from the United States, 8 percent from other European countries and sometimes from Japan, and 1 percent from developing countries. Although these examples are not dominant forms of sourcing practices, they substantiate the claim that global sourcing has become a reality. The following section explores the relationships between various sourcing strategies and their market performance.

The Product's Market Performance (PERFORM)

Table 2–4 shows the analysis of covariance (ANCOVA) results for the product's market performance (PERFORM). A covariance-controlled t-ratio for each variable was computed to determine whether each of the variables was statistically significant in explaining the product's market performance after accounting for the impact of the other variables. The extent of internal sourcing (INTSORC) was found to be a significant variable (p = .02) with a positive sign, while assembly location (AS-BLLOC) was not significant (p > .80). Internal assembly (INTASBL) is not significant in explaining the product's market performance (p > .60).

The extent of internal sourcing of major components is positively related

Table 2–4
Analysis-of-Covariance Results for the Product's Market Performance

PARAMETER		ESTIMATE[a]	STANDARD ERROR	t	SIGNIFICANCE
intercept		5.75	1.41	4.08	<.01
INTSORC		.02	.01	2.29	.02
INTASBL[b]	0	.31	.61	.51	.61
	1	.00	-	-	- -
ASBLLOC[c]	1	-.12	1.05	-.12	.91
	2	-.16	1.04	-.15	.88
	3	.00	-	-	-
SIZE		-.13	.17	-.75	.46
PLC		.26	.27	-.96	.34
ADAPT		-.49	.19	-2.59	.01
REGION[d]	0	.35	.45	.78	.44
	1	.00	-	-	-
TYPE[e]	0	.79	.67	1.18	.24
	1	.00	-	-	-

[a]Estimated coefficients are covariance-adjusted and in unstandardized form.

[b]0 = external assembly; 1 = internal assembly

[c]1 = assembly in the home country; 2 = assembly in the United States; 3 = assembly in the developing country (or countries). Also note that, for European firms, the home country includes their home bases and other European countries in the European Community; while for Japanese firms, the home country is Japan only.

[d]0 = European firms; 1 = Japanese firms

[e]1 = durable product; 0 = nondurable product

to the product's market performance, whereas the extent of internal assembly has no bearing on the product's market performance. Internal sourcing of major components appears to positively affect the product's market performance, whether the product is assembled by the internal members (e.g., subsidiaries, majority-owned joint ventures, or parent itself) of the multinational firm or by the external members (e.g., licensees, minority-participated joint ventures, or contracted independent manufacturers).

Internalization theory offers interesting insight into these findings. This theory views that as some markets (such as in complex components and intangible proprietary knowledge) are imperfect, the firm will bypass them and create an internal governance structure within the corporate system. The firm brings under its common ownership and control the activities which are linked by the markets (Buckley and Casson 1976; Williamson 1979). Imperfect markets, thus costly transactions, stem from barriers to the transfer of technology, tariff and nontariff barriers, inappropriately valued exchange rates, and information imperfections (Dunning 1977). Casson (1982) also stresses the importance of the firm's internal management of the quality specification of components used for manufacture in order to retain the goodwill and confidence of consumers.

This point can be elaborated on a little further from a viewpoint of the value-added chain. The most important advances in quality originate not from final assembly, but from production of components and subassemblies. Also, since most of the technology content of end products is in components and subassemblies, where earnings tend to be low, major manufacturers of technologically sophisticated products will have to compete more aggressively for world leadership in the development and production of key components (Kumpe and Bolwijn 1988).

The findings indicate that internalization of major components sourcing is more likely than is internalization of final product assembly. In other words, to maintain competitiveness, multinational firms tend to procure major components from within the corporate system around the world, while they may more likely contract out final assembly without hurting their competitiveness. It is also suggestive that unless manufacturers of end products strive to take over the components end of the business, they could be gradually outdone by those who dominate in development and production of sophisticated components. Such seems to be the case in the computer industry, where NEC, Hitachi, Toshiba, Motorola, Texas Instruments, and Intel, among others (all dominant integrated-circuit producers), are gradually edging into the computer assembly business.

The size (SIZE) of the multinational firm, the product life cycle stage (PLC), the product type (TYPE), and the national origin of the firm (NATION) have little significant bearing on the product's market performance ($p > .20$ for all). Particularly noteworthy is the result for PLC. By definition, PLC is indicative of the product's market performance on a global basis. PLC was expected to be negatively related to the product's market performance, but was found statistically insignificant. While there may be other explanations, this unexpected finding is compatible with Leroy's (1976) conclusion that the concept of international product cycle may be applicable at the aggregate industry level, but not at the firm level—a focal point of this research.

Interestingly, the level of product adaptation (ADAPT) is a very significant variable ($p = .01$) with a negative sign, indicating that the higher the level of product adaptation to the U.S. market, the lower the product's market performance. Although product adaptation is often a means by which to effectively meet the different needs and wants of foreign customers, the high level of product adaptation apparently worsens the product's market performance. This is true for both consumer and industrial durable products. The possible reasons for this result are several. Product adaptation may be viewed as a reactive, rather than proactive, strategic concept (Keegan 1969). As noted earlier, competitive reactions may be sufficiently swift as to nullify transitory market-customized advantages. Further, a high level of product adaptation may make it difficult for the multinational firm to reap economies of scale in production and marketing on a global basis. This finding strongly supports an argument for the development of a globally acceptable product that would not require any major adaptation to foreign markets (Levitt 1983).

CONCLUSIONS AND IMPLICATIONS

In response to the primary objectives in this chapter, the following two major findings are reported. First, categorization of sourcing practices by European and Japanese multinational firms shows a limited number of sourcing strategies are in actual use. As expected, Japanese firms are somewhat more export-oriented than European firms.

Second, the relationship between sourcing strategies and the product's market performance involves several interesting findings. A product's market performance in the United States is influenced by the extent to which major components are sourced internally. However, performance is neither affected by the source (internal/external) of assembly nor by the assembly locations. Whether the product is finally assembled by the internal members (e.g., subsidiaries) of the multinational firm or by the external members (e.g., licensees, minority-owned affiliates, or subcontractors) does not appear to affect the product's market performance. Neither does the assembly location.

The findings provide two major managerial implications. They involve the nature of global sourcing strategies and the role of those strategies in determining the product's market performance.

Nature of Global Sourcing Strategies

It is widely recognized that the expansion of European and Japanese firms into U.S. production through direct investment has been staggering, while that of U.S. firms' direct investment abroad has slowed since the 1970s (Negandhi and Baliga 1981; U.S. Department of Commerce 1982). Now that many European and Japanese multinational firms have affiliates established in many parts of the world, they have become capable of tapping various resources on a global scale, if they opt to do so. Global strategy mandates that the affiliates of the multinational firm become part of a system in manufacturing, marketing, and financial management rather than operating independently of others.

Global sourcing strategy has been conceived of as a set of alternative ways of serving foreign markets. In fact, many firms simultaneously use a mix of multiple sourcing strategies in marketing their products in the United States. Multiple sourcing generally requires a high level of coordination between parent firms and their foreign affiliates when setting corporate product policies and production schedules on a global scale. More than 80 percent of the firms participating in this study have a parent company policy of developing either standardized products worldwide or standardized products worldwide with some specific adaptation for some markets, if necessary. A high level of product standardization within the corporate system facilitates the parent and its foreign affiliates' coordination of their worldwide production schedule in a way that the U.S. market can be served from various sourcing locations, depending upon the level of U.S. demand for the product.

Market Performance

The product's life cycle stage is determined by competitive and market forces. Contrary to the prediction of the international product cycle paradigm, this study has found that a product's market performance is neither related to its assembly location nor is it influenced by who assembles the product. If the parent's continuing control over the manufacturing process is not necessary, some form of external assembly (such as minority-participated joint venture or licensing) may lead to a level of product performance not different than if the parent or its subsidiary assembled the product. This indicates that some configurations of sourcing strategies exist that do not sacrifice market performance. However, this study did not examine to what extent product adaptation is required due to any possible uniqueness (or lack thereof) of the U.S. market. In general, the finding is consistent with the argument calling for standardization on a global scale to the extent possible in order to increase market performance.

Global sourcing appears to be strongly supported by standardization of the core components and the product. The results suggest that standardization enhances the firms' economies of scale and scope and thus their ability to integrate the resources of various countries into a global sourcing strategy. Despite a small degree of components sourcing and product assembly in developing countries, the products sourced from the developing countries enjoyed high market performance in the United States.

Overall, the results generally point toward the viability of global sourcing strategies. While certain cross-national sourcing strategies can enhance market performance, there is no guarantee that specific sourcing strategy implementation will always yield superior results. However, this study empirically confirms that competitive advantage can be gained through global sourcing, *provided* that managers can skillfully execute it.

This chapter has focused on the market performance implications of various sourcing strategies employed by European and Japanese multinational firms serving the U.S. market. These foreign multinational firms have stepped up international sourcing of components and finished products. An increasing portion of global competition is shaped by the European and Japanese multinational firms with due emphasis on product quality and manufacturing. Thus, it is an opportune time to examine the link among their product development, manufacturing, and sourcing activities. This issue will be explored in Chapter 3.

LIMITATIONS

This study was cross-sectional in nature and presented the results based on a snapshot of the sourcing strategies of European and Japanese multinational firms. Cross-sectional research may not truly represent the dynamic nature of global sourcing strategy, which could change over time. The inclusion of a life cycle variable may not have fully accounted for time-dependent changes. Thus, a longitudinal study of sourcing practices is strongly called for. Given the usual methodological and budgetary constraints, such an effort will likely be a descriptive case-study type of research, tracing the development over time of a product with a strong focus on how and from where components are sourced.

A second limitation relates to the nature of the sample. This study has found that a high level of product adaptation worsens market performance for consumer and industrial durable products. However, nondurable products (such as packaged food products) may not be as easily subject to standardization policy as durable products because nondurable products are more likely to be culture-bound and associated with older consumption pattern (Whitelock 1987).

Finally, a third limitation is an implicit methodological assumption that the parent firm can effectively control its affiliates only if the parent owns

more than 50 percent of their outstanding corporate stocks. The parent
firm's long-lasting contractual relationships with independent firms could
prove to be equally effective in controlling the operations of these inde-
pendents, as evidenced by Japanese "keiretsu" or industrial groups (Kotabe 1984).

In a keiretsu arrangement, the core firm usually owns a nominal to
moderate portion of its affiliates, and is capable of administering them as
if they were virtually satellite subsidiaries. If components sourcing from
these nominally owned firms had been considered "internal," particularly
in the case of Japanese firms, then the strategic importance of internal
sourcing could have been all the more conspicuous. For the interested
reader, the issue of keiretsu-sourcing will be critically examined in the
appendix that follows.

APPENDIX: SOURCING TRANSACTIONS IN A JAPANESE INDUSTRIAL GROUP

At a recent conference on Japanese business, several prominent Japanese businessmen from a number of giant electronics companies affiliated
with Japan's much-touted keiretsu, or industrial groups, appeared puzzled
by American academicians' perception that the inner workings of industrial groups are nearly as cohesive as those of pre-war Zaibatsu. The
cohesive relationships among member companies (i.e., a major bank, a
major trading company, and several major manufacturing companies) in
a keiretsu are considered to have greatly contributed to Japan's dramatic
postwar economic growth by dispersing risk through the accumulation of
relationships to cushion shock in times of economic downturn as well as
by establishing a virtual barrier to entry to Japan by foreign competitors
(Saso and Kirby 1982; Nakatani 1984; Prestowitz 1988). The Japanese
businessmen thought that the Americans' understanding of the cooperative nature of keiretsu arrangements was blown out of proportion. This
led me to wonder why the American perception, or understanding, differs
from Japanese businessmen's.

Numerous books have been published on Japanese business management approaches and strategies in recent years (e.g., Prestowitz 1988;
Christopher 1983; Clark 1979; Davidson 1983; DeMente 1981; Gibney
1975; Kahn and Pepper 1980; Ohmae 1982; Ouchi 1981; Pascale and Athos
1981; Vogel 1979). These books and others have helped us understand
the Japanese culture, language, and the historical development of Japanese businesses and industrial groups as well as their corporate strategies.
In general, the development of industrial groups is considered to be rooted
in such unique sociocultural factors as the vertical and group-oriented
structure of Japanese society (Nakane 1970). Measures such as intercorporate shareholdings, interlocking directorates and "old boy" networks

of major university graduates are often used to demonstrate close working relationships within an industrial group. However, Japanese businessmen involved in day-to-day business deals both within and outside their industrial groups see something different than those measures convey.

In this appendix, we will examine business relationships within an industrial group from the perspective of a member company's business transactions with other group members in order to bridge a perceptual gap between Japanese businessmen and American academicians. This will help us better understand the nature of Japan's industrial groups. First, historical development and significance of keiretsu arrangements will be reviewed. Then, to illustrate business transactions within an industrial group, focus will be placed on a major electronics company considered to be a "star" company in an industrial group that originated from one of the major prewar Zaibatsu.

The Origin of the Keiretsu Arrangement

Until the end of World War II, the Zaibatsu, or the powerful financial combines, had owned and controlled key industries including railroads, communication facilities, mining, and shipbuilding—all strategically important for Japan's push for industrialization. Strongly influenced by Japan's "trade-or-die" mentality, Zaibatsu-affiliated trading companies functioned as core trading arms for the Zaibatsu to sustain the lifeline of the burgeoning, resource-scarce Japanese economy by importing raw materials for manufacturing firms and exporting those manufacturers' finished products (Kotabe 1984).

Soon after the war, the Zaibatsu groups and their affiliates were dissolved by the Allied Occupation Authorities for two significant reasons. First, Zaibatsu-affiliated trading companies in close collaboration with other Zaibatsu members through collective decision making had served as a means of nationalistic interest supporting Japan's militarism during World War II. Second, the Zaibatsu had also virtually monopolized prewar Japanese international commerce through their trading companies. However, because of a series of postwar political events, including the Cold War between the United States and the Soviet Union and the Korean War, the reunification of the Zaibatsu was implicitly encouraged by the Occupation Authorities as a means of mobilizing Japan's industrial resources to meet the supply needs of the Allies (Kojima and Ozawa 1984). The postwar Japanese government subsequently abolished the Occupation ban on intercorporate shareholdings and interlocking directorates and allowed a new form of alliances called keiretsu or industrial groups to be formed.

Industrial groups that emerged from this reunification were more loosely affiliated than the original Zaibatsu. Each industrial group is led by a

general trading company, a major bank, and a number of leading manufacturing firms. In contrast with the direct corporate governance of the
prewar Zaibatsu family with a close tie with the government, the postwar
industrial groups have a more indirect means of coordination among leading member companies. Each industrial group has established a Presidents' Council consisting of CEOs of member companies that meets on
a regular basis, not only for socialization purposes but also for exchange
of ideas and informal discussion of their corporate planning and coordination. Occasionally, government representatives from the Ministry of
International Trade and Industry participate in an informal Presidents'
Council meeting. Today, six leading industrial groups (i.e., Mitsui, Mitsubishi, Sumitomo, Sanwa, Fuyo, and Dai-Ichi Kangyo) alone account
for about a quarter of the total assets and sales of all Japanese business
corporations.

Therefore, the size and economic influence of these industrial groups
are undoubtedly enormous. Their economies of scale in financing, production, and marketing and those of scope in pooling of technology and
know-how form a formidable threat to foreign competition in Japan as
well as abroad. To Americans, keiretsu arrangements are unfair and thus
are a form of nontariff barrier. In the United States, the Glass-Steagall
Act of 1934 still prohibits bank holding companies from owning a commercial business venture (except for an international trading company
involved principally in exports, thanks to the Export Trading Company
Act of 1984), while the Clayton Act of 1914 prohibits certain monopolistic
practices such as exclusive dealing, intercorporate shareholdings, and
interlocking directorates. Not only are these practices common in Japan
but, above all, they allegedly represent the crux of the inner workings of
industrial groups.

If member firms in an industrial group do function as a collective organization for its collective good with a coordinated set of objectives, two
inferences about Japanese markets could be made. First, it could be extremely difficult to establish a business relationship with any keiretsu
member because of its tendencies to deal with other keiretsu members.
Second, once a foreign company established a relationship with a keiretsu
member, it should facilitate this foreign company's access to other keiretsu members for increased business (Coughlan and Scheer 1987).

If a keiretsu company sources a significant amount of raw materials
and components from, and reciprocally sells its products to other member
companies, then a case may be made that the industrial group is insulated.
If this is the case, then it will be difficult for foreign firms to enter the
Japanese market successfully without somehow aligning themselves with
one or more of the industrial groupings. Often when foreign firms experience difficulty in developing ties with Japanese firms to gain market

entry into Japan, they consider such industrial groupings a form of non-tariff barrier (Lawrence 1987).

A Case of an Electronics Company in an Industrial Group

Takeshita Kogyo (a disguised name[2]), founded in 1878, is a leading global supplier of a broad range of communications systems and equipment, computers and industrial electronic systems, and semiconductor devices as well as home electronics products. With a total work force of 120,000, Takeshita Kogyo and its subsidiaries and affiliates operate 53 plants in Japan and 32 plants in 15 other countries.

Takeshita Kogyo is affiliated with the Maekawa Group. Typical of Japan's keiretsu, the Maekawa Group has major companies in such fields as banking, insurance, trading, steel, electronics, glass, oil, forestry, and metals, with overall group sales exceeding $200 billion. Some 30 percent of Takeshita Kogyo's stock is held by other Maekawa keiretsu companies, and Takeshita Kogyo returns the favor by keeping more than 35 percent of its own shareholdings in other group members. In addition, some 30 percent of its long- and short-term loans are provided by group institutions. These percentages differ for other companies, but the pattern is generally similar.

CEO's of leading companies of the Maekawa Group are represented in a Presidents' Council, called the "Hasu-no-Kai" (Water Lily Council), and hold regular meetings for purposes of social interaction and informal dissemination of strategic information among the member companies. A tendency toward group autonomy generally results in strong competition among industrial groups. Therefore, the Maekawa Group, like other keiretsu, attempts to have a strong position in every major sector of the economy. Since Takeshita Kogyo is viewed as a star high-technology company within the Maekawa Group, the company has been provided with financial as well as moral support by the Group.

Takeshita Kogyo sources supply of various materials from as well as sells finished products to other member companies. These intrakeiretsu business transactions are shown in Table 2–5. Of its total materials purchase of $16.5 billion in 1987, Takeshita Kogyo's purchases from other member companies accounted for $0.3 billion. In other words, Takeshita Kogyo's intrakeiretsu sourcing ratio was merely 1.6 percent. Maekawa Trading Company was the most important materials supplier for Takeshita Kogyo. Although the breakdown of original sources of materials purchased from the member trading company is unknown, the trading company's role as a materials supplier appears limited. Similarly, Takeshita's total sales in 1987 were $19.5 billion, of which about 0.4 billion, or a meager 1.9 percent, was accounted for by its sales to member companies.

Table 2–5
Takeshita Kogyo's Business Transactions in 1986 Inside and Outside the
Maekawa Keiretsu (in millions of dollars: 130 yen/$)

	Sales to	Purchase from
MAEKAWA KEIRETSU		
Maekawa Bank	14	0
Maekawa Metal	92	1
Maekawa Life Insurance	34	0
Maekawa Marine & Fire Insurance	29	0
Maekawa Trust & Banking	25	0
Yoshida Sheet Glass	16	3
Maekawa Chemical	15	1
Maekawa Trading	12	145
Maekawa Heavy Industries	10	35
Maekawa Electric Industries	9	47
Maekawa Cement	3	0
Maekawa Metal Mining	2	23
Other Member Companies	5	14
Total Transactions within Maekawa Group	365 (1.9%)	269 (1.6%)
Transactions within Takeshita Kogyo Group	19,112 (98.1%)	6,675 (40.5%)
Transactions outside the Groups		9,546 (57.9%)
TOTAL TRANSACTIONS	19,477	16,489

Maekawa Bank, Maekawa Metal, Maekawa Life Insurance, and Maekawa
Trust & Banking have been considered the group's "key accounts" by
Takeshita Kogyo and absorbed over 70 percent of its intra-keiretsu sales.

Despite the intercorporate shareholdings and interlocking directorates,
among others, between Takeshita Kogyo and the rest of the Maekawa
Group member companies, their business transactions have been ex-

tremely far from significant. To further investigate this weak transactional relationship, Takeshita Kogyo's intrakeiretsu sales of computers was examined. Over the years, Takeshita Kogyo has focused its corporate effort on integration of computers and communications, and is increasingly well positioned to meet diverse needs in worldwide markets. Yet, Takeshita Kogyo's "key account" companies still heavily rely on IBM and other computer makers, while many other members of the Maekawa Group have adopted Takeshita Kogyo's computer systems. For example, Maekawa Bank uses IBM, NCR, and UNIVAC, among others, as well as Takeshita Kogyo's. On the other hand, Maekawa Metal and Maekawa Trust & Banking operate only on IBM computers. Despite the strategic importance of computers and communications business to Takeshita Kogyo, its computers have not become mainstream in the Maekawa Group, although there is always a possibility that they will. In addition, a number of member companies including Maekawa Life Insurance have established a consortium with IBM Japan to develop a new communications network independently. This further illustrates rather independent relationships among member companies within the same keiretsu.

All in all, it may be concluded that the Maekawa Group does not constitute any measurable barrier to entry by foreign competitors, barring Japanese cultural tendency that Japanese companies prefer domestic vendors to foreign vendors. Even this cultural tendency may be questioned on the basis of inferior quality of components and products from abroad (*Fortune* 1986b).

Where Does Takeshita Kogyo Source Supply of Materials and Components?

This question casts an important dimension to keiretsu arrangements. A keiretsu not only exists across industries (e.g., the Maekawa Group), but also exists within nonfinancial industries. The keiretsu arrangement within a nonfinancial industry is often called "shihon keiretsu" (capital group) or "kigyo keiretsu" (enterprise group). Kigyo keiretsu consists of a nonfinancial parent company and a set of subsidiary firms tied by ownership, management interlockings, and credit policy to the parent (Hadley 1970). In a way, kigyo keiretsu constitutes a vertically, yet loosely, integrated manufacturing network.

Takeshita Kogyo has its own vertically integrated group of affiliates. As of 1988, Takeshita Kogyo Group consists of Takeshita Kogyo as the parent company and a total of 94 affiliates (28 manufacturing companies, 31 software development companies, and 35 sales companies). What is intriguing about Takeshita Kogyo Group is the way affiliates are formed. Although Takeshita Kogyo itself is an integrated electronics company, performing all manufacturing, software development, and sales within the company is not necessarily the most efficient and cost-effective. There is a point in every aspect of productive activity beyond which diseconomies of scale set in (see, for example, Mallen 1973). Takeshita Kogyo has centrifugally spun off various activities when diseconomies have set in. As a result, Takeshita Kogyo has formed a consortium of specialized affiliates. Takeshita Kogyo's spin-off policy has solved the following two major problems: (1) functional specialization is made possible for technical as well as cost efficiency: (2) such resource bottlenecks as limited plant size and labor are reduced as spun-off affiliates have been relocated throughout Japan and abroad.

This spinoff-based integration contrasts sharply with integrations observed in the United States, which are based mostly on mergers and buyouts. It is no wonder Takeshita Kogyo's affiliates are intimately linked to the parent company through interlockings of personnel and mutual trust as employees at the parent company have been spun off and assigned to affiliates.

As a result of this integration, Takeshita Kogyo has purchased $6.7 billion worth of supplies of materials and components from member affiliates of the Takeshita Kogyo Group in 1986 (see Table 2–5). This internal sourcing amounted to over 40 percent of Takeshita Kogyo's total supply needs worth $16.5 billion in 1986. Takeshita Kogyo's reliance on its affiliates for materials and components also has been increasing steadily over the years. One possible reason for increased reliance can be found in Takeshita's increased R&D-intensity. R&D-intensive firms are likely to create an internal governance structure within the corporate system and internalize transactions involving proprietary knowledge and components to maximize value added by them (Buckley and Casson 1976; Dunning 1977; Williamson 1979). A second reason for internalization is the importance of the firm's internal management of the quality specification of components used for manufacture in order to retain the goodwill and confidence of consumers (Casson 1979). Thus, the more R&D-intensive the firm becomes, the more internal transactions occur within its integrated corporate structure.

In addition, loyalty of affiliates to the parent company is further reinforced by the just-in-time manufacturing system, which often extends beyond the subsidiary line and includes a group of firms that have come to accept the leader company's goals as their own through socialization and compensation according to length of service and other nonperformance criteria (Ouchi 1980). It is also true with sales affiliates that organize distribution channels for Takeshita Kogyo's products. For example, Takeshita Kogyo sells about 90 percent of its semiconductor output through two captive distributors in Japan. Therefore, those foreign competitors that are anticipating entry to or have already entered Japan face a formidable entry barrier as they have to establish their own distribution networks.

Increase in internal transactions due to increase in R&D intensity, just-in-time vertical arrangement, and captive distribution systems, among others, are what foreign firms are afraid of as impenetrable competitive threats and also criticize as nontariff barriers to entry. However, they may not be considered either an unfair or illegal means of blocking out foreign competition. It is not simply because the same barriers face Japanese firms outside the arrangement, but more importantly because *they represent functional relationships which help reduce transactional uncertainty and opportunism among members, thus assuring mutual trust and efficiency* (Williamson 1979).

Summary and Conclusions

We have examined the Japanese keiretsu arrangement from one company's perspective. Keiretsu exist in two ways: interindustry and intraindustry. Maekawa Group is a keiretsu of an interindustry kind to which Takeshita Kogyo belongs. Takeshita Kogyo itself has its own vertically arranged intraindustry kigyo keiretsu or enterprise group of firms functionally related along the value-added chain. Although reminiscent of prewar Zaibatsu in the form of intercorporate shareholdings, interlocking directorates, and an "old boy" network of major university graduates, a interindustry keiretsu appears to have lost substance to a much larger extent than is commonly thought. As one Japanese businessman admits, *higoro no kankei* (literally, daily relationships implying golfing, social drinking after work, among others, as well as high-level Presidents' Council meetings) somewhat facilitates business relations among member companies, but constitutes little more than neighborly friendship.

We have shown that vertically arranged enterprise groups, such as Takeshita Kogyo Group, have become more significant in Japan. An enterprise group is made up mostly of both component affiliate firms that have been spun off from a parent company and those that have come into long-term working relationships so as to achieve economies of scale through specialization. This type of vertical integration (more aptly, vertical disintegration-cum-reintegration) contrasts sharply with those observed in the United States through buyouts and mergers. Long-term working relationships and resultant mutual trust likely emerge more strongly in Japan's enterprise groups than in vertically integrated companies in the United States.

This enterprise group arrangement may form an invincible barrier to foreign competitors entering Japanese markets since it literally controls all phases of the value added chain from components sourcing to manufacturing to distribution.[3] The importance of attaining competitive strength in various phases of the value added chain has been well documented elsewhere (Kogut 1985; Porter 1986; Robinson 1987). Japanese firms have started extending their enterprise group strategy to foreign markets, as exemplified by Japanese suppliers of automobile components investing in the United States to follow Japanese auto manufacturers operating in the United States. This is one of the sources of Japanese competitiveness both in Japan and abroad.

NOTES

1. This variable was originally defined in two ways. INTSORC1 represented the percentage of the value of all the components in the product sourced internally, while INTSORC2 excludes from INTSORC1 the value of the components that are "standardized." Since a preliminary analysis indicated that INTSORC2 was a better predictor than INTSORC1 of the product's market performance (PER-FORM), INTSORC2 (INTSORC, henceforth) was used in the analysis.

2. All data are disguised to assure confidentiality. Disguised values shown here are derived by multiplying real values by a certain common factor so as to preserve ratios. For example, Company A's sale to Companies B and C of $10 million and $5 million, respectively, might be represented by multiplying these values by a common factor of .8. The reported data would then show sales of $8 million and $4 million, respectively. This system of computation preserves all *ratios* in that Company A sold twice as much to Company B as to Company C.

3. A good example of a European enterprise group is Benetton SpA of Italy, for which much of the above discussion holds. Benetton owns or strongly influences the value chain right from knitting to retailing of sweaters and other clothes. In this respect, Italy is becoming known as the "Japan of Europe."

REFERENCES

Armstrong, J. Scott and Terry S. Overton (1977). "Estimating Nonresponse Bias in Mail Surveys." *Journal of Marketing Research,* 14 (August), 396–402.

Bartlett, Christopher A. and Sumantra Ghoshal (1989). *Managing Across Borders: The Transnational Solution.* Boston: Harvard Business School Press.

Buckley, Peter J. (1979). "The Foreign Investment Decision." *Management Bibliographies and Reviews,* 5.

Buckley, Peter J. and Mark Casson (1976). *The Future of the Multinational Enterprise.* London: MacMillan.

Business International (1982). *The Effects of U.S. Corporate Foreign Investment 1970–1980.* New York: Business International Corporation, May.

Buzzell, Robert D., Bradley T. Gale, and Ralph G.M. Sultan (1975). "Market Share—A Key to Profitability." *Harvard Business Review,* January–February.

Casson, Mark (1979). *Alternatives to Multinational Enterprise.* New York: Holmes & Meier.

——— (1982). "Transaction Costs and the Theory of the Multinational Enterprise." In *New Theories of the Multinational Enterprise,* Alan M. Rugman, ed. London: Croom Helm, 24–54.

Christopher, Robert C. (1983). *The Japanese Mind.* New York: Linden Press.

Clark, Rodney (1979). *The Japanese Company.* New Haven, CT: Yale University Press.

Coughlan, Anne T. and Lisa K. Scheer (1987). "Keiretsu Strength in Japanese Industrial Organization: Empirical Evidence on the Decision Participation Framework." A Working Paper, Northwestern University.

Davidson, William H. (1982). *Global Strategic Management.* New York: John Wiley.

——— (1983). *The Amazing Race: Winning the Technorivalry with Japan.* New York: John Wiley.

Dell'Osso, Fillipo (1990). "Defending a Dominant Position in a Technology Led Environment." *Business Strategy Review,* Summer, 77–86.

DeMente, Boye (1981). *The Japanese Way of Doing Business.* Englewood Cliffs, NJ: Prentice-Hall.

Dunning, John H. (1977). "Trade, Location of Economic Activity and the MNE: A Search for an Eclectic Approach." In *The International Allocation of Economic Activity,* Bertil Ohlin, Per-Ove Hesselborn, and Per Magnus Wijkman, eds. New York: Holmes and Meier, 395–418.

Edwards, Anthony (1984). *How to Make Offshore Manufacturing Pay.* Special Report no. 171. London: The Economist Publications.

Fayerweather, John (1969). *International Business Management: A Conceptual Framework.* New York: McGraw-Hill.

Fortune (1986a). "The FORTUNE International 500 and the World Economy," August 4, 169–200.

——— (1986b). "Are Japanese Managers Biased Against Americans?" September 1, 72–75.

Franko, Lawrence G. (1978). "Multinationals: The End of U.S. Dominance." *Harvard Business Review,* 56 (November–December), 93–101.

Gibney, Frank (1975). *Japan: The Fragile Superpower.* Rutland, VT: Charles E. Tuttle.

Graham, Edward M. and Paul R. Krugman (1989). *Foreign Direct Investment in the United States.* Washington, DC: Institute for International Economics.

Grosse, Robert (1985). "An Imperfect Competition Theory of the MNE." *Journal of International Business Studies,* 16 (Spring), 57–80.

Hadley, Eleanor M. (1970). *Antitrust in Japan.* Princeton, NJ: Princeton University Press.

Helleiner, Gerald K. (1981). *Intra-Firm Trade and the Developing Countries.* New York: St. Martin's Press.

International Directory of Corporate Affiliations 1985/1986 (1985). Wilmette, IL: National Register Publishing.

Kahn, Herman and Thomas Pepper (1980). *The Japanese Challenge: The Success and Failure of Economic Success.* New York: William Morrow.

Keegan, Warren J. (1969). "Multinational Product Planning: Strategic Alternatives." *Journal of Marketing,* 33 (January), 58–62.

Kogut, Bruce (1985). "Designing Global Strategies: Comparative and Competitive Value-Added Chains." *Sloan Management Review,* 26 (Summer), 15–28.

Kojima, Kiyoshi and Terutomo Ozawa (1984). *Japan's General Trading Companies: Merchants of Economic Development.* Paris: OECD.

Kotabe, Masaaki (1984). "Changing Roles of the Sogo Shoshas, the Manufacturing Firms, and the MITI in the Context of the Japanese 'Trade or Die' Mentality." *Columbia Journal of World Business,* 19 (Fall), 33–42.

Kotler, Philip, Liam Fahey, and Somkid Jatusripitak (1985). *The New Competition.* Englewood Cliffs, NJ: Prentice-Hall.

Kumpe, Ted and Piet T. Bolwijn (1988). "Manufacturing: The New Case for Vertical Integration." *Harvard Business Review,* 66 (March–April), 75–81.

Lawrence, Robert Z. (1987). "Imports in Japan: Closed Markets or Minds?" *Brookings Papers on Economic Activity,* 21, 517–548.

Leroy, Georges (1976). *Multinational Product Strategy: A Taxonomy for Analysis of Worldwide Product Innovation and Diffusion.* New York: Praeger.

Levitt, Theodore (1983). "The Globalization of Markets." *Harvard Business Review,* 61 (May–June), 92–102.

Mallen, Bruce (1973). "Functional Spin-Off: A Key to Anticipating Change in Distribution Structure." *Journal of Marketing,* 37 (July), 18–25.

Moxon, Richard W. (1974). *Offshore Production in the Less Developed Countries,* Bulletin No. 98–99. New York: New York University Institute of Finance.

Nakane, Chie (1970). *Japanese Society.* Berkeley: University of California Press.

Nakatani, Iwao (1984). "The Economic Role of Financial Corporate Grouping." In *The Economic Analysis of the Japanese Firm,* M. Aoki, ed. Amsterdam: Elsevier Science Publishers, 227–258.

Negandhi, Anant R. and B. R. Baliga (1981). *Tables Are Turning: German and Japanese Multinational Companies in the United States.* Cambridge, MA: Oelgeschlager, Gunn, and Hain.

Negandhi, Anant R. and Martin Welge (1984). *Beyond Theory Z.* London: JAI Press.

Ohmae, Kenichi (1982). *The Mind of the Strategist: The Art of Japanese Business.* New York: McGraw-Hill.

——— (1985). *Triad Power.* New York: The Free Press.

OECD (1985). *OECD Environmental Data: Compendium 1985.* Paris.

Ouchi, William (1980). "Markets, Bureaucracies, and Clans." *Administrative Science Quarterly,* 25 (March), 129–141.

——— (1981). *Theory Z: How American Business Can Meet the Japanese Challenge.* Boston: Addison-Wesley.

Pascale, Richard T. and Anthony G. Athos (1981). *The Art of Japanese Management.* New York: Simon & Schuster.

Porter, Michael E., ed. (1986). *Competition in Global Industries.* Boston, MA: Harvard Business School Press.

Prestowitz, Clyde V., Jr. (1988). *Trading Places: How We Allowed Japan to Take the Lead.* New York: Basic Books.

Robinson, Richard D., ed. (1987). *Direct Foreign Investment: Costs and Benefits.* New York: Praeger.

Root, Franklin R. (1987). *Entry Strategies for International Markets.* Lexington, MA: Lexington Books.

Saso, Mary and Stuart Kirby (1982). *Japanese Industrial Competition to 1990.* Cambridge, MA: Abt Books.

Schlender, Brenton R. (1990). "Who's Ahead in the Computer Wars." *Fortune,* February 12, 59–66.

Servan-Schreiber, J.-J. (1968). *The American Challenge.* New York: Atheneum.

United Nations Center on Transnational Corporations (1988). *Transnational Corporations in World Development: Trends and Perspectives.* New York: United Nations.

U.S. Department of Commerce (1982). *Survey of Current Business,* April, 34–36.

Vernon, Raymond (1966). "International Investment and International Trade in the Product Cycle." *Quarterly Journal of Economics,* 80 (May), 190–207.

—————— (1974). "The Location of Economic Activity." In *Economic Analysis and the Multinational Enterprise,* John H. Dunning, ed. London: George Allen and Unwin, 89–114.

—————— (1979). "The Product Cycle Hypothesis in a New International Environment." *Oxford Bulletin of Economics and Statistics,* 41 (November), 255–267.

Vogel, Ezra F. (1979). *Japanese Number One: Lesson for America.* Cambridge, MA: Harvard University Press.

Whitelock, Jeryl M. (1987). "Global Marketing and the Case for International Product Standardization." *European Journal of Marketing,* 21, 32–44.

Williamson, Oliver E. (1979). "Transactions-Cost Economics: the Governance of Contractual Relations." *Journal of Law and Economics,* 22 (October), 233–261.

Yoshino, Michael Y. (1976). *Japan's Multinational Enterprises.* Cambridge, MA: Harvard University Press.

Chapter 3

Product and
Process Innovations

Global competition has become a central issue for many multinational firms, irrespective of nationality. The emergence of European and Japanese multinational firms has created a new competitive environment, calling for globalization of corporate strategy (Kotler, Fahey, and Jatusripitak 1985; Levitt 1983; Ohmae 1985; Porter 1986). Numerous advantages are increasingly recognized in creating and integrating various business operations across national boundaries (Kogut 1985; Porter 1986; Robinson 1987; Prahalad and Doz 1987). This has resulted in an increasing number of multinational firms engaged in sourcing of components and products on a global scale. Indeed, cross-national marketing transactions encompass both the buying (i.e., sourcing) and selling (i.e., market selection) aspects of the exchange process. Although marketing institutions are examined primarily in their roles as sellers rather than as buyers, the buying side of the exchange process should not be ignored (Kotler and Levy 1973).

As demonstrated in Chapter 2, European and Japanese multinational firms have been pursuing integrated sourcing to a greater extent than before, because such an operation enables them to exploit not only their competitive advantages but also comparative advantages of various countries more efficiently than would otherwise be possible (Kogut 1985). The configuration and coordination necessary for successful sourcing strategy have of late received an increasing amount of research attention (Porter 1986). However, there is no empirical study investigating sourcing coordination issues centering on management of innovative activities in product and manufacturing process development on a global basis. In this chapter, sourcing strategy is examined from a perspective of a strategic arrangement by which to coordinate product innovations, manufacturing process innovations, and sourcing of components supplied for production. Furthermore, it is expected that successful management of these three related activities will jointly determine corporate performance.

PURPOSE OF THE CHAPTER

A wide range of sourcing strategy patterns or *configurations* was discussed in detail in Chapter 2. Sourcing configurations are suggestive of the firm's market performance, but they may not offer sufficient conditions for causal interpretation. Therefore, in order to explore underlying reasons for sourcing performance, this chapter delves deeper into the intricacies of global sourcing strategy.

The purpose of this chapter is twofold. First, a taxonomy of sourcing strategies developed in Chapter 2 will be reformulated for examining a wide range of alternative sourcing strategies linking product development and manufacturing activities (innovation-sourcing linkages). This is necessary in order to highlight coordination issues involving such linkages. Second, performance implications of management of innovation-sourcing linkages will be empirically explored.

It is to be noted, however, that not all multinational firms can pursue sourcing strategy on a global scale (Toyne and Walters 1989, pp. 5–7). First, some firms are newcomers in international marketing and treat foreign markets primarily as secondary outlets for their products. For such firms "going international" for the first time, integrated sourcing activities may well be beyond their means and scope—at least for the time being. Second, multinational firms marketing highly culture-bound products (such as packaged food products) may neither be conducive to nor benefit from global integration of sourcing activities as tastes are vastly different (Boddewyn, Soehl, and Picard 1986; Whitelock 1987). Also, by definition, "global" service companies (e.g., McKinsey, Federal Express, and McDonald's) are constrained in their serving options.

An increasing portion of global competition is shaped by European and Japanese multinational firms with due emphasis on product quality and manufacturing (Franko 1978; Negandhi and Welge 1984; Kotler et al. 1985; Vernon 1986). Therefore, it is an opportune time to examine the link among their product development, manufacturing, and sourcing activities in pursuit of rationalization advantages on a global basis. Those European and Japanese multinational firms marketing products (excluding highly culture-bound products) in the United States are subjects of this chapter.

AN OVERVIEW

As discussed in Chapter 2, sourcing strategy has reemerged as an important strategic issue in response to global competition in recent years.

Some conceptual justifications for integrated sourcing have been developed along the value chain concept in recent years (see, for example, Kogut 1985 and Porter 1986). So far, most of the recent research in sourcing strategy has dealt with various managerial issues, ranging from structural complexity (Starr 1984) and operational complexity of international sourcing (Mascarenhas 1984) to reasons for international sourcing (Monczka and Giunipero 1984) and to cost advantage/disadvantage arguments (Hahn, Kim, and Kim 1986), among others.

To maintain competitive advantage, multinational firms, both U.S. and foreign alike, have begun looking beyond their national boundaries for sourcing of components and/or finished products. There are many alternative sourcing options for these firms to choose from. They range from establishing a buyer/seller relationship across national boundaries to investing directly in overseas production facilities. In between purely contractual and full ownership modes there is an option to enter into a joint venture agreement with an existing foreign company.

In developing viable sourcing strategies on a global scale, firms must consider not only manufacturing costs, the costs of various resources, and exchange rate fluctuations, but also availability of infrastructure (including transportation, communications, and energy), industrial and cultural environments, the ease of working with foreign host governments, and so on (Hefler 1981; Caddick and Dale 1986).

The complex nature of sourcing strategy on a global scale spawns many barriers to its successful execution. Monczka and Giunipero (1984) have reported that logistics/inventory/distance, nationalism, and lack of working knowledge about foreign business practices, among others, are major problems identified by both U.S. and foreign multinational firms engaging extensively in international sourcing. They further argue that sourcing development programs should be established within the organization to foster a positive attitude regarding international purchases. Thus, the implementation of such sourcing strategy calls for a well-integrated and efficient global corporate system (Fayerweather 1981; Porter 1986).

Unfortunately, little research has been conducted to date bearing directly on the performance implications of global sourcing activities. However, there exists some related literature that adds to our understanding of global sourcing and its performance implications. Threads of insight can be found in various theoretical treatises, particularly in those related to international product life cycle, specialized competence, intra-firm transactions, and product and process innovations.

International Product Cycle

Despite its conceptual limitations (as discussed in Chapter 1), the international product cycle model provided a compelling description of dynamic patterns of international trade of manufactured products by U.S.-based multinational firms in the 1960s and 1970s (Vernon 1966, 1974, 1979). The international product cycle model generally describes the evolutionary pattern of the diffusion of a new product or technology across national boundaries. Recognizing the importance of integrated sourcing on a global basis, Vernon (1974, p. 106) argues:

> [A multinational firm is] familiar with the operating conditions of some countries where the materials or components can be produced at low cost; indeed, it may already have manufacturing subsidiaries in such a country. When that is so, the parent may elect to enlarge the scale and function of the existing subsidiary so that it can supply materials or components to other parts of the system . . . . [Thus,] multinational enterprises farmed out the manufacture of all sorts of components to their foreign subsidiaries, components which eventually would find their way into assembled electric razors, toys, automobiles, radios, and many other products in which costs and price were of importance.

Grunwald and Flamm (1985) have also witnessed the large-scale overseas production of manufactured products by multinational firms for the U.S. markets. They claim that this strategy allows those firms to retain their cost competitiveness after their products have entered the later stages of the product cycle. The firms that developed the product are able to continue producing economically by eventually relocating to or subcontracting assembly production facilities in low-wage developing countries. Drucker (1979) referred to this arrangement as "production sharing" in which production activities are coordinated vertically across national boundaries in order to withstand the onslaught of low-cost high-quality competition from around the world. For example, semiconductors alone account for about 40 percent of the value of U.S.-made components reimported into this country after overseas assembly, and more than 80 percent of the U.S. semiconductor production is probably assembled abroad.

Specialized Competence

In response to the decline in productivity and business failures in the United States in the last decade, Miles and Snow (1986) have argued that many successful firms have developed a dynamic organizational network through increased use of joint ventures, subcontracting, and licensing activities across international borders. This flexible network system allegedly allows each participant to pursue its particular competence. Therefore, each network participant can be seen as complementing rather than competing with the other participants for the common goals. They claim that the advantage of adopting a dynamic network is its structural flexibility. A dynamic network can accommodate a vast amount of complexity while maximizing the specialized competence of each member, and it provides much more effective use of human resources that would otherwise have to be accumulated, allocated, and maintained by a single organization. In other words, a firm can concentrate on performing the task at which it is most efficient. This approach is increasingly applied on a global basis with countries participating in a dynamic network as multinational firms configure and coordinate product development, manufacturing, and sourcing activities around the world.

Intra-Firm Transactions

It has not been not until recently, however, that some researchers have paid attention to the benefit of intra-firm sourcing transactions on a global scale. For example, the market performance implications of various sourcing strategies were explored in Chapter 2. It is discovered that the extent of intra-firm sourcing of major components—that is, the firm's ability to procure major components from within its corporate system on a global basis—appears to be a crucial determinant of its market performance, while sourcing and production locations do not. In other words, these empirical findings cast serious doubt on the alleged benefits (i.e., cost competitiveness and specialization) of integrated international sourcing discussed in the previous arguments, *unless* the international sourcing of major components is of an intra-firm nature.

Some anecdotal evidence further supports the importance of intra-firm sourcing of major components regardless of their procurement locations. Hayes and Wheelwright (1984) contend that U.S. firms are losing their competitiveness despite going offshore for procurement of components and products *from* independent suppliers on a contractual basis. A few examples may be cited to support their case. In 1983, Japanese television manufacturers dominated several U.S. market segments even though many U.S. manufacturers enjoyed the same low labor cost advantages of offshore production or procurement of finished products from local suppliers. Also, German machine tool and automotive producers have secured a big portion of the U.S. market even though their labor rates have risen above those in the United States. Similarly, Swatch decided to make the whole watch in Switzerland despite its high costs, in order to keep control of crucial design and production and avoid giving away profit margins to subcontractors. In addition, Kim's (1986) study has revealed that Japanese firms, rather than U.S. firms, have been the major suppliers of complex components for the Asian Four Tigers (Hong Kong, South Korea, Singapore, and Taiwan). Moreover, Japanese firms export to the United States through these countries by supplying them intermediate goods that are then assembled into finished products to be sold in the United States. It appears that U.S. firms' increased dependence on major components from independent foreign suppliers did not alleviate, but rather accelerated, their competitive decline.

The sourcing of major components and products by multinational firms thus takes place in two ways: (1) from independent suppliers on a "contractual" basis (external sourcing) and (2) from the parents or their foreign subsidiaries on an intra-firm basis (internal sourcing). When studying the relationship between sourcing and competitiveness of multinational firms, it is crucial to distinguish between sourcing on a "contractual" basis and sourcing on an intra-firm basis, for these two types of sourcing will have a different impact on their competitiveness.

Sourcing from independent suppliers on a "contractual" basis, whether domestically or from abroad, appears to have three long-term consequences for multinational firms. First, they tend to forsake part of the most important value-creating activities to, and also become dependent on, independent operators for assurance of components quality (Kumpe and Bolwijn 1988). Second, those multinational firms tend to promote competition among independent suppliers, ensure continuing availability of materials in the future, and exploit full benefits of changing market conditions. However, individual suppliers are forced to operate in an uncertain business environment that inherently necessitates a shorter planning horizon. The uncertainty about the potential loss of orders to competitors often forces individual suppliers to make operating decisions that will likely increase their own long-term production and material costs (Hahn et al. 1986). In the process, it tends to adversely affect the multinational firms sourcing components and/or finished products from independent suppliers.[1]

Third and of utmost importance, those multinational firms tend to lose sight of emerging technologies and expertise in the long run that could be incorporated into the development of new manufacturing processes as well as new products (Imai 1986). Thus, continual sourcing from independent suppliers is likely to forebode those firms' long-term loss of the ability to manufacture at competitive cost and, as a result, loss of their global competitiveness. However, if technology and expertise developed by a multinational firm are exploited within its multinational corporate system (i.e., by its foreign affiliates and by the parent firm itself), the firm can retain its technological base to itself without unduly disseminating them to competitors as though it were a public good. The benefit of such internalization is great, particularly when technology is highly idiosyncratic or specific with limited alternative use, or when it is novel in the marketplace. It is because its true economic value to the firm tends to be undervalued in the marketplace due to uncertainty associated with the technology as perceived by potential buyers (Buckley and Casson 1976; Dunning 1977; Rugman 1982).

In addition, by getting involved in design and production on its own, the multinational firm can keep abreast of emerging technologies and innovations originating anywhere in the world for potential use in the future. Furthermore, management of the quality of major components is required to retain the goodwill and confidence of consumers in the products (Casson 1982). As a result, intra-firm sourcing of major components and finished products between the parent firm and its affiliates abroad and between its foreign affiliates themselves would enable the firm to retain a long-term competitive edge in the world market.

Product and Process Innovations

Recently, there has been a renewed interest in manufacturing that was long ignored in traditional considerations of development as a strategic weapon in the United States (Hayes and Wheelwright 1984; Cohen and Zysman 1987). As a result of the aggressive competition from European and Japanese multinational firms with due emphasis on manufacturing and concomitant product quality, U.S. firms have come to grips with the crucial supportive role of manufacturing ingenuity once the initial competitive edge brought about by product innovations is threatened (Hayes and Abernathy 1980; Wheelwright 1985; Utterback 1987).

Although the ability to deliver a high volume of products of satisfactory quality at a reasonable price was once the hallmark of many successful U.S. firms, an increasing number of global suppliers have eventually rendered the delivery of volume in an acceptable time no longer a competitive weapon. There has since occurred a strategic shift from *quantity* to *quality* of products as a determinant of competitive strength (Starr and Ullman 1988).

Ignoring manufacturing as a strategic weapon, U.S. firms have historically placed emphasis on product innovations (i.e., product proliferation and modifications). Product innovations alone, however, could not sustain the firm's long-term competitive advantage, since the U.S. technological lead over foreign competition has virtually evaporated (Davidson and Harrigan 1977; Mansfield and Romeo 1984; Mansfield 1988). Thus, there will be fewer products that U.S. firms can export simply because no one else has the technology to manufacture the products (Thurow 1985). Stressing the historical linkage of imitation and product innovations, Brooks (1983) and Starr and Ullman (1988) further contend that imitation (manufacturing process learning), followed by more innovative adaptation, leading to pioneering product innovation, forms the natural sequence of industrial development. In other words, product and process innovative activities are intertwined such that continual improvement in manufacturing processes can enable the firm not only to maintain product innovation-based competitiveness, but also to improve its product innovative abilities in the future (Imai 1986).

The importance of product and process innovations is also manifest at the national level. Take a look at the U.S. semiconductor industry. Because advances in semiconductor technology are closely linked to equipment and materials capabilities, the competitive decline of these suppliers suggests that the United States is not only suffering production losses to foreign competitors, but it is also losing the ability to stay at the leading edge of semiconductor technology and is becoming increasingly dependent on Japan for the technology critical to its entire defense industry (Prestowitz 1988). It is not necessarily equipment makers' lackluster technological development that is causing the U.S. semiconductor industry to flounder. Rather, it is due in a major part to U.S. semiconductor makers that have not pushed themselves to innovate internally on their manufacturing equipment. Unlike Japanese semiconductor makers, many U.S. makers have relied too much on external equipment makers for necessary manufacturing process innovations.

This renewed interest in manufacturing necessitated differentiation of product innovation from manufacturing process innovation (or process innovation) (Abernathy and Townsend 1975). In a broad sense, innovation may be defined as know-how composed of product technology (the set of ideas embodied in the product) and process technology (the set of ideas involved in the manufacture of the product or the steps necessary to combine new materials to produce a finished product) (Abernathy and Utterback 1978; Capon and Glazer 1987; Acs and Audretsch 1988).

By emphasizing marketing strategy centered around product proliferations and modifications, U.S. firms have been reluctant to invest heavily in the development of new manufacturing processes. Rather, they are increasingly "hollowing-out" and adopting a designer role of offering innovations in product and product design without investing in manufacturing process innovations, while allowing independent firms in Japan, South Korea, and Singapore (among others) to improve on their manufacturing technology much faster than U.S firms can (Teece 1987).

Somewhat different situations exist in the leading nations of West European countries and Japan. Many European and Japanese firms have made a strong commitment to increasing market share through internal development of advanced process technology, complementing the value of product technology (Mansfield 1988). This *interactive* nature of product and process technology has given major foreign competitors a competitive advantage over U.S. firms.

Unfortunately, few firms are willing to openly discuss their long-term technology strategy. As a result, not much is known about how individual

European and Japanese firms successfully manage and integrate their technological capabilities for global competitiveness. One notable exception is NEC, a giant Japanese electronics firm. To stress the importance of the need for continual quest for product and process innovations, the case of this Japanese company is illustrated here.

This company manufactures over 15,000 different products marketed in more than 140 countries. NEC has openly publicized its technology strategy with a long-term vision into the future. Its technological vision has been known as the "Computer and Communications" (C&C) concept, which illustrates the importance of understanding the past, present, and future linkages of on-going technological evolution and that of manufacturing process evolution. In NEC's term, R&D is a composite of short- and medium-term strategies to develop products for "today and tomorrow" and long-term strategies to develop basic ideas and technologies for "the day after tomorrow." The company is constantly upgrading its production engineering capabilities in order to apply its technological abilities to products that will meet the high standards its customers have come to expect.

As shown in Figure 3-1, the Japanese company has a balanced combination of four major operations—communications, computers, electron devices, and home electronics—all synergistically integrated under the umbrella of the C&C concept. The dark lines with an arrow connecting technological advancements show how manufacturing process innovations will also evolve. The C&C concept was advocated by NEC as early as 1977, to anticipate the industrial evolution and the strategic direction for the company, characterized by such technological developments as digitalization of communications, distributed data processing, and advances in microelectronics technology (NEC Corporation 1990).

NEC is a high-tech company in a high-tech industry. Similar examples can also be found in a mature industry. Richardson Sheffield, a British cutlery manufacturer, offers an interesting example in a mature industry. Many features of the U.K. cutlery industry have not changed over a century. The postwar history of the industry is characterized as one of near-continuous decline due to an influx of low-cost imports from South Korea, Taiwan, Japan, and also from other West European countries.

Richardson Sheffield has finally come out of the doldrums since 1980, when the "Laser" kitchen knife, an innovative product that needs no sharpening, was introduced. By 1986, the company was exporting finished knives to more than 70 countries. The original Laser brand was followed by a successive introduction of new improved knives, the Laser 5 in 1982 and the Laser 7 in 1986. The new knives featured continual improvements in handles and blades. Despite the strong engineering orientation of the company, Richardson gives meticulous attention to the design of its knives to suit consumers' different needs around the world. The company's com-

Figure 3–1
NEC Strategic Horizon

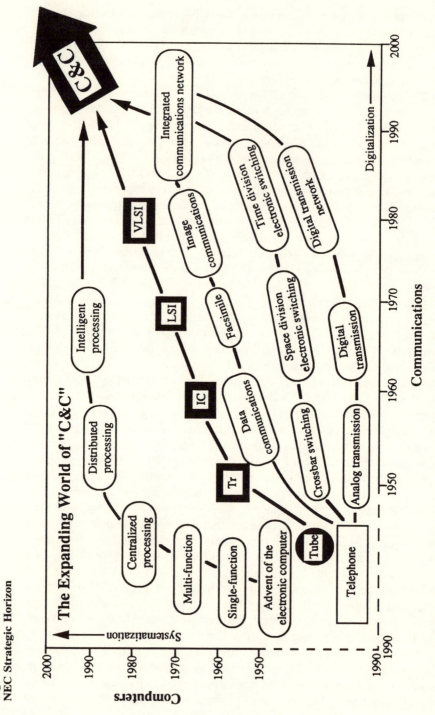

Source: NEC Corporation, "This Is NEC 1990" (Tokyo: NEC, 1990), used with permission.

mitment to excellence is recapitulated by the following statement: "We don't know what the knife of the year 2000 will look like. But you can bet your bottom dollar that the Japanese are working on some ideas. We are staying one jump ahead."

Richardson Sheffield puts equal efforts into its manufacturing operations. Most of its continual process improvement has been in the application of electrics and pneumatics to semiautomate existing processes. Virtually all the manufacturing process improvement, including blade-grinding technology, has taken place in-house and almost all Richardson's machinery has been developed and built in its own plant. Indeed, this British company is fully aware that both product and process innovations are the "success producers" even in a mature industry (Grant and Fuller 1988).

DEVELOPMENT OF A TAXONOMY AND A PRIMARY PROPOSITION

For a taxonomy of innovation-sourcing linkages to be conceptually and managerially meaningful, performance implications should be obtainable. The literature has revealed three factors addressing performance implications for various forms of innovation-sourcing linkages: (1) the degree of product innovation, (2) the degree of process innovation, and (3) the mode of components sourcing—the extent to which major components are procured from independent suppliers on a contractual (external) basis or within the corporate system on an intra-firm (internal) basis.

Based on these three major factors, the different types of innovation-sourcing linkages can be denoted as $D_i C_j M_k$ where:

D_i = Product innovation; i = 1,2 (low, high),

C_j = Process innovation; j = 1,2 (low, high), and

M_k = Mode of sourcing; k = 1,2 (external, internal).

As shown in Table 3–1, eight alternative innovation-sourcing linkages can be identified. For example, $D_1 C_1 M_1$ represents a sourcing strategy in which a less-innovative product is manufactured in a less-innovative manufacturing facility with a large portion of major components being sourced externally from independent suppliers operating on a contractual basis. Similarly, $D_1 C_1 M_2$ illustrates a situation in which a product of low degrees of product and process innovations is manufactured with major components sourced internally within the corporate system. At a low degree of product and process innovations, the firm may be indifferent between internal and external sourcing as long as products are procured at low cost, since cost is a major determinant of competitiveness. On the other hand, $D_2 C_2 M_1$ and $D_2 C_2 M_2$ both involve high degrees of product and

Table 3–1
A Framework for the Development of a Taxonomy of Innovation-Sourcing Linkages

	Process Innovation (C_j)	
	Low	High
Product innovation (D_i)		
Low	Internal (M_1)	Internal (M_1)
	External (M_2)	External (M_2)
High	Internal (M_1)	Internal (M_1)
	External (M_2)	External (M_2)

process innovations, but differ in the way the product is procured. At a high degree of product and process innovations, internal sourcing of major components ($D_2C_2M_2$) may provide a firm with a higher competitive advantage than external sourcing ($D_2C_2M_1$). Components sourcing on an intra-firm basis at a high degree of product and process innovations would allow a firm not only to keep its technological base to itself but also to keep abreast of emerging technologies and innovations inside and outside the firm; therefore, it enables the firm to maintain its competitive edge for a long period of time. For those strategies that lie in between the two extremes ($D_2C_1M_1$, $D_2C_1M_2$, $D_1C_2M_1$, and $D_1C_2M_2$), the literature fails to provide a coherent explanation of their impact on a firm's competitiveness. For example, $D_2C_1M_1$ symbolizes a highly innovative product manufactured in a not-so-innovative manufacturing facility with a majority of major components sourced from independent suppliers. $D_1C_2M_2$ represents a product with a low degree of product innovation manufactured in a highly innovative plant with internally sourced components.

The real test of a taxonomy lies in its ability to explain scores on dimensions, such as performance, other than those originally used to formulate it (Miller 1978). Thus, the taxonomy of innovation-sourcing linkages will be useful for three reasons. First, the highly criticized "hollowing-out" argument may well be misleading as one is led to think of this issue dichotomously either as good or as bad. The taxonomy helps identify a range and diversity of innovation-sourcing linkages. Second, the taxonomy can be used to examine how various international innovation-sourcing linkages are associated with a firm's performance measures, such as market share, sales growth, and pre-tax profitability. Third, the taxonomy of innovation-sourcing linkages provides a framework for future studies for the evaluation of different innovation-sourcing linkages on the sustainability of a multinational firm's long-term competitiveness.

At the current level of knowledge, mostly anecdotal, of these innovation-sourcing relationships, empirical investigations are strongly called for to provide some generalizable evidence to the literature. In this chapter, such an attempt is made to compare and contrast among various types of innovation-sourcing linkages in terms of some performance measures such as market share, sales growth, and profitability. The primary hypothesis in this chapter is, therefore, that *market performance is explained jointly by the levels of product and process innovations and the extent of internal sourcing.*

MEASURES

A few variables have been identified for the development of a taxonomy. A taxonomy is essentially a simplification of complex reality. Therefore, the variables in our taxonomy should be more salient in explaining market performance than other variables not identified in the taxonomy.

There are several strategically and characteristically important variables that are not addressed in the taxonomy but that might have some bearing on market performance. Namely, they are the year of product introduction, product type (consumer versus industrial), and nationality (European versus Japanese). These variables are incorporated into the performance analysis as control variables.

The measures used in this chapter are presented in Table 3–2. Some of the variables were assessed by using multiple-item measures, for which Cronbach's internal consistency alphas are reported.

Criterion Variable

Market Performance (PERFORM): Market performance, or relative competitive strength, is a multifaceted construct, often represented by relative market share and profitability, among others (Abell and Hammond 1979). Based on Burke's (1984) market performance analysis, a measure of market performance in this chapter was expanded from the previous measure employed in Chapter 2 such that the product's market performance was more encompassing, which included sales growth rate in addition to relative market share and pretax profitability.[2] The three items are measured on a 5-point scale (0–4; Cronbach's alpha = .55).

Explanatory Variables in the Taxonomy

Product and Process Innovations (PRODUCT and PROCESS): As Utterback (1987) stated, it is difficult to differentiate between product and process innovations since they are inextricably interdependent. Objective measures of R&D intensity as a proxy for innovativeness generally lump

Table 3–2
Measurement

Variables	Measure	Cronbach's Alpha

Market Performance	A 3-item measure:
	Relative to competition
	    Your Market Share is... (Very Low 0-4 Very High)
	    Your Sales Growth Rate is... (Very Low 0-4 Very High)
	    Your Pretax Profitability is... (Very Low 0-4 Very High)
		.55

Product Innovations	A 3-item measure:
	In terms of the following aspects of *technology* for your firm, is this product
	    Product-related patents... 0. Not applicable
	                                1. Minor change of a previous product in your product line,
	                                2. Major change of a previous product in your product line, or
	                                3. Totally new to your firm?
	As a *technical development*, how would you rate the product in terms of its competitive impact on the U.S. market for the following aspects of technology?
	    Product-related patents... 0. Not applicable
	                                  1. Minor,
	                                  2. hard to appaise, or
	                                  3. Major.
	How many alternative *applications* (or uses) are there of the technology incorporated in this product in terms of the following aspects of technology?
	    Product-related patents... 0. Not applicable
	                                    1. Few,
	                                  2. Several, or
	                                  3. Many.
		.78

Process Innovations	A 3-item measure: The same as above, asked for proprietary methods of production	.79
Degree of Internal Sourcing	A single-item measure: Total market value of components less the market value of "standard" components. The value of standard components is estimated by asking, "Ignoring transportation costs, approximately what percent of the total purchased vlaue of components in the product could be sourced form local firms in newly industrializing countries such as Taiwan, South Korea, and Brazil, without technical assistance from your firm?	n.a.
Product Policy	A single-item measure: For product development, the parent company policy is to attempt to have 1. Unique Product Designed for Each Country 2. Standard Products with Specific Adaptation for Some Markets, or 3. Standardized Products Worldwide	n.a.
Year of Product Introduction	A single-item measure: When was the product initially marketed in the United States? 19__	n.a.
Type of Product	Consumer Durables (0) or Industrial Durables (1)	n.a.
Nationality	European (0) or Japanese (1)	n.a.

product and process innovations together. Besides, many studies (e.g., Hufbauer 1970) have used aggregate industry data, which may not disclose strategic variations among different products. Therefore, aggregate industry data may not fully reflect management's view of innovations.

There is extensive evidence to indicate that managerial decisions are driven by perceptions (Einhorn and Hogarth 1981; March 1978; Slovic, Fischhoff, and Lichtenstein 1977). As a result, insights can be gained into the innovative activities of European and Japanese multinational firms by investigating executives' perceptions regarding their innovation policies.

Therefore, following Leroy's (1976) seminal study, management's perception of what constitutes product and process innovations is introduced to gain more managerial insight into product and process innovations. The degree of innovations can be measured by product-related patents, proprietary methods of production, trade secrets, and the product's functional performance (Leroy 1976; Buzzell and Gale 1987). Initially, 12 items (i.e., 3 items on each aspect of innovation) on a 4-point scale (0–3) were developed. Subsequent principal components analysis reduced the number of usable items to 6. These 6 items were the degree of product and process innovations to the firm (2 items) and the degree of product and process innovations to the competition (2 items), and the versatility of product and process innovations (2 items).

Varimax-rotated principal components analysis on these 6 items confirmed the tenability of the dichotomy of product and process innovations. To increase reliability of each measure, a summated variable was subsequently developed to represent product innovation and process innovation, respectively (Cronbach's alpha = .78 and .79).

Extent of Internal Sourcing (INTSORC): The extent of internal sourcing is measured as the market value of major components in the product procured within the corporate system, or the total market value of components less the market value of "standard" components. Standard components are defined as components that could be produced by local firms in newly industrialized countries. NICs have increasingly become a supplier of components and products that lost the initial innovative advantage enjoyed by the developed countries (Vernon 1974; Helleiner 1981). The percentage of standard components in the product was estimated by asking respondents a hypothetical question: "Ignoring transportation costs, approximately what percent of the total purchased value of components in the product could be sourced from local firms in newly industrializing countries such as Taiwan, South Korea, and Brazil, without technical assistance from your firm?" (Kotabe and Omura 1989).

Control Variables Not in the Taxonomy

Year of Product Introduction (YEAR): In an era of global competition, new product innovations are relatively easily reverse-engineered, improved upon, and invented around by competitors without violating patents and other proprietary protections bestowed on them (Levin et al. 1987; Starr and Ullman 1988). Domestic and foreign competitors will begin to produce similar components and products in due time. Hence, it may be argued that until others have developed the expertise to become a supplier, the innovator will have to rely on its own manufacturing processes and its own components. Therefore, one may argue that the year of product introduction, rather than process innovations or the extent of internal sourcing, is a primary determinant of market performance.

Type of the Product (TYPE): Because industrial buyers are more rational in their purchase decisions than consumers, product standardization is more feasible for industrial durable products than for consumer durable products (Boddewyn et al. 1986). Although the authors are not aware of any study examining how the type of the product affects the level of product and process innovations, the potential impact on innovations of the ease of standardization was suspected. Therefore, TYPE is a dichotomous variable representing either consumer durable (0) or industrial durable products (1).

Nationality of the Multinational Firm (NATION): The nationality of multinational firms was identified either as European (0) or as Japanese (1) in this chapter.

ANALYSIS AND RESULTS

The research interest is in confirming the robustness of the variables in the taxonomy in accounting for various aspects of market performance. First, the way the set of all variables (i.e., variables in the taxonomy and control variables) operate together in determining market performance is examined. Second, once the robustness of the variables in the taxonomy is confirmed, performance implications of various innovation-sourcing linkages identified in the taxonomy are investigated. The correlation matrix is presented in Table 3–3 to provide the full information contained in the data about the relationships among the variables investigated.

Performance Implications of Various
Innovation-Sourcing Linkages

It was suspected that different measures of market performance (i.e., relative market share, sales growth rate, and pretax profitability) might be affected differently by the independent variables. Initially, each of the performance measures was regressed on the explanatory and control variables. Product and process innovations (PRODUCT and PROCESS) and the extent of internal sourcing (INTSORC) were consistently significant (at least at the .10 level) in all three performance measures. Consequently,

Table 3–3
Correlation Matrix of Variables

		PERFORM	PRODUCT	PROCESS	INTSORC	POLICY	YEAR	TYPE	NATION
PERFORM	Market Performance	1.000	.293[b]	-.113	.329[a]	.034	.029	-.063	.173
PRODUCT	Product Innovation		1.000	.436[a]	.321[a]	.271[b]	.267[b]	-.145	.503[a]
PROCESS	Process Innovation			1.000	.153	.168	.158	-.048	.399[a]
INTSORC	Degree of Internal Sourcing				1.000	.013	.353[a]	-.272[b]	.278[a]
POLICY	Corporate Product Policy					1.000	-.166	.167	.055
YEAR	Year of Product Introduction						1.000	-.054	.125
TYPE	Product Type							1.000	-.457[a]
NATION	Nationality of Firm								1.000

[a]significant at the .01 level
[b]significant at the .05 level

Table 3–4
Regression Analysis for Market Performance, without an Interaction Term

Variables	Regression Equation [a]		
	Beta Coefficient	t-Value	Significant Level
PRODUCT	.34	2.40	.02
PROCESS	-.30	-2.24	.03
INTSORC	.27	2.08	.04

[a]R^2=22.1% (adjusted R^2=17.7%), significant at the .004 level.

regression analysis performed on an aggregate performance measure (PERFORM) is reported here.

As two-way and three-way interactions were anticipated in the taxonomy, not only the main effects but also all possible interaction effects were considered in the model. As discussed earlier, it was suspected that the year of product introduction (YEAR), product type (TYPE), and nationality (NATION) might have a bearing on market performance above and beyond the innovative and sourcing policies of the firms. These variables were also included in the model as control variables.

Although, as shown in Table 3–3, there existed statistically insignificant correlations between the YEAR, TYPE, and NATION control variables and market performance (PERFORM), it was suspected that some significant correlations among the independent variables (i.e., a multicollinearity problem) might produce erroneous results in regression analysis. Therefore, it was necessary to examine how the set of explanatory and control variables operated together in explaining market performance. If significant results were obtained for the explanatory variables after accounting for the impact of the control variables in the model, then it could be argued that the importance of the explanatory variables outweighed that of the control variables in the model (Perreault, Behrman, and Armstrong 1979).

Initial regression analysis indicated that none of the control variables was significant. The finding also implies that none of the control variables has a significant impact on market performance beyond the explanatory variables identified in the taxonomy. Therefore, the control variables were dropped from subsequent analysis.

Our interest is in examining how the explanatory power (as measured by the coefficient of determination or R^2) of the regression model would be improved by adding interaction terms. First, regression analysis was performed without interaction terms among PRODUCT, PROCESS, and INTSORC. Table 3–4 shows the regression results without the interaction terms. PRODUCT, PROCESS, and INTSORC were all statistically significant (p < .05 for each) in the model, accounting for 22.1 percent (or adjusted 17.7 percent, p = .004) of the variation in market performance. As expected, PRODUCT and INTSORC are positively related to PERFORM.

It is noteworthy that PROCESS is negatively related to PERFORM in the model. A correlation coefficient between PROCESS and PERFORM was negative, but not statistically significant, as shown in Table 3–3. However, PROCESS is highly correlated with PRODUCT (r = .44, p < .01). This high correlation between product and process innovative activities is indicative that the role of process innovations should not be assessed independently of product innovations in explaining market performance. Therefore, an immediate causal interpretation of the impact of PROCESS on PERFORM may not be made.

The literature offers a justification for it. As Imai (1986) and Utterback (1987), among others, separately pointed out, product innovations and manufacturing process innovations are interdependent. It is suggested that the shortened innovational lead time makes it difficult for firms to rely solely on product innovations as a source of long-term competitive advantage. The decreased salience of product innovations will have to be compensated for by the increased investment in process innovations so as to maintain the initial competitive advantage. Thus, it is likely that a negative relationship can be observed between PROCESS and PERFORM.

Interaction terms were subsequently introduced into the model. The only statistically significant interaction term was between PRODUCT and PROCESS (p < .01). It is to be noted that this interaction term virtually replaced the main effect of PRODUCT on PERFORM. As expected, this result indicates that market performance is *jointly* determined by the interaction of product and process innovations. The rest of the interaction terms and the main effect of PRODUCT were subsequently dropped from further analysis. The results of the modified regression analysis with an interaction term (PRODUCT × PROCESS) are presented in Table 3–5.

The resultant model is highly significant (p < .001), accounting for 27.2 percent (or adjusted 23.1 percent) of the variation in market performance. The model with an interaction term has improved the explanatory power by 5.1 percent (or adjusted 5.4 percent) over the model with the main effects only. A highly significant interaction term (PRODUCT × PROCESS; p < .01) suggests that erroneous conclusions would be drawn if the impact of product and process innovations were assessed independently. In other words, the negative slope coefficient associated with PROCESS no longer indicates the negative change in the mean response for a unit increase in PROCESS. *That effect in this model depends on the level of product innovation (PRODUCT)* (Neter, Wasserman, and Kutner 1985, p. 232). This point is explored in detail later in this chapter.

Table 3–5
Regression Analysis for Market Performance, with an Interaction Term

	Regression Equation [a]		
Variables	Beta Coefficient	t-Value	Significant Level
PRODUCT	-.64	-3.35	.002
PROCESSxPROCESS	.63	3.15	.003
INTSORC	.23	1.85	.07

[a]R^2=27.2% (adjusted R^2=23.1%), significant at the .001 level.

On the other hand, the extent of internal sourcing (INTSORC) is shown to explain market performance independently of innovative activities (PRODUCT and PROCESS). Although attenuated by product and process innovation terms, a positive impact of the extent of internal sourcing (INTSORC) on market performance (p = .07; or p = .03 on a unidirectional test) is consistent with the result confirmed in Chapter 2. It is thus concluded that the results attest to the robustness of PRODUCT, PROCESS, and INTSORC in the taxonomy.

Next, in order to closely examine the nature of the interaction between product and process innovations, PERFORM was regressed on PROCESS and PRODUCT × PROCESS, assuming away the impact of INTSORC. The results of the reduced-form model are shown in Figure 3–2. The reduced form is statistically significant at the .001 level, accounting for 22.5 percent (or adjusted 19.6 percent) of the variation in market performance.

Based on these findings, we can offer tentative conclusions to the performance implications of various innovation-sourcing linkages. As stated earlier, the level of internal sourcing of major components appears to positively affect market performance independently of the product policies of the firms. In the following discussion, the extent of internal components sourcing ($\bar{M}$) is assumed away as an error term.

The results suggest that when the degree of a product innovation is relatively high (PRODUCT > 5), the more effort the firm puts into manufacturing process innovations, the higher its market performance is likely to be. Manufacturing process innovations provide a competitive boost for highly innovative products in the form of lower price and improved quality, among other things. This finding offers statistical support to the strategic importance of simultaneously taking on product and process innovations. When the degree of a product innovation is high, it pays to embark on process innovations concurrently rather than to wait until the decline in novelty of the product innovation necessitates improvement on manufacturing processes. Thus, $D_2C_2\bar{M} > D_2C_1\bar{M}$.

Figure 3–2
Interactive Nature of Product and Process Innovations for Market Performance

$PERFORM = 6.9 - 0.5 \times (PROCESS) \times 0.1 \times (PRODUCT*PROCESS)$ [a]

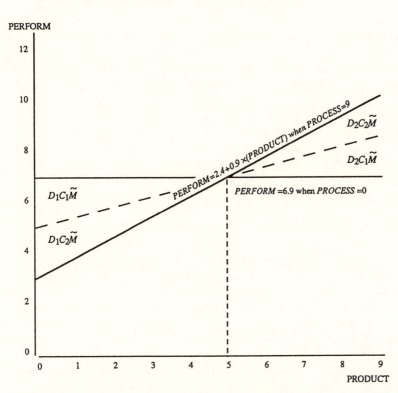

Note: PRODUCT, PROCESS and PERFORM are summated variables. PRODUCT and PROCESS range from low (0) to high high (9) in magnitude. PERFORM ranges from low (0) to high (12).

[a]$R^2 = 22.5\%$ (adjusted $R^2 = 19.6\%$), significant at the .001 level.

On the other hand, when the degree of a product innovation is relatively low (PRODUCT $\leqq$ 5), the emphasis on manufacturing process innovations is negatively related to the firm's market performance. Thus, $D_1C_1\tilde{M} > D_1C_2\tilde{M}$. Two plausible alternative explanations may be offered. First, the decline in the strategic value of a product innovation will prompt the firm to step up efforts at manufacturing process innovations in order to maintain its competitive position and/or keep it from deteriorating (Utterback 1987). If so, then a causal relationship should rather be the opposite of what this regression analysis implies. Second, if the product innovation is relatively low, stepped-up efforts at manufacturing process innovations may not bring about as much improvement in market performance as could justify the cost of such efforts. Such efforts could result in higher costs and lower the profit margin, resulting in lower market performance. Either case as it may be, one thing appears to be clear: product innovation is a necessary, but not sufficient, determinant of market performance.

If these four sourcing strategy types are evaluated simultaneously, the ideal sourcing strategy would be $D_2C_2\bar{M}$ (a high degree of product and process innovations and using internal sourcing) with the highest market performance. On the other hand, $D_1C_2\bar{M}$ (a low degree of product innovations and a high level of process innovation) represents the worst scenario with the lowest market performance. For the remaining two sourcing types, $D_2C_1\bar{M}$ (a high degree of product innovation and a low level of process innovation) outperforms $D_1C_1\bar{M}$ (a low level of both product and process innovations). Combining these evaluations provides the following conclusion: $D_2C_2\bar{M} > D_2C_1\bar{M} > D_1C_1\bar{M} > D_1C_2\bar{M}$

CONCLUDING REMARKS

In response to the primary objectives of this chapter, a taxonomy of innovation sourcing linkages and subsequent regression analysis on performance implications of various innovation-sourcing linkages have uncovered two noteworthy relationships among innovative activities, components sourcing, and market performance. First, as Imai (1986) has stressed, it appears that product and process innovations are intertwined such that continual improvement in manufacturing processes lead to product innovations.[3] Regression analysis has confirmed that product innovations or process innovations alone may not be used as direct causal evidence of the firm's market performance. Rather, their interaction is.

Second, the taxonomy showed that when either one of the innovative activities was low while the other was high, the extent of internal sourcing of major components appeared generally low. Subsequent regression analysis has shown that although no significant interaction effect on market performance is observed between either of the innovative activities and internal components sourcing (i.e., PRODUCT × INTSORC, PROCESS × INTSORC), the extent of internal components sourcing has a positive impact on market performance. In other words, the firm's *ability* to source a majority of its major components needs within its corporate system will help improve its performance level independently of its innovative activities. It is further suggestive of the benefits of vertical integration (i.e., critical stage for quality assurance and high value added in components and subassembly stages of the value chain), and it is consistent with views expressed by Kumpe and Bolwijn (1988).

Third, the hollowing-out or outsourcing strategy, which is the opposite of internal sourcing, is therefore related to lower market performance.

The hollowing-out of U.S. firms in pursuit of a short-term profit over a long-term market performance has of late received a strong criticism as "an economics of instant gratification, an abdication of responsibility to future [American] investors, workers, and consumers" (*Business Week* 1986). This criticism appears to apply equally to foreign multinational firms. The issue of hollowing-out will be further explored in Chapter 7.

Fourth, when a high level of product innovation is backed simultaneously by a high level of manufacturing process innovations, such strategy will provide by far the strongest competitive advantage to the firm. As Thurow (1985) cautioned, since an increasing number of European and Japanese multinational firms are emphasizing both product and process innovations today, U.S. firms' historical emphasis on product innovations may no longer engender a strong competitive position that they used to enjoy.

In Chapter 4, the product policies of European and Japanese multinational firms will be examined from a perspective of product and process innovations. We will also investigate linkages between corporate product policy and manufacturing strategy and their implications on product and process innovations in an era of global competition.

LIMITATIONS

The same limitations apply as described in Chapter 2. First, this study was cross-sectional in nature and presented the results based on a snapshot of the product and process innovations of European and Japanese multinational firms, while the linkage of product and process innovations is dynamic. A cross-sectional study may not capture all the implications of a dynamic system, which could change over time. Therefore, longitudinal time-series studies of product and process innovations are strongly called for.

Second, limitations in the sample should be noted. The sample consisted of relatively large European and Japanese multinational firms. It is speculative whether or not the findings of this study apply to U.S. firms. A relatively low response rate was obtained because of the nature of the questionnaire, which required from the respondents a fair amount of knowledge of innovative activities and sourcing practices. Furthermore, only consumer and industrial durable products were subjects of this study. It is known that durable products can be more globally marketed than culture-bound consumer nondurable products (Boddewyn et al. 1986; Whitelock 1987). Therefore, the findings of this study are limited to durable products, and overgeneralization of the findings should not be made. Replication of similar studies, involving different sets of multinational firms and products—including U.S. multinational firms, smaller multinational firms, and nondurable products—is called for so as to further provide cumulative evidence in marketing implications of product and process innovations.

Finally, although this study has offered a number of interesting findings on European and Japanese multinational firms' sourcing strategies, it has ignored the notion of strategic alliance, which is a relatively amorphous organizational setup in which two or more firms contribute their respective superior technology and know-how to make synergistically possible what could not otherwise be achieved by each individual firm (Jain 1987; Buckley and Casson 1988; Hamel, Doz, and Prahalad 1989). Innovative activities that are jointly developed in a consortium of competing firms have not been considered. As the number of strategic alliances is recently on the dramatic increase, it will be interesting to examine the impact of innovative activities and components sourcing on the market performance of strategic alliances vis-a-vis that of independent firms.

NOTES

1. There are exceptions to this argument. As explained in the last section of Chapter 2, it is known that some Japanese firms have been able to manage independent suppliers operating on a "contractual" basis as if they were "permanent" members of the integrated firms, thereby eliminating transactional uncertainty associated with business relationships with independent suppliers. A frequently cited example is Toyota Motors' working relationships with its subcontractors.

2. After the study report discussed in Chapter 2 was published in the Spring 1989 issue of the *Journal of International Business Studies,* the use of a 3-item measure of market performance was deemed important so as to explore the encompassing nature of performance implications that could be extracted from this present study. It is to be reported that whether a 2-item measure or a 3-item measure was employed, the results were essentially identical.

3. Conscious effort at continual improvement in manufacturing processes has come to be known as *Kaizen* as exercised by many Japanese firms.

REFERENCES

Abell, Derek F. and John S. Hammond (1979). *Strategic Market Planning.* Englewood Cliffs, NJ: Prentice-Hall.
Abernathy, William J. and Phillip L. Townsend (1975). "Technology, Productivity and Process Change." *Technological Forecasting and Social Change,* 7 (August), 379–396.
Abernathy, William J. and James M. Utterback (1978). "Patterns of Industrial Innovation." *Technology Review,* 80 (June–July), 40–47.
Acs, Zoltan J. and David B. Audretsch (1988). "Innovation in Large and Small Firms: An Empirical Analysis." *American Economic Review,* 78 (September), 678–690.

Armstrong, J. Scott and Terry S. Overton (1977). "Estimating Nonresponse Bias in Mail Surveys." *Journal of Marketing Research*, 14 (August), 396–402.

Boddewyn, Jean J., Robin Soehl, and Jacques Picard (1986). "Standardization in International Marketing: Is Ted Levitt In Fact Right?" *Business Horizons*, 29 (November–December), 69–75.

Brooks, Harvey (1983). "Japanese Technological Advances and Possible United States Responses Using Research Joint Ventures." Presented at House Subcommittee on Investigations and Oversight and the Subcommittee on Science, Research, and Technology of the Committee on Science and Technology, 98th Congress, 1st session, June 29–30.

Buckley, Peter J. and Mark Casson (1976). *The Future of the Multinational Enterprise*. London: Macmillan.

―――― (1988). "A Theory of Cooperation in International Business." In *Cooperative Strategies in International Business*, Farok J. Contractor and Peter Lorange, eds. Lexington, MA: Lexington Books, 31–53.

Burke, Marian C. (1984). "Strategic Choice and Marketing Managers: An Examination of Business-Level Marketing Objectives." *Journal of Marketing Research*, 21 (November), 345–359.

Business Week (1986). "Special Report: The Hollow Corporation," March 3, 56–59.

Buzzell, Robert D. and Bradley T. Gale (1987). *The PIMS Principles* New York: The Free Press.

Caddick, J. R. and B. G. Dale (1986). "Sourcing from Less Developed Countries: A Case Study." *Journal of Purchasing and Materials Management*, 22 (Fall), 17–23.

Capon, Noel and Rashi Glazer (1987). "Marketing and Technology: A Strategic Coalignment." *Journal of Marketing*, 51 (July), 1–14.

Casson, Mark C. (1982). "Transaction Costs and the Theory of the Multinational Enterprise." In *New Theories of the Multinational Enterprise*, Alan M. Rugman, ed. London: Croom Helm, 24–54.

Cohen, Stephen S. and John Zysman (1987). "Why Manufacturing Matters: The Myth of the Post-Industrial Economy." *California Management Review*, 29 (Spring), 9–26.

Davidson, William H. and Richard Harrigan (1977). "Key Decisions in International Marketing: Introducing New Products Abroad." *Columbia Journal of World Business*, 12 (Winter), 15–23.

Drucker, Peter F. (1979). "Production Sharing, Concepts and Definitions." *Journal of the Flagstaff Institute*, 3 (January), 2–9.

Dunning, John H. (1977). "Trade, Location of Economic Activity and the MNE: A Search for an Eclectic Approach." In *The International Allocation of Economic Activity*, Bertil Ohlin, Per-Ove Hesselborn and Per Magnus Wijkman, eds. New York: Holmes and Meier, 395–418.

Einhorn, Hillel J. and Robin M. Hogarth (1981). "Behavioral Decision Theory: Processes of Judgment and Choice." *Annual Review of Psychology*, 32, 53–88.

Fayerweather, John (1981). "Four Winning Strategies for the International Corporation." *Journal of Business Strategy*, 2 (Fall), 1981.

Franko, Lawrence G. (1978). "Multinationals: The End of U.S. Dominance." *Harvard Business Review,* 56 (November–December), 93–101.

Grant, Robert M. and Charles B. Fuller (1988). *The Richardson Sheffield Story: A British Winner.* London: London Business School.

Grunwald, Joseph and Kenneth Flamm (1985). *The Global Factory: Foreign Assembly in International Trade.* Washington, DC: The Brookings Institution.

Hahn, Chan K., Kyoo H. Kim, and Jong S. Kim (1986). "Costs of Competition: Implications for Purchasing Strategy." *Journal of Purchasing and Materials Management,* 22 (Fall), 2–7.

Hamel, Gary, Yves L. Doz, and C. K. Prahalad (1989). "Collaborate with Your Competitors and Win." *Harvard Business Review,* 67 (January–February), 133–139.

Hayes, Robert H. and William J. Abernathy (1980). "Managing Our Way to Economic Decline." *Harvard Business Review,* 58 (July–August), 67–77.

Hayes, Robert H. and Steven C. Wheelwright, eds. (1984). *Restoring Our Competitive Edge: Competing through Manufacturing.* New York: John Wiley.

Hefler, Daniel F. (1981). "Global Sourcing: Offshore Investment Strategy for the 1980s." *Journal of Business Strategy,* 2 (Summer), 7–12.

Helleiner, Gerald K. (1981). *Intra-Firm Trade and the Developing Countries.* New York: St. Martin's Press.

Hufbauer, G. C. (1970). "The Impact of National Characteristics and Technology on the Commodity Composition of Trade in Manufactured Goods." In *The Technology Factor in International Trade,* Raymond Vernon, ed. New York: Columbia University Press, 145–231.

Imai, Masaaki (1986). *Kaizen.* New York: Random House Business Division.

Jain, Subhash C. (1987). "Perspectives on International Strategic Alliances." In *Advances in International Marketing,* vol. 2., S. Tamer Cavusgil, ed. Greenwich, CT: JAI Press, 103–120.

Kim, W. Chan (1986). "Global Production Sharing: An Empirical Investigation of the Pacific Electronics Industry." *Management International Review,* 26 (2), 62–70.

Kogut, Bruce (1985). "Designing Global Strategies: Comparative and Competitive Value Added Chains." *Sloan Management Review,* 26 (Summer), 15–28.

Kotabe, Masaaki and Glenn S. Omura (1989). "Sourcing Strategies of European and Japanese Multinationals: A Comparison." *Journal of International Business Studies,* 20 (Spring), 113–130.

Kotler, Philip, Liam Fahey, and S. Jatusripitak (1985). *The New Competition.* Englewood Cliffs, NJ: Prentice-Hall.

Kotler, Philip, and S. J. Levy (1973). "Buying is Marketing, Too." *Journal of Marketing,* 37 (January), 54–59.

Kumpe, Ted and Piet T. Bolwijn (1988). "Manufacturing: The New Case for Vertical Integration." *Harvard Business Review,* 66 (March–April), 75–81.

Leroy, Georges (1976). *Multinational Product Strategy: A Typology for Analysis of Worldwide Product Innovation and Diffusion.* New York: Praeger.

Levin, Richard C., Alvin K. Klevorick, Richard R. Nelson, and Sidney G. Winter (1987). "Appropriating the Returns from Industrial Research and Development." *Brookings Papers on Economic Activity,* Issue 3, 783–831.

Levitt, Theodore (1983). "The Globalization of Markets." *Harvard Business Review,* 61 (May–June), 92–102.

Mansfield, Edwin (1988). "Industrial R&D in Japan and the United States: A Comparative Study." *American Economic Review,* 78 (May), 223–228.

———— and Anthony Romeo (1984). "Reverse Transfers of Technology from Overseas Subsidiaries to American Firms." *IEEE Transactions on Engineering Management,* EM–31 (3) (August), 122–127.

March, J. G. (1978). "Bounded Rationality, Ambiguity, and the Engineering of Choice." *Bell Journal of Economics and Management Science,* 9 (Autumn), 587–608.

Mascarenhas, Briance (1984). "The Coordination of Manufacturing Interdependence in Multinational Companies." *Journal of International Business Studies,* 15 (Winter), 91–106.

Miles, Raymond E. and Charles C. Snow (1986). "Organizations: New Concepts for New Forms." *California Management Review,* 28 (Spring), 62–73.

Miller, Danny (1978). "The Role of Multivariate Q-Techniques in the Study of Organizations." *Academy of Management Review,* 9 (July), 515–531.

Monczka, Robert M. and Larry C. Giunipero (1984). "International Purchasing: Characteristics and Implementation." *Journal of Purchasing and Materials Management,* 20 (Fall), 2–9.

NEC Corporation (1990). *This is NEC 1990.* Tokyo: NEC.

Negandhi, Anant R. and Martin Welge (1984). *Beyond Theory Z.* London: JAI Press.

Neter, John, William Wasserman, and Michael H. Kutner (1985). *Applied Linear Statistical Models,* 2nd ed. Homewood, IL: Richard D. Irwin.

Ohmae, Kenichi (1985). *Triad Power.* New York: The Free Press.

Perreault, William D., Jr., Douglas N. Behrman, and Gary M. Armstrong (1979). "Alternative Approaches for Interpretation of Multiple Discriminant Analysis in Marketing Research." *Journal of Business Research,* 7, 151–173.

Porter, Michael E. (1986). *Competition in Global Industries.* Boston: Harvard Business School Press.

Prahalad, C. K. and Yves L. Doz (1987). *The Multinational Mission.* New York: The Free Press.

Prestowitz, Clyde V., Jr. (1988). *Trading Places: How We Allowed Japan to Take the Lead.* New York: Basic Books.

Robinson, Richard D., ed. (1987). *Direct Foreign Investment: Costs and Benefits* New York: Praeger.

Rugman, Alan M. (1982). "Internalization and Non-Equity Forms of International Involvement." In *New Theories of the Multinational Enterprise,* Alan M. Rugman, ed. London: Croom Helm.

Slovic, P., B. Fischhoff, and Sarah Lichtenstein (1977). "Behavioral Decision Theory." *Annual Review of Psychology,* 28, 1–39.

Starr, Martin K. (1984). "Global Production and Operations Strategy." *Columbia Journal of World Business,* 19 (Winter), 17–22.

———— and John E. Ullman (1988). "The Myth of Industrial Supremacy." In *Global Competitiveness,* Martin K. Starr, ed. New York: W. W. Norton.

Teece, David J. (1987). "Capturing Value from Technological Innovation: Integration, Strategic Partnering, and Licensing Decisions." In *Technology and*

Global Industry, Bruce R. Guile and Harvey Brooks, eds. Washington, DC: National Academy Press, 65–95.

Thurow, Lester C. (1985). *The Management Challenge.* Cambridge, MA: MIT Press.

Toyne, Brian and Peter G.P. Walters (1989). *Global Marketing Management: A Strategic Perspective.* Boston: Allyn and Bacon.

Utterback, James M. (1987). "Innovation and Industrial Evolution in Manufacturing Industries." In *Technology and Global Industry,* Bruce R. Guile and Harvey Brooks, ed. Washington, DC: National Academy Press, 16–48.

Vernon, Raymond (1966). "International Investment and International Trade in the Product Cycle." *Quarterly Journal of Economics,* 80 (May), 190–207.

—— (1974). "The Location of Economic Activity." In *Economic Analysis and the Multinational Enterprise,* John H. Dunning, ed. London: George Allen and Unwin, 89–114.

—— (1979). "The Product Cycle Hypothesis in a New International Environment." *Oxford Bulletin of Economics and Statistics,* 41 (November), 255–267.

—— (1986). "Can U.S. Manufacturing Come Back?" *Harvard Business Review,* 64 (July–August) 98–106.

Wheelwright, Steven C. (1985). "Restoring the Competitive Edge in U.S. Manufacturing." *California Management Review,* 27 (Spring), 26–42.

Whitelock, Jeryl M. (1987). "Global Marketing and the Case for International Product Standardization." *European Journal of Marketing,* 21, 32–44.

Chapter 4

Corporate Product Policy

Innovation-sourcing linkages represent the interactive roles of product and process innovations and internal sourcing of major components as joint determinants of market performance. Innovation-sourcing linkages were the major research focus of Chapter 3. European and Japanese multinational firms that stress the strategic importance of both product and process innovations simultaneously are found to enjoy a higher level of market performance in the U.S. market than other firms.

Figure 4-1 shows determinants of innovative behavior and performance. It is posited that the multinational firm's corporate-wide product policy acts either as an institutional opportunity or as an institutional barrier to determining to what extent the firm can take advantage of innovation-sourcing linkages and market opportunities on a global scale. This chapter will focus on the product policies of European and Japanese multinational firms as they affect the firms' innovative activities.

It is clear by now that global competitive strategy has become increasingly important for many multinational firms as they have come to realize the advantages of coordinating and integrating operations across national boundaries (Kogut 1985; Porter 1986). Globalization of competition is triggered both by the emergence of Triad industrialized markets with relatively homogeneous demands, comprising the United States, the European Community, and Japan (Ohmae 1985) and by the realization of sourcing components and products on a global basis (as examined in Chapter 2).

In response to global competition, successful companies are evolving from a product policy of offering customized products to that of offering globally standardized ones (Levitt 1983). While the marketing standard-

Figure 4–1
Determinants of Innovative Behavior and Market Performance in Global Competition

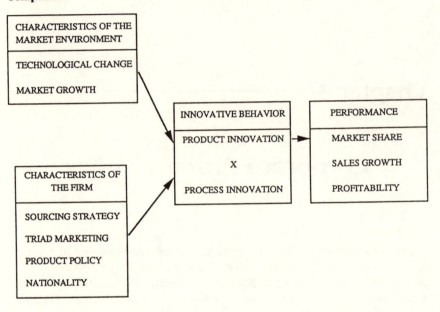

ization argument is not new (e.g., Bartels 1968; Buzzell 1968; Aylmer 1970; Sorenson and Wiechmann 1975), Theodore Levitt's "global product" thesis has rekindled a great deal of controversy over what can be standardized in global marketing and to what extent it can be done (Walters 1986; Douglas and Wind 1987; Jain 1989).

The quintessence of Levitt's global product thesis lies in his call for proactive identification of similar market segments around the world, rather than ethnocentric extension of a domestic product to foreign markets or reactive response to differing needs and wants of customers in various parts of the world. In other words, developing a standard in the home country and using it as a model for the world (an ethnocentric approach) or adapting it if necessary (a reactive approach) is different from getting market information from all marketplaces around the world in which the firm wishes to sell the product and using that to make a standard (a proactive approach).

Unfortunately, Levitt's thesis for "intermarket" segmentation has been interpreted erroneously by many business researchers and practitioners to mean standardization of all marketing activities including marketing research, pricing, product policy, promotion, and distribution. He clearly argues in favor of proactive marketing strategy: "Success in a world with homogenized demand requires a search for sales opportunities in similar segments across the globe in order to achieve the economies of scale necessary to compete" (Levitt 1983, p. 94).

After a series of heated debates that ensued, one consensus has emerged that a distinction should be made between standardization of marketing programs (i.e., marketing mix) and that of the managerial process through which these programs are developed. It is not clear, however, whether these two standardization aspects are independent of each other, or how they interact with each other.

Sorenson and Wiechmann (1975) argue that successful multinational firms have better systems for planning and implementing their local marketing efforts than their competitors do. Those firms tend to have a uniform system for annual marketing planning with a uniform reporting format for their subsidiaries around the world. This way, the marketing decision making process can be standardized across all subsidiaries under the guidelines set by the world headquarters office. Actual marketing programs (i.e., pricing, promotion, product assortment, and distribution channels) are left to a large extent to the judgment of regional managers. On the other hand, Kotler, Fahey, and Jatusripitak (1985), observing Japanese multinational firms' successful product policies, contend that successful global marketers establish plants around the world and decide which plants should manufacture which products for which markets to obtain the lowest costs of production and distribution.

It is clear that the success of global marketing strategy depends on how uniformly a short list of pivotal decisions essential to attaining the aims of standardization are implemented. For multinational firms operating with a traditional polycentric, country-by-country approach, a successful switchover to a global marketing strategy requires their local subsidiaries' acceptance and cooperation. Although it is beyond the scope of this book to elaborate on the difficulty of switchover due to organizational inertia, two examples will be illustrated here: (1) a case of Philips, a Dutch consumer electronics company, which has found it almost impossible to adopt a global strategy; and (2) a case of Parker Pen, an American pen maker, which had difficulty managing a global strategy.

Philips is essentially made up of national subsidiaries that have long operated independently of each other in R&D, product development, and manufacturing. At a time when major successful competitors in consumer electronics, such as Matsushita and Sony, are consolidating their R&D and product development on a global basis, Philips still remains vulnerable because of the difficulties in weaving disparate national subsidiaries into a coherent global competitive team.

Similarly, an abrupt switchover will also likely fail, as experienced by Parker Pen. A well-intended global standardization decision by Parker Pen Company went awry exactly because of its local subsidiaries' resis-

tance to a sudden product policy change introduced in 1982 from its
traditional polycentric decision-making process to a geocentric, head-
quarters-controlled one. Parker Pen's product line was slashed from 500
to the 100 most profitable ones, its manufacturing facilities were also
reduced, and the number of its advertising agencies went from 40 to 1—
unfortunately, all too fast!

Successful global product policy mandates the development of universal
products or products that require no more than a cosmetic change for
adaptation to differing local needs and use conditions (Takeuchi and Porter
1986). A few examples illustrate the point; Seiko watches are the best
example of this core component standardization. Seiko, a Japanese watch-
maker, offers a wide range of designs and models, but based only on a
handful of different operating mechanisms. Similarly, the best-performing
German machine tool-making companies are found, according to a
McKinsey study, to have a narrower range of products, use up to 50
percent fewer parts than their less successful rivals, and make continual,
incremental product and design improvement, with new developments
passed rapidly on to customers (*Economist* 1991).

For companies marketing an extremely wide range of products due to
cultural differences in product-use patterns around the world, it is also
possible to reap economies-of-scale benefits. For example, Electrolux, a
Swedish appliance manufacturer, has adopted the concept of "design
families," offering different products under four different brand names,
but using the same basic designs. A key to such product design standardization lies in standardization of components, including motors,
pumps, and compressors. Thus, White Consolidated in the United States
and Zanussi in Italy, Electrolux's subsidiaries, have the main responsibility for component production within the group.

Competitive advantage can result from such standardization in two
other ways (Takeuchi and Porter 1986). First, standardized components
will make it possible to develop a universal product with all the features
demanded anywhere in the world. Japan's Canon has done so successfully
with its Canon AE-1 cameras and newer models that ensued. Alternatively, Honda is marketing its almost identical Accord cars around the
world by positioning them differently from country to country (more on
this later).

These four ways of developing a global product policy are considered
an effective means to streamline manufacturing, thus lowering manufacturing cost, without sacrificing marketing flexibility. They are summarized
as follows: (1) core components standardization, (2) product design families, (3) universal product with all features, and (4) universal product with
different positioning.

Recently, there has been an increasing amount of interest in the strategic
linkages between product policy and manufacturing long ignored in tra-

ditional considerations of global strategy development (e.g., Hayes and Wheelwright 1984; Cohen and Zysman 1987). With the aggressive competition from European and Japanese multinational firms emphasizing corporate product policy and concomitant manufacturing, U.S. firms have realized that product innovations alone cannot sustain their long-term competitive position without an ingenious product policy linking product and manufacturing process innovations (Wheelwright 1985). Since an increasing portion of global competition is shaped by European and Japanese multinational firms (Franko 1978; Negandhi and Welge 1984; Kotler et al. 1985; Vernon 1986), it is worthwhile to examine their corporate product policies.

DETERMINANTS OF INNOVATIVE BEHAVIOR

A large body of research conducted during the last two decades, under the general rubric of the international product cycle model, has increased our understanding of the diffusion of product innovations in international commerce over time and space. To explain the phenomenon of overseas direct investment in relation to international trade, the international product cycle model has incorporated into a dynamic framework the timing of product innovation, the characteristics of markets, the effects of scale economies, and the role of ignorance and uncertainty in influencing trade patterns (e.g., Wells 1968; Vernon 1966, 1974, 1979). In the first stage of the model, it is suggested that firms (typically of U.S. origin) favored by their domestic market size, innovation acceptance, R&D resources, and strong marketing expertise dominate global markets. In later stages, firms from less favored countries increase their competitiveness by controlling, first their own markets, second third-country markets, and finally the original entrant's (U.S.) market.

Many U.S. firms tend to recognize that their growth and profits come largely from new products (Booz, Allen & Hamilton 1982). Because of the international product cycle model's emphasis on product innovations and marketing implications across national boundaries, the evolution of manufacturing process innovations has not been explicitly considered (Hays and Wheelwright 1979). The issue of the interactive role of product and process innovations was explored in Chapter 3.

In the United States, this product-innovation orientation has put undue emphasis on research-intensive product innovations as a source of competitive advantage, neglecting improvements on products and on manufacturing process (i.e., process innovations) as an "imitation" strategy (Brooks 1983). It is to be noted that the concept of process innovations differs somewhat from the experience curve concept.

The experience curve effect has been discussed from a cost-reduction perspective in the strategy literature (e.g., Hedley 1976; Day and Montgomery 1983). Typically, it includes a broad range of costs that are expected to decrease as cumulative production volume increases along with increased levels of learning, economies of scale and specialization, and modification of product for lower production costs in a stable competitive environment. As Abernathy and Wayne (1974) argued, the experience curve concept becomes inoperative in a competitive environment where rapid technological changes bring about a great deal of product or process design changes. Indeed, today's global competition represents such a competitive environment. Emphasis on the experience curve effect could discount the importance of innovations as an integral part of corporate strategy.

It has been argued that imitation, followed by more innovative adaptation leading to pioneering innovation, forms the natural sequence of industrial development (Brooks 1983; Starr and Ullman 1988). Process innovations should be considered not simply as a means for the firm to capture the experience curve effect, but as a means to improve product quality and performance (Phillips, Chang, and Buzzell 1983; Gale and Klavans 1985; Imai 1986). In many product categories, Japanese firms absorbed U.S. product innovations and improved on product quality and manufacturing process more significantly than U.S. innovators (Buffa 1984; Hayes 1985). Once the product reaches maturity, U.S. firms usually find themselves entrenched in both price and quality competition from European and Japanese firms.

For top managers of U.S. firms to ignore the production function when formulating corporate strategy has been recognized as a grave mistake (Skinner 1969; Cohen and Zysman 1987). Not until recently, however, was the evolutionary relationship between product innovations and manufacturing process innovations explored explicitly for linking technological innovation and productivity improvement within an organization (e.g., Abernathy and Townsend 1975; Abernathy and Utterback 1978; Utterback 1987).

This new perspective differs from the international product cycle model in a crucial respect. The strategic importance of innovations in the production process is a focal point. The international product cycle model emphasizes product innovations and marketing implications, but tends to ignore other important factors, particularly the change in manufacturing process technology (Hayes and Wheelwright 1979). U.S. firms have often been successful abroad because they happened to be marketing a product for the U.S. market that the rest of the world could not make itself because of its lack of necessary technology (Thurow 1985). A product's technological superiority alone may be of short-lived economic significance unless it is backed by complementary process capacities that allow a firm to capture returns from product innovation for a longer period of time.

Thus, the interactive nature of product design and manufacturing process has become increasingly crucial to maintain market performance.

As described in Figure 4–1, the characteristics of the market environment in which European and Japanese multinational firms operate and those of the firms bearing on product policies are considered in this chapter. The market environmental factors will be discussed first, followed by the product policy-related factors as determinants of the firms' innovative behavior.

Characteristics of the Market Environment

Technological Change. The recent emphasis on manufacturing process innovations offers a different perspective on technological change and production locations than the international product cycle model implies. Product innovations are a critical determinant of a firm's competitive advantage at an initial stage as the fluid nature of innovations limits their diffusion to competition. When the product becomes mature, competition begins to shift to product price and production efficiency. According to the international product cycle model, as price competition increases, the locus of competitive production location shifts from developed to less developed countries, and the multinational firm will establish manufacturing facilities overseas to take advantage of inexpensive labor. Such a substitution of labor for capital may provide some temporary respite from price competition, but will cost the firm an opportunity to improve on manufacturing technology in a rapidly changing technological environment (Markides and Berg 1988). Rather, it should be argued that process innovations have become all the more necessary for an increase in productivity to maintain the product's competitiveness, while a plant relocation is not (Stobaugh and Telesio 1983). Therefore, it is expected that *the more rapid the technological change in the marketplace, the more emphasis will be placed on process innovations* (Hypothesis 1).

Market Growth. For many foreign multinational firms, the United States represents a pivotal market in implementing their global strategies. In a study of *Fortune*-listed multinational firms, Dunning and Pearse (1985) found that almost half of the foreign multinational firms' total worldwide sales in 1982 was generated abroad (or, more specifically, over 60 percent for European and about 40 percent for Japanese multinational firms). Much of their foreign sales is attributed to sales in the United States.

A high level of market attractiveness, a prime determinant of which is the market growth rate, provides the firm a strong incentive to adopt a strategy of building market share (Burke 1984). Since many foreign multinational firms use the U.S. market growth as a benchmark for their global strategy, a high level of U.S. market growth rate encourages European and Japanese multinational firms to increase investment in both product and process innovative activities. Therefore, it is anticipated that *the higher the growth rate of the U.S. market, the more emphasis will be placed on product and process innovations* (Hypothesis 2).

Characteristics of the Firm

Outsourcing. The 1960s saw foreign competitors gradually catching up in a productivity race with U.S. firms that had commanded an unbeatable position in international trade (Starr 1973). This coincided with U.S. corporate strategic emphasis drifting from manufacturing to finance and marketing (Buffa 1984). As a result, manufacturing management gradually lost its organizational influence.[1] Production managers' decision-making authority was reduced such that R&D personnel prepared specifications with which production complied and marketing imposed its own delivery, inventory, and quality conditions, but not productivity considerations. In a sense, production managers gradually took on the role of outside suppliers within their own firms. Production managers' reduced influence in the organization further led to an erroneous belief that manufacturing functions could, and should, be transferred easily to independent operators and subcontractors, depending upon cost differential between in-house and contracted-out production. Thus, in order to lower production costs under competitive pressure, U.S. multinational firms turned increasingly to outsourcing of components and finished products from abroad, particularly from newly industrialized countries, including South Korea, Taiwan, Singapore, Hong Kong, Brazil, and Mexico (Moxon 1974; Markides and Berg 1988).

Outsourcing strategy is receiving an increasing amount of attention, as it affects domestic employment and economic structure. As discussed in Chapter 3, U.S. firms using such strategy have been described pejoratively as "hollow corporations." Teece (1987) cautions that U.S. firms are increasingly adopting a "designer role" in global competition—offering innovations in product design without investing in manufacturing process technology. This widespread outsourcing practice is considered to have a deleterious impact on the ability of U.S. firms to maintain their initial competitive advantage based on product innovations (Hayes and Abernathy 1980; Markides and Berg 1988). Indeed, keeping abreast of emerging technology through continual improvement in R&D and manufacturing is the *sine qua non* for the firm's continued competitiveness (Imai 1986).

Foreign multinational firms engage in outsourcing to a lesser extent than U.S. multinational firms due to various legal constraints (Grunwald and Flamm 1985). Outsourcing by U.S. firms for the U.S. market is encouraged by the U.S. tariff provisions for products imported under items 806.30 and 807.00 (renamed 9802.00.60 and 9802.00.80 under the Harmonized Tariff Schedule since 1989). These tariff provisions permit duty-free reentry to the United States of U.S. components sent abroad for further processing or assembly as further-in-process components or finished products. The European Community and Japan also have similar tariff arrangements, though much more restrictive in effect than the U.S. tariff provisions. Despite the difficulties, outsourcing by European and Japanese multinational firms is increasing (UN Center on Transnational Corporations 1983). Little is known, however, about the impact of outsourcing on foreign multinational firms' innovative activities. It is our thesis that *the increase in outsourcing retards multinational firms' process innovative activities regardless of nationality* (Hypothesis 3).

Triad Marketing. Mature multinational firms have come to learn the strategic importance and benefit of global strategy in increasingly homogenized markets, in particular, of the Triad regions of the world (Ohmae 1985). The Triad regions with a total combined population of 630 million people, including the United States (250 million), the European Community (260 million), and Japan (120 million), represent a very attractive and competitive market where more than 80 percent of world production is consumed by about 15 percent of world population.

It is further argued that the Triads are forming with such speed that multinational firms with significant product innovations can no longer approach Triad markets on a country-by-country basis because of the immediate threat from potential entrants (Ohmae 1985). If they do, competition on a global scale through syndicated competitors will overcome the innovator's initial competitive advantages. This global orientation will prompt the multinational firms to simultaneously invest in manufacturing process innovations to maintain their product-based competitive advantage. Thus, it is anticipated that *the products that are marketed in all three Triad regions of the world represent a higher level of product and process innovations than those that are not* (Hypothesis 4).

Product Policy. In growing global competition, sourcing of components and finished products around the world within the multinational firm has increased (UN Center on Transnational Corporations 1983; Dunning and Pearse 1985). The development of global sourcing and marketing strategies across different foreign markets has become a central issue for many multinational firms. Traditionally, a polycentric approach to organizing operations on a country-by-country basis allowed each country manager to tailor marketing strategy to the peculiarities of local markets. As such, product adaptations were considered a necessary strategy to better cater to the different needs and wants of customers in various countries (Keegan 1969).

As early as 1972, Stopford and Wells (1972) recognized that global coordination calls for products standardized to some extent in world markets. Porter (1986) further argues that coordination among increasingly complex networks of activities dispersed worldwide is becoming a prime source of competitive advantage. As discussed earlier, it can be argued that product adaptation tends to be a reactive, rather than a proactive, strategic response to the market. Therefore, a high level of product adaptation may make it difficult for multinational firms to reap economies of scale in production and marketing and to coordinate their networks of activities on a global scale.

Product standardization, however, does not necessarily imply either production standardization or a narrow product line. For example, Japanese automobile manufacturers have gradually stretched out their product line offerings, while marketing them with little adaptation in many parts of the world (Kotler et al. 1985). This strategy requires manufacturing flexibility, which is a form of process innovation (Miles and Snow 1986). The crux of global product standardization rather calls for proactive identification of homogeneous segments around the world, and is different from the concept of marketing abroad a product originally developed for the home market.

A proactive approach to product policy has gained momentum in recent years, as spearheaded by Levitt's (1983) call for global products made possible by intermarket segmentation. Takeuchi and Porter (1986), among others, offer a more balanced view of intermarket segmentation for global markets. In addition to clustering of countries and identification of homogeneous segments in different countries, targeting different segments in different countries with the same products is another way to maintain a product policy of standardization (e.g., Honda Accords to the second or commuter car buyer segment in the United States, the family car segment in Japan, and the highly engineered sports car segment in some European countries). These intermarket segmentation approaches require a product policy by which to develop a product that has all the features demanded anywhere in the world or in a region, or to develop a universal product with optimal functions and features that balance market needs and costs of its development and production.

If the firms wish to gain market share in global markets, management must learn to combine product and process innovations for global leadership in cost and value. Mansfield and Romeo (1984) have found that increased expenditures on R&D activities by both parents and their overseas subsidiaries have begun to produce technology for application throughout the world, increased reciprocal technology transfer between them, and consequently shortened a technology application lag at home and abroad. This is a strategic response to global competition by making it possible to "sprinkle major markets of the world with a new product" (Ohmae 1985).

As a result, a corporate product policy pursuing standardized products worldwide requires a high level of management and R&D commitment to capitalizing on commonalities across national boundaries rather than debating the differences of customers based on nationalities. Therefore, it is believed that *multinational firms with a corporate product policy pursuing worldwide standardized products place a higher level of emphasis on product and process innovations than do those with a product policy pursuing adaptation* (Hypothesis 5).

European and Japanese Difference in Innovations. During the postwar period from the 1950s to 1960s, Japanese firms relied heavily on U.S. or European technology through licensing for product development and improved on product quality by investing heavily in manufacturing processes in order to garner differential advantage over the foreign competitors with initial product innovations (e.g., Kotler et al. 1985). However, it is increasingly evident that Japan's non military R&D spending has caught up with and even surpassed that of (then) West Germany, France, and Britain (Japan Science & Technology Agency 1981). The quality and productivity of Japanese R&D activities are also reported to have surpassed those of West European countries (*Fortune* 1986).

This technological evolution is of the kind the United States had once experienced at the dawn of this century, known as Yankee ingenuity, and heralds Japan's technological maturation (Brooks 1983; Starr and Ullman 1988). Japanese firms may have reached a point where they put an increasing amount of R&D earmarked for product innovations, although the Japanese were once imitators through licensing of product innovations introduced abroad. It is our hypothesis that *given Japanese multinational firms' mastering of manufacturing processes, they may outperform European competitors in both product and process innovations* (Hypothesis 6).

MEASURES

The measures used for analysis in this chapter are presented in Table 4–1. Since product and process innovations were defined and measured in Chapter 3, this section describes the explanatory variables that will be used to account for the variation in levels of product and process innovative activities by European and Japanese multinational firms.

Technological Change (TECHCH)

A two-item measure was used. First, respondents were asked whether there had been major technological changes in the product or in the methods of production since the introduction of the product in the United States. Second, they were also asked whether there would be major technological changes within the next three years. The two items were highly

Table 4–1
Measurement

Variables	Measure	Cronbach's Alpha[a]
Technological Change	A 2-item measure: Have there been major technological changes in the product offered by your firm and/or major competitors, or in the methods of production, since the introduction of your product? (yes 1/0 no) Is it likely that there will be major technological changes in the product offered by your firm and/or major competitors, or in the methods of production, within the next 3 years? (yes 1/0 no)	.86
Market Growth Rate	A 2-item measure: Short-term (3-year) future market growth rate is... (very low 1/5 very high) Long-term (3-year) future market growth rate is... (very low 1/5 very high)	.87
Outsourcing Definition 1	A single-item measure Actual percentage of the total purchased value of components sourced from all independent suppliers	n.a.
Definition 2	Actual percentage of the total purchased value of components sourced from independent suppliers in NICs	n.a.
Definition 3	Without technical assistance from your firm, approximately what percentage of the total purchased value of components in the product could be sourced from local firms in newly industrializing countries such as Taiwan, South Korea, and Brazil	n.a.
Triad Markets	A single-item measure: In which regions (countries) is the product currently marketed? (1 if all Triad regions are identified; 0 otherwise)	n.a.
Product Policy	A single-item measure: For product development, the parent company policy is to attempt to have... 1) Unique product designed for each country, 2) Standard products with specific adaptation for some markets, or 3) Standardized products worldwide	n.a.
Nationality	European (0) or Japanese (1)	n.a.
Type of Product	Consumer durables (0) or industrial durables (1)	n.a.

[a]n.a. indicates alpha is not applicable.

correlated ($r = .76$, $p < .0001$; Cronbach's alpha $= .86$), and were added together to create TECHCH.

U.S. Market's Growth Rate (GROWTH)

Initially, a broader measure of U.S. market attractiveness was attempted. Based on multinational portfolio analysis (Channon and Jalland 1978; Wind and Douglas 1981), Burke's (1984) 6-item measure of market attractiveness on a 5-point scale was modified for the international context. However, the modified measure yielded a very low internal consistency. Since market growth rate is the most important determinant of market attractiveness, two items measuring short-term (3-year) and long-term (10-year) expected market growth rates were retained and added together to represent GROWTH (Cronbach's alpha $= .87$).

Outsourcing (OUTSORC1, OUTSORC2, and OUTSORC3)

Outsourcing broadly refers to components and finished products supplied to the multinational firm by independent suppliers from around the world (OUTSORC1). Outsourcing is also narrowly defined, and more frequently used, to indicate the extent of components and finished products supplied to the firm by independent suppliers located in developing countries such as South Korea, Taiwan, Singapore, Hong Kong, and Mexico (OUTSORC2). As mentioned earlier, because of various legal constraints on outsourcing faced by European and Japanese multinational firms, the actual level of outsourcing may not fully represent its implications on innovative behavior. It is conjectured that the extent to which the executives of the foreign multinational firms believe components and finished products can be procured from those LDCs (OUTSORC3) may more adequately represent its impact on the foreign firms' innovative activities (i.e., outsourceability).

Respondents were asked a series of questions regarding (1) what percentage of the total purchased value of components comes from each of the following locations including the United States (US), West European countries (WE), Japan (JP), other developed countries (DC), and newly industrializing countries (LDC) ($SOURCE_i$), and (2) of the components sourced in each of those locations, what percent is supplied by internal members (i.e., fully owned subsidiaries or majority-owned affiliates) of the parent system ($INTERNAL_i$). Therefore,

$OUTSORC1 = \Sigma \, SOURCE_i \times (1 - INTERNAL_i)$; i = US to LDC, and

$OUTSORC2 = SOURCE_{LDC} \times (1 - INTERNAL_{LDC})$.

To measure OUTSORC3, the respondents were also asked the question: "Without technical assistance from your firm, approximately what percent of the total purchased value of components in the product could be sourced from local firms in newly industrializing countries such as Taiwan, South Korea, and Brazil?"

Triad Markets (TRIAD)

This is a dichotomous variable constructed by asking the following question: "In which regions (countries) is the product currently marketed?" This variable represents whether or not the product is marketed in all Triad regions. If all Triad regions are identified, then this variable is 1; otherwise, 0.

Corporate Product Policy (POLICY)

The literature has provided general support that standardization of all or parts of marketing strategy in industrialized countries is increasingly possible because of "homogenization" of needs and wants despite cultural differences. Particularly, a high degree of standardization appears to exist in product-related areas of marketing strategy, including brand names, physical characteristics, and packaging. Although corporate product policy established by the parent firm may not be adopted by subsidiaries without modification due to local market conditions, the parent's product policy nonetheless reflects corporate goals. Respondents were asked to identify their parent company's global product policy in the following range: standardized products worldwide (3), standard products with specific adaptation for some markets (2), or unique product designed for each country (1).

Nationality of the Multinational Firm (NATION)

The nationality of multinational firms was identified either as European (0) or as Japanese (1) in this study.

Type of the Product (TYPE)

Because industrial buyers are more rational in their purchase decisions than consumers, product standardization is more feasible for industrial products than for consumer products (Boddewyn, Soehl, and Picard 1986). Although I am not aware of any study examining how the type of the product affects the level of product and process innovations, the potential impact on innovations of the ease of standardization was suspected.

Therefore, TYPE is a dichotomous variable representing either consumer durable (0) or industrial durable products (1).

ANALYSIS AND RESULTS

The hypotheses explaining the variation in the levels of product and process innovations were tested by regression analysis. Preliminary regression analysis indicated that the first two of the three alternative definitions used for outsourcing (i.e., OUTSORC1 and OUTSORC2) did not have any significant impact on innovative activities. As speculated, outsourceability (OUTSORC3) was a more salient variable in explaining their innovative activities. In subsequent analysis, therefore, the concept of outsourceability was employed. The results of the analysis are presented in Table 4–2.

Technological Change

It was expected in Hypothesis 1 that the rapid technological change in the marketplace will prompt the multinational firms to invest more in process innovations in order to keep their initial competitive advantage based on product innovations from being quickly eroded, while its impact on product innovations is not consistent. As expected, technological change is significant ($p = .05$) in the process innovation model, but not strongly significant ($p = .20$) in the product innovation model. Therefore, support is obtained for the first hypothesis.

Incidentally, it is noted that although technological change was not significant in the product innovation model, a positive slope coefficient was observed. It is suspected that the rapid technological change in the marketplace may have a weak but positive impact on the magnitude of product innovations.

Market Growth

Hypothesis 2 explored the pivotal role of the U.S. market in the Triad regions for European and Japanese multinational firms to implement a global strategy. It is anticipated that a high growth rate of the U.S. market will prompt the foreign multinational firms to increase investment in both innovative activities. Growth rate is found to be significant ($p = .04$) in both product and process innovation models, in support of the hypothesis.

Outsourcing

As noted earlier, the actual degree of outsourcing (OUTSORC1 and OUTSORC2) was not significantly related to any of the innovative activ-

Table 4–2
Multiple Regression Analysis for Product and Process Innovations

Variable		Product Innovations[a]			Product Innovations[b]		
		Beta Coefficient	t-Value	Significance Level	Beta Coefficient	t-Value	Significance Level
TECHCH	Technological change	.14	1.29	.20	.22	1.95	.05
OUTSORC3	Outsourceability	-.06	-.58	.57	-.20	-1.73	.09
GROWTH	U.S. market growth rate	.25	2.16	.04	.25	2.10	.04
TRIAD	Triad markets	.26	2.19	.03	.04	.32	.75
POLICY	Product policy	.30	2.72	.01	.24	2.13	.04
NATION	Nationality of firm	.35	2.72	.01	.33	2.45	.02
TYPE	Product type	.10	.74	.47	.16	1.16	.25

[a]$R^2 = 40.0\%$, significant at the .0002 level.

[b]$R^2 = 36.2\%$, significant at the .0008 level.

ities. Instead, it was examined how outsourceability from LDCs (OUTSORC3) would affect the multinational firms' innovative activities. Hypothesis 3 expects that easy outsourceability tends to slacken the multinational firms' effort at continual improvement in manufacturing processes, if not their new product development activities. Outsourceability is weakly significant (p = .09) and has a negative impact on process innovations, while it is not the case with product innovations (p > .20). These findings are generally consistent with the hypothesis.

Triad Marketing

Hypothesis 4 probed how the growing demand homogenization in Triad regions and the shortened product life cycle in global competition will affect the multinational firms' marketing strategy. It is posited that the products that are marketed in all Triad regions represent a higher level of product and process innovations than those that are not.

As expected, this variable is significantly related (p = .03) to product innovations. The average magnitude of product innovations was measured at 4.6 on a 9-point summated scale for Triad marketers, while it was 3.0 for non-Triad marketers. The same variable, however, failed to be significantly related (p > .50) to process innovations. The average magnitudes of process innovations were 4.4 for Triad marketers and 4.0 for non-Triad marketers. This unexpected finding may be reconciled by considering that not all foreign multinational firms that market in all Triad regions will simultaneously put an equal amount of effort on process innovations. As Abernathy and Utterback (1978) argued, process innovations may still lag behind product innovations, at least for some multinational firms. Therefore, the hypothesis is partially supported.

Product Policy

Hypothesis 5 looked into the relationship of product and process innovations with the firm's corporate product policy. As expected, product policy is significant in both product and process innovation models (p = .01 and p = .04, respectively), confirming that corporate product policy has a strong impact on both innovative activities. The average magnitude of product innovations for each of the three levels of product policy (i.e., worldwide standardized product policy, standard product policy with specific adaptation for some markets, and policy of unique product for each country) was measured at 6.0, 4.0, and 2.6 on a 9-point summated scale, respectively. Similarly, the magnitude of process innovations averaged at 6.1, 4.1, and 3.3, respectively.

Thus, the firm's commitment to R&D effort at product and process innovations tends to be accompanied by its pursuit for global leadership and its commitment to capitalizing on commonalities across national boundaries. Furthermore, since a high level of R&D commitment is a costly endeavor, the firm has to take advantage of scale economies by pursuing global markets so as to recoup its R&D investment in a shorter period of time than would be possible with a corporate policy requiring a higher level of product adaptation.

Nationality

Hypothesis 6 focused on a recent turnaround of Japanese firms' policy on innovations. Nationality is also highly significant in both product and process models ($p = .01$ and $p = .02$, respectively). Japanese firms had an average magnitude of product and process innovations measured at 5.5 and 5.3, with European firms at 3.2 and 3.6. The results support the hypothesis, suggesting that Japanese multinational firms have become increasingly oriented toward product innovations as well as they have been adept at process innovations.

CONCLUSIONS AND IMPLICATIONS

All the hypotheses are generally supported, regardless of product type. Findings strongly represent a number of major changes in the competitive environment that will have a significant impact on the way U.S. as well as foreign multinational firms should operate in global markets.

Corporate Product Policy and Triad Markets

This chapter has found that corporate policy for globally standardized products is associated with a higher level of product and process innovations than is corporate product policy allowing product adaptation to some or a large extent. Multinational firms' corporate policy for globally standardized products is concomitantly backed by a high level of management's commitment to R&D activities in pursuit of major product and process innovations.

It has been found in Chapter 2 that a high level of product adaptation is associated with low performance. This finding may be construed by the concomitant relationship that exists between global product policy and corporate commitment to R&D. Product adaptation may be viewed as a reactive, rather than proactive, strategic concept. As noted earlier, competitive reactions may be sufficiently swift as to nullify transitory market-customized advantages. Further, a high level of product adaptation may make it difficult for the firm to reap economies of scale in production and marketing on a global basis. This finding generally supports Levitt's (1983) argument for the development of a globally acceptable product that would not require any more than cosmetic adaptation to foreign markets.

It is to be noted that global products should not automatically be equated to standardization of other aspects of the marketing mix—namely, promotion, pricing, and distribution channels. As long as firms take a proactive approach to product development, product standardization is probably the most feasible (i.e., manageable) in contrast with standardization of other marketing mix variables that tend to be more market-constrained. Therefore, although such nonproduct standardization is surely hoped for, differences in market requirements may not warrant such an all-round standardization policy. Yet the potential benefits of product standardization are economies of scale, consistent product image around the world, and streamlined product management that could result in huge savings and market power, among other things.

However, global product policy does not automatically imply that the product will be marketed in all three Triad markets, as evidenced by an extremely low correlation between POLICY and TRIAD ($r = -.04$, $p = .79$). Products that are marketed in all three Triad regions are found to represent a higher level of product innovations than those that are not. However, no such difference has been observed in process innovations between the Triad and the non-Triad products.

It implies that not all European and Japanese multinational firms put an equal amount of effort on both product and process innovative activities. As the literature suggests, while some foreign multinational firms do pursue a strategy of simultaneously developing product and process innovations, others may still follow a more gradual approach to global competition by putting an increasing amount of effort on process innovations once their product innovation-based competitive advantage has been threatened. Because of the interactive nature of product and process innovations, the former group of European and Japanese multinational firms is likely to enjoy a higher level of market performance than the latter group because of the positive interactive and compensatory nature of product and process innovations.

Nature of Component Sourcing and Innovative Behavior

In a global marketplace crowded with a myriad of competitive firms from both developed and developing countries, it has become easier for any multinational firm to source an increasing percentage of its components for manufacture from outside suppliers. While there are exceptions, as shown in Excerpt 4–1, many U.S. multinational firms increasingly outsource from independent foreign suppliers those components and finished products often made to their specifications. In this process, however, U.S. multinational firms' ability to manufacture cost-efficiently is

Excerpt 4–1

Black & Decker: An Un-American Way

Not all U.S. firms got themselves into the dilemma of losing long-term innovative ability in exchage for short-term cost advantage, of course. In the mid-1970s, Black & Decker, for example, confronted rapidly rising wage costs in the United States and an incessant on-slaught of foreign competition in consumer power tool industry *not* by increasing components sourcing from independent suppliers abroad, *but* by redesigning its product development and whole pro-duction policy. Black & Decker introduced the program called "Dou-ble Insulation." The program's ultimate goal was to redesign the product line and develop a family look, simplify the product offerings, reduce manufacturing costs, automate manufacturing, standardize components, incorporate new material and new product features, im-prove product performance, and provide for worldwide product spec-ifications. Behind the company's successful transition was collaborative effort among design, engineering, and manufacturing divisions. Not only did this program reduce production and marketing costs (and as a result, increased market share and profitability), but also *it further improved the company's manufacturing and new prod-uct development capability.*

Source: Alvin P. Lehnerd, "Revitalizing the Manufacture and Design of Mature Global Products," in *Technology and Global Industry: Companies and Nations in the World Economy*, Bruce R. Guile and Harvey Brooks, eds. (Washington, DC: National Acad-emy Press, 1987), 49–64.

likely to suffer in the long run as they lose touch with emerging manu-facturing know-how and technology that may eventually find their way into process innovations. Although European and Japanese multinational firms are not yet engaged in outsourcing as extensively as are U.S. firms, this chapter has shown that there appears to be a sign of the negative relationship between outsourceability and the magnitude of process in-novations in the foreign multinational firms.

Technological Trajectory

This chapter has also shown the highly competitive technological state of Japanese multinational firms. As indicated earlier, Yankee ingenuity once referred to Americans successfully imitating and improving upon British technology at the dawn of this century. Recently, the Japanese have gone through the same stage of technological development on to a new stage where they have skills and originality in many areas of science and technology. As a result, U.S. as well as European competitors can no longer disregard Japanese creativity, which brings about new product and process innovations.

This point was further demonstrated recently in a report that several Japanese electronics giants (closely followed by European firms) have perfected HDTV (high definition television) technology after more than 20 years of endeavor, promising to usher in a new electronic age before the turn of the century (*Business Week* 1987). U.S. competitors are experiencing tremendous difficulty meeting the Japanese competition for two major reasons. First, they had balked at the idea of developing such technology long ago as they did not see a ready market for it. Second, because they could not manufacture cost-effectively, they have outsourced video cassette recorders (VCRs) from Japanese and other original equipment manufacturers, which were the harbinger of HDTV technology. This example, although of an anecdotal nature, further illustrates the importance of keeping abreast of emerging technology through continual improvement in product and manufacturing processes.

In conclusion, the era of global competition has arrived, at least for consumer and industrial durable products. As Levitt (1983) and Ohmae (1985), among others, separately anticipated, it has become increasingly important to capitalize on expanding commonalities across national boundaries rather than to focus on the differences of customers based on nationalities. By doing so, multinational firms will be capable of capitalizing both on economies of scale in production and marketing and on economies of scope in technological frontiers for future innovations.

LIMITATIONS

This chapter is an extension of the studies conducted in Chapters 2 and 3. Therefore, the same limitations apply and will not be repeated here. However, there is one caveat to be shared with the readers. The subsidiaries of European and Japanese multinational firms operating in the United States, thus their products marketed in (either exported to or manufactured in) the United States, were considered in the study. Although the United States is a pivotal market in the Triad for the foreign multinational firms, not all of their products are marketed in the United States. The author's informal conversation with executives of a number of foreign multinational firms indicates that about 80 percent of products introduced within the last ten years found their way into the U.S. market. If this were reflective of the population, one could argue that some 20 percent of the products had not been represented in this study.

NOTE

1. The lack of emphasis on manufacturing in the United States was manifested in MBA programs across the country. In the 1970s and much of the 1980s, the MBA program was made up of every functional area (i.e., accounting, finance,

marketing, management, and technology) *but* manufacturing. Only in recent years has manufacturing caught the attention of a growing number of business researchers and attained a research area status comparable to the other functional areas of business (see, for example, Cohen and Zysman 1987).

REFERENCES

Abernathy, William J. and Phillip L. Townsend (1975). "Technology, Productivity and Process Change." *Technological Forecasting and Social Change,* 7 (August), 379–396.

Abernathy, William J. and James M. Utterback (1978). "Patterns of Industrial Innovation." *Technology Review,* 80 (June–July), 40–47.

Abernathy, William J. and Kenneth Wayne (1974). "Limits of the Learning Curve." *Harvard Business Review,* 52 (September–October), 109–119.

Aylmer, R. J. (1970). "Who Makes Marketing Decisions in the Multinational Firm?" *Journal of Marketing,* 34 (October), 25–30.

Bartels, Robert (1968). "Are Domestic and International Marketing Dissimilar?" *Journal of Marketing,* 32 (July), 56–61.

Boddewyn, J. J., Robin Soehl, and Jacques Picard (1986). "Standardization in International Marketing: Is Ted Levitt in Fact Right?" *Business Horizons,* 29 (November–December), 69–75.

Booz, Allen & Hamiltion, Inc. (1982). *New Products Management for the 1980s.* New York: Booz, Allen & Hamilton.

Brooks, Harvey (1983). "Japanese Technological Advances and Possible United States Responses Using Research Joint Ventures." Presented at House Subcommittee on Investigations and Oversight and the Subcommittee on Science, Research, and Technology of the Committee on Science and Technology, 98th Congress, 1st session, June 29–30.

Buffa, Elwood S. (1984). "Making American Manufacturing Competitive." *California Management Review,* 26 (Spring), 29–46.

Burke, Marian C. (1984). "Strategic Choice and Marketing Managers: An Examination of Business-Level Marketing Objectives." *Journal of Marketing Research,* 21 (November), 345–359.

Business Week (1987). "Television Makers Are Dreaming of a Wide Crispness." December 21, 108–109.

Buzzell, Robert D. (1968). "Can You Standardize Multinational Marketing?" *Harvard Business Review,* 46 (November–December), 102–113.

Channon, Derek and Michael Jalland (1978). *Multinational Strategic Planning.* New York: AMACOM.

Cohen, Stephen S. and John Zysman (1987). "Why Manufacturing Matters: The Myth of the Post-Industrial Economy." *California Management Review,* 29 (Spring), 9–26.

Day, George S. and David B. Montgomery (1983). "Diagnosing the Experience Curve." *Journal of Marketing,* 47 (Spring), 44–58.

Douglas, Susan P. and Yoram Wind (1987). "The Myth of Globalization." *Columbia Journal of World Business,* 22 (Winter), 19–30.

Dunning, John H. and R. D. Pearse (1985). *The World's Largest Industrial Enterprises 1962–1983.* New York: St. Martin's Press.

Economist (1991), "Less is More," May 25, 75–76.

Fortune (1986). "Where the U.S. Stands," October 13, 28–40.

Franko, Lawrence G. (1978). "Multinationals: The End of U.S. Dominance." *Harvard Business Review,* 56 (November–December), 93–101.

Gale, Bradley T. and Richard Klavans (1985). "Formulating Quality Improvement Strategy." *Journal of Business Strategy,* 5 (Winter), 21–32.

Grunwald, Joseph and Kenneth Flamm (1985). *The Global Factory: Foreign Assembly in International Trade.* Washington, DC: The Brookings Institution.

Hayes, Robert H. (1985). "Strategic Planning—Forward in Reverse?" *Harvard Business Review,* 63 (November–December), 111–119.

—— and William J. Abernathy (1980). "Managing Our Way to Economic Decline." *Harvard Business Review,* 58 (July–August), 67–77.

Hayes, Robert H. and Steven C. Wheelwright (1979). "Link Manufacturing Process and Product Life Cycles." *Harvard Business Review,* 57 (January–February), 133–140.

—— eds. (1984). *Restoring Our Competitive Edge: Competing Through Manufacturing.* New York: John Wiley.

Hedley, Barry (1976). "A Fundamental Approach to Strategy Development." *Long Range Planning,* 9 (December), 2–11.

Imai, Masaaki (1986). *Kaizen.* New York: Random House Business Division.

Jain, Subhash C. (1989). "Standardization of International Marketing Strategy: Some Research Hypotheses." *Journal of Marketing,* 53 (January), 70–79.

Japan Science and Technology Agency (1981). *White Paper on Science and Technology.* Tokyo.

Keegan, Warren J. (1969). "Multinational Product Planning: Strategic Alternatives." *Journal of Marketing,* 33 (January), 58–62.

Kogut, Bruce (1985). "Designing Global Strategies: Comparative and Competitive Value-Added Chains." *Sloan Management Review,* 26 (Summer), 15–28.

Kotabe, Masaaki. "Corporate Product Policy and Innovative Behavior of European and Japanese Multinational Firms: An Empirical Investigation." *Journal of Marketing,* 54, April 1990, 19–33.

Kotler, Philip, Liam Fahey, and Somkid Jatusripitak (1985). *The New Competition.* Englewood Cliffs, NJ: Prentice-Hall.

Lehnerd, Alvin P. (1987). "Revitalizing the Manufacture and Design of Mature Global Products." In *Technology and Global Industry: Companies and Nations in the World Economy,* Bruce R. Guile and Harvey Brooks, eds. Washington, DC: National Academy Press, 49–64.

Levitt, Theodore (1983). "The Globalization of Markets." *Harvard Business Review,* 61 (May–June), 92–102.

Mansfield, Edwin and Anthony Romeo (1984). " 'Reverse' Transfers of Technology from Overseas Subsidiaries to American Firms." *IEEE Transactions on Engineering Management,* EM–31(3) (August), 122–127.

Markides, Constantinos and Norman Berg (1988). "Manufacturing Offshore Is Bad Business." *Harvard Business Review,* 66 (September–October), 113–120.

Miles, Raymond E. and Charles C. Snow (1986). "Organizations: New Concepts for New Forms." *California Management Review,* 28 (Spring), 62–73.

Moxon, Richard W. (1974). *Offshore Production in the Less Developed Countries.* Bulletin No. 98–99. New York: New York University Institute of Finance.

Negandhi, Anant R. and Martin Welge (1984). *Beyond Theory Z.* London: JAI Press.

Ohmae, Kenichi (1985). *Triad Power.* New York: The Free Press.

Phillips, Lynn W., Dae Chang, and Robert D. Buzzell (1983). "Product Quality, Cost Position, and Business Performance: A Test of Some Key Hypotheses." *Journal of Marketing,* 47 (Spring), 26–43.

Porter, Michael E., ed. (1986). *Competition in Global Industries.* Boston: Harvard Business School Press.

Skinner, Wickham (1969). "Manufacturing—Missing Link in Corporate Strategy." *Harvard Business Review,* 47 (May–June), 136–145.

Sorenson, Ralph Z. and Ulrich E. Wiechmann (1975). "How Multinationals View Marketing Standardization." *Harvard Business Review,* 53 (May–June), 38–56.

Starr, Martin K. (1973). "Productivity is the USA's Problem." *California Management Review,* 15 (Winter), 32–36.

————— and John E. Ullman (1988). "The Myth of Industrial Supremacy." In *Global Competitiveness.* Martin K. Starr, ed. New York: W.W. Norton.

Stobaugh, Robert and Piero Telesio (1983). "Match Manufacturing Policies and Product Strategy." *Harvard Business Review,* 61 (March–April), 113–120.

Stopford, John M. and Louis T. Wells, Jr. (1972). *Managing the Multinational Enterprise.* New York: Basic Books.

Takeuchi, Hirotaka and Michael E. Porter (1986). "Three Roles of International Marketing in Global Strategy." In *Competition in Global Industries,* Michael E. Porter, ed. Boston: Harvard Business School Press, 111–146.

Teece, David J. (1987). "Capturing Value from Technological Innovation: Integration, Strategic Partnering, and Licensing Decisions." In *Technology and Global Industry,* Bruce R. Guile and Harvey Brooks, eds. Washington, DC: National Academy Press, 65–95.

Thurow, Lester C. ed. (1985). *The Management Challenge.* Cambridge, MA: MIT Press.

United Nations Center on Transnational Corporations (1983). *Transnational Corporations in World Development, Third Survey.* New York: United Nations.

Utterback, James M. (1987). "Innovation and Industrial Evolution in Manufacturing Industries." In *Technology and Global Industry,* Bruce R. Guile and Harvey Brooks, eds. Washington, DC: National Academy Press, 16–48.

Vernon, Raymond (1966). "International Investment and International Trade in the Product Cycle." *Quarterly Journal of Economics,* 80 (May), 190–207.

————— (1974). "The Location of Economic Activity." In *Economic Analysis and the Multinational Enterprise,* John H. Dunning, ed. London: George Allen and Unwin, 89–114.

————— (1979). "The Product Cycle Hypothesis in a New International Environment." *Oxford Bulletin of Economics and Statistics,* 41 (November), 255–267.

————— (1986). "Can U.S. Manufacturing Come Back?" *Harvard Business Review,* 64 (July–August), 98–106.

Walters, Peter G. (1986). "International Marketing Policy: A Discussion of the
    Standardization Construct and its Relevance for Corporate Policy." *Journal of International Business Studies,* 17 (Summer), 55–69.
Wells, Louis T., Jr. (1968). "Product Life Cycle for International Trade?" *Journal of Marketing,* 32 (July), 1–6.
Wheelwright, Steven C. (1985). "Restoring the Competitive Edge in U.S. Manufacturing." *California Management Review,* 27 (Spring), 26–42.
Wind, Yoram and Susan Douglas (1981). "International Portfolio Analysis and
    Strategy: The Challenge of the 80s." *Journal of International Business Studies,* 11 (Fall), 69–82.

Chapter 5 ─────────────────────────

Marketing Strategy

The research findings reported in the previous chapters have unequivocally revealed the importance of the corporate drive to pursue product standardization and internal sourcing of core components on a global basis and the role of product and process innovations as the key determinants of European and Japanese multinational firms' market performance in the United States. These are all "supply-side" arguments. Thus far, our discussion has been predicated on a "demand-side" assumption that the firms capitalize on commonalities across national boundaries. This chapter attempts to show that corporate drive toward successful standardization strategy involves not simply supply-side manufacturing creativity but, more importantly, demand-side marketing ingenuity. Indeed, they cannot be considered separately for successful implementation of corporate strategy.

The presence of European and Japanese firms has continued to escalate in the United States (Boyer 1986; Herr 1988; Johnson 1987). Japanese firms, in particular, have dramatically increased their presence both by establishing their manufacturing plants and by taking over existing businesses in recent years. As shown in Figure 5–1, while Britain still has the largest cumulative investment position of over $120 billion in the United States as of 1990, Japanese direct investment has increased substantially over the past five years, making it the second largest investor nation with a cumulative investment of over $70 billion in the United States (*Fortune* 1990). European investments (led by British, Dutch, and German firms) are still substantial.

The increase in foreign direct investments in the United States has been attributed to a variety of factors, including the large U.S. market size

Figure 5–1
Cumulative Foreign Direct Investment Positions in the United States

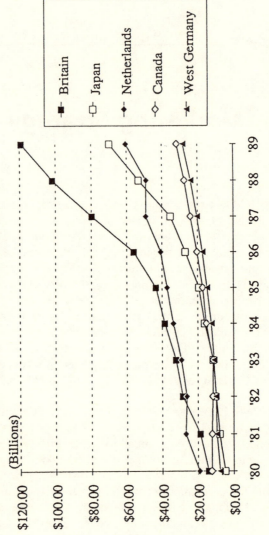

(Billions)

$120.00

$100.00

$80.00

$60.00

$40.00

$20.00

$0.00

'80 '81 '82 '83 '84 '85 '86 '87 '88 '89

■— Britain
□— Japan
◆— Netherlands
◇— Canada
◄— West Germany

Source: U.S. Bureau of Economic Analysis, *Survey of Current Business*, August 1990, and earlier issues.

(Ajami and Ricks 1981; Daniels 1970; Kim and Lyn 1987), oligopolistic competition between a small number of large firms (Flowers 1975; Knickerbocker 1973), "return of threat" strategy (Graham 1974), acquisition of U.S. technology (Ajami and Ricks 1981; Franko 1976), and consumer demand (Faith 1972). More recent studies have attributed the increase to the cheaper dollar and relatively liberal U.S investment policies (Skrzycki 1987).

Whatever their motives have been, European and Japanese multinational firms have enjoyed varying degrees of market success in the United States (Furstenberg 1974). Concomitant with their market success has been the increased interest in their marketing strategies (Japanese marketing strategies in particular). However, much of the research interest has been in Japanese management styles (England 1983), production philosophies (Hayes and Abernathy 1980), and sourcing strategies (Kotabe and Omura 1989), among others, rather than marketing strategies. A few exceptions can be found in studies that have focused on only certain aspects of Japanese firms' marketing strategies (Johansson and Nonaka 1983; Sims 1986) or European marketing strategies (Doyle, Saunders, and Wong 1986; Ward 1973a, 1973b).

Despite their increased presence in the United States, however, there is little research comparing strategic differences in their marketing strategies. Above all, no empirical study exists of how the different marketing strategies of a comparable group of European and Japanese firms affect their market performance in the United States. The role of marketing variables in their strategy development cannot be ignored, since it is a source of competitive advantage (Porter 1980). This chapter does not intend to address all aspects of marketing strategy development. Rather, it highlights a number of major marketing strategy decisions made by European and Japanese firms serving the U.S. market. Specifically, two primary research objectives are:

1. To investigate hypotheses relating to the differences in marketing strategies of European and Japanese firms in the U.S. market. It is expected that marketing strategies of European and Japanese multinational firms differ in varying degrees in the U.S. market.

2. To empirically determine the relationships between these marketing strategies and market performance. In other words, to determine if differences in marketing strategies (i.e., performance criteria, product adaptation/standardization, customer satisfaction, and market selection) of European and Japanese firms are explanatory factors of their market performance in the U.S. market.

FOUNDATION

Market share, standardization, customer service, market selection, and market entry decisions, among other things, form the crux of international marketing strategy (Terpstra 1987). It is widely debated whether marketing strategies that generally have to be adapted to the idiosyncrasies of customers, competition, and distribution systems are delegated to local subsidiaries with considerable autonomy (Doyle, et al. 1986; Sorenson and Wiechmann 1975). This necessitates understanding the marketing strategies of European and Japanese multinational firms operating in the United States.

Performance Criteria

Market share, sales, and profits are commonly used market performance criteria (Aaker 1988; Keegan 1989; Kotler and Armstrong 1989). Market share and sales are relevant to the extent that they determine business strengths, since scale and experience effects enhance marketing efficiency, hence profitability (Buzzell and Gale 1987).

A recent listing of the top 1,000 global corporations showed that eight out of the top ten are Japanese firms (*Business Week* 1988a). Also, evidence based on sales performance of the top 15 global firms indicates that seven are Japanese (including the top four), six are U.S. firms, while only two are British (*Business Week* 1988b). In addition, Japanese firms have enjoyed a dominant market share in industries they targeted (e.g., motorcycles, automobiles, consumer electronics, cameras, etc.) (Takitani 1973). A whopping 87 percent of the British subsidiaries of Japanese firms in Doyle, Saunders, and Wong's (1986) sample gave "aggressive growth" or "market domination" as their goal, compared to only 25 percent of the British firms that claim to have such a goal. They have also found that while British firms are more concerned about short-term profitability in Britain, the British subsidiaries of Japanese counterparts are more sales-growth-oriented.

Therefore, it is expected that sales and market share orientation are more prevalent with Japanese firms operating in the United States, while profit orientation is with European counterparts. In other words, *European firms tend to place more emphasis on short-term profitability in the U.S. market than do Japanese firms* (Hypothesis 1). Contrarily, *Japanese firms place more emphasis on sales and market share goals in the U.S. market than do European firms* (Hypothesis 2).

Product Adaptation/Standardization

In response to global competition, sourcing of components and finished products around the world within the multinational firm has increased

(Dunning and Pearse 1981, 1985; UN Center on Transnational Corporations 1983). As amply demonstrated in the previous chapters, the coordination of global sourcing and marketing strategies across different foreign markets has become a crucial determinant of market performance for many multinational firms. As such, product adaptations that were once considered a cornerstone of marketing strategy across national boundaries should not necessarily be the driving force any longer for strategy development on a global basis.

It is not intended to deny the principle that products need to be adapted to better cater to the different needs and wants of customers in various countries (Keegan 1969). The product adaptation principle is still needed by the local subsidiaries to adapt their offerings to local market conditions, although to a lesser degree today than in the past. However, it should be built into implementation of global marketing programs. Today, there is also a growing realization of the cost and resource advantages to be acquired by coordinating and integrating operations across national boundaries (Kogut 1985; Ohmae 1985; Porter 1986; Robinson 1987). Johnson Wax's guiding corporate principle illustrates the contemporary view of this globalization-localization issue shared by many other multinational firms: "As unified as possible; as diversified as necessary."

As early as 1972, Stopford and Wells (1972) recognized that global coordination calls for products standardized to some extent in world markets. Porter (1986) further argues that coordination among increasingly complex networks of activities dispersed worldwide is becoming a prime source of competitive advantage. In Chapter 2, we found that Japanese multinational firms engage more extensively in coordination of their networks of sourcing activities on a global scale to reap economies of scale in production and marketing than do European multinational firms. Therefore, it is expected that *Japanese firms tend to adapt their products for the U.S. market less than European firms* (Hypothesis 3).

Customer Satisfaction

Customer satisfaction is the ultimate goal of the firm's marketing efforts (Aaker 1988; Houston 1986). To motivate marketers, customer satisfaction goals have to be attainable. Hence, goals are set in light of the firm's characteristics and marketplace opportunities.

Historically, European and U.S. firms have placed more emphasis than Japanese firms on introduction of research-intensive product innovations as a chief source of competitive advantage, and have tended to ignore improvements on products and on manufacturing process as an "imitation" strategy (Abegglen and Stalk 1985; Brooks 1983). In many product categories, Japanese firms absorbed product innovations in particular from the United States and improved on product quality and manufacturing processes more significantly than European and U.S. competitors (Buffa 1984; Hayes 1985; Kotler, Fahey, and Jatusripitak 1985).

As a result, Japanese firms' emphasis on product quality and manufacturing process innovations encourages them to pursue customer satisfaction by way of continual improvement in the product line to meet customer needs as well as, or better than, previously. On the other hand, European firms tend to pursue customer satisfaction by offering products to satisfy needs not met by their existing products. Therefore, it is expected that *European firms tend to introduce products such that they satisfy customer needs not met by their existing products, while Japanese do so such that they satisfy customer needs as well as, or better than, existing products in their product line* (Hypothesis 4).

Market Selection

Firms typically select foreign markets via systematic analysis (Ayal and Zif 1979; Harrell and Keifer 1981) or by simply choosing psychologically close countries (Johansson and Vahlne 1977). European firms have been known to enter psychologically close countries first (i.e., other European markets and the U.S. market). This may account for the fact that European firms have historically been the major investor group in the United States. Japanese firms carefully analyze market opportunities through exhaustive market feasibility studies before entering any market (Sims 1986), and simultaneously attempt to establish a sourcing network for marketing globally (Kotler et al. 1985). As Ohmae (1985) noted, Japanese firms are increasingly marketing products in all major Triad regions of the world simultaneously to move down the experience curve faster than their competitors. Therefore, it is expected that *Japanese firms are more likely to market products simultaneously not only in the United States but also in the rest of the Triad regions than are European firms* (Hypothesis 5).

Market Performance

Marketing strategy is a crucial determinant of the firm's market performance (Porter 1980). Abundant research exists on the relationships between marketing strategy and market performance in the purely U.S. domestic context. In particular, the Profit Impact of Marketing Strategy (PIMS) Project has been instrumental in empirically identifying a large number of business principles regarding relationships between marketing strategy and performance in the United States, such as a positive relationship between market share and profitability, the importance of new products in gaining market share, and so on (Buzzell and Gale 1987).

While a number of studies exist on the relationships for U.S. and non-U.S. firms in foreign markets (Banting and Ross 1973; Craig, Douglas, and Reddy 1987; Douglas and Craig 1983; Samiee 1982), empirically little is known of performance implications of European and Japanese firms' marketing strategies in the United States. If their marketing strategies have bearing on market performance, the differences in marketing strategies should be able to account for the performance differences between European and Japanese firms more than their nationality could. Therefore, it is expected that *differences in marketing strategies, rather than the nationality of the firm, account for market performance differences between European and Japanese firms* (Hypothesis 6).

The Variables

Performance Criteria (Sales Volume, Market Growth, Current and Future Profitability). Respondents were asked to rate six items measuring various market factors that the foreign firms considered important in achieving corporate goals in the United States on a 5-point scale. Burke's (1984) measures developed for the domestic context were modified for the international context in this chapter. Based on multinational portfolio analysis argued in Channon and Jalland (1978) and in Wind and Douglas (1981), sales volume was added to, and the stage of product life cycle was removed from, Burke's measure. Therefore, the items used in this chapter are U.S. sales volume (MKT1), average gross margin (MKT2), average gross pretax margin in dollars (MKT3), short-term future market growth rate (MKT4), long-term future market growth rate (MKT5), and prospect for three-year future profit (MKT6).

Varimax-rotated principal components factor analysis indicated that there were four discrete factors. Since MKT4 and MKT5 formed one factor, the mean of the two variables was used to represent the importance of expected future market growth rate. Likewise, MKT2 and MKT3 formed another factor, and the mean value was computed to represent the importance of current profitability in the U.S. market. The others (MKT1 and MKT6) were used as is.

Product Adaptation. As in the PIMS Project, the level of product adaptation was measured on a 4-point scale, ranging from "not at all" to "substantially," in the question: "For the U.S. market, has this product been modified . . . ?" (Buzzell and Gale 1987).

Customer Satisfaction. Following Leroy (1976), it is considered from the firm's point of view that customer needs may be satisfied in three ways by product offerings. The product may (1) satisfy customer needs equally as well as a pre-existing product in the firm's product line, (2) satisfy customer needs better than a pre-existing product in the firm's product line, and (3) satisfy customer needs not met by the firm's existing product. Respondents were asked to identify a chief means of customer satisfaction used for the product under investigation from among the above three.

Market Selection. Respondents were asked: "In which regions (countries) is the product currently marketed?" If West European countries and Japan were identified in addition to the United States, then the firm was considered a Triad marketer (1); otherwise, not (0). In other words, for a Triad marketer, the U.S. market was selected as part of the firm's global marketing strategy.

Market Performance. The marketing strategies described above are expected not simply to describe European and Japanese multinational firms' current market share and profitability in the United States, but, more importantly, they represent a corporate strategy to bring about such market performance as a result. Since the static aspect of market performance (i.e., market share and profitability) of European and Japanese multinational firms in the United States was examined in Chapter 2, the dynamic aspect of market performance will be investigated in this chapter. Therefore, the foreign firm's ability to gain market share and sales growth rate relative to competition in the United States was measured on a 5-point scale (very low–very high). Since these two items were highly correlated ($r = .69$, $p < .0001$), a summated variable was developed to represent the firm's market performance.

Nationality of the Multinational Firm. The nationality of multinational firms was identified either as European (0) or Japanese (1).

Type of the Product. Product type was used as a control variable. It is a dichotomous variable representing either consumer durable (0) or industrial durable products (1). As there were five cases in which the same products were marketed both as industrial and as consumer durable products, they were classified as one of the two product types on the basis of difference in sales volume between the two.

ANALYSIS AND RESULTS

Hypotheses 1, 2, and 3 were tested by t-test for comparison of the two means on each variable between European and Japanese firms. The results of the t-tests are presented in Table 5–1. Similarly, hypotheses 4 and 5 were tested by chi-square contingency analysis, and the results are shown in Table 5–2.

Hypothesis 1

This hypothesis states that European firms place a higher level of importance than Japanese firms in short-term profitability (i.e., current profitability and prospect for near future profit). As expected, the prospect of near future profit is rated as more important by European firms than

Table 5–1
Comparison of the Means

VARIABLES	NATIONALITY OF FIRM[a]		
	EUROPEAN		JAPANESE
IMPORTANCE OF PERFORMANCE CRITERIA			
CURRENT PROFITABILITY	2.77	>	1.33[d]
PROSPECT FOR (3-YEAR) FUTURE PROFIT	3.29	>	2.84[c]
SALES VOLUME	3.04	<	3.76[b]
FUTURE MARKET GROWTH RATE	3.13		3.40
LEVEL OF PRODUCT ADAPTATION	2.16		2.48

[a]The scale ranges from 1=very low to 5=very high.
[b]The difference is significant at the .01 level.
[c]The difference is significant at the .05 level.
[d]The difference is significant at the .10 level.

Japanese firms (3.29 vs. 2.84 on a 5-point scale; $p < .05$). The difference in the mean level of importance given to current profitability is in the expected direction, and weakly significant (2.77 for Europeans vs. 1.33 for Japanese; $p < .10$). Interestingly, however, both European and Japanese firms perceive that current profitability is of less importance than the prospect for near future profit. Therefore, support is obtained for the hypothesis.

Hypothesis 2

This hypothesis deals with the frequently argued notion of Japanese firms' sales and market share-orientation. In the absolute sense, sales volume and future market growth rate are thought to be somewhat important by both European and Japanese firms. As expected, sales volume is considered to be relatively more important by Japanese firms than by European firms. No such difference is observed with future market growth rate. Therefore, the hypothesis is partially supported.

Hypothesis 3

This hypothesis states that European firms tend to adapt their products more than Japanese firms. As shown in Table 5–1, the absolute level of product adaptation is relatively low for both European and Japanese firms.

Table 5–2
Customer Satisfaction, Market Selection, and Nationality of the Firm

	NATIONALITY OF FIRM[a]	
MEANS OF CUSTOMER SATISFACTION	EUROPEAN	JAPANESE
Satisfying customer needs as well as, or better than, a pre-existing product in the firm's product line[b]	48.8%	82.1%
Satisfying customer needs not met by a pre-existing product in the firm's product line	51.2%	17.9%
COLUMN TOTAL (%)	100.0%	100.0%

[a]χ^2=7.98 and significant at the .01 level.
[b]Two cells were combined as they had expected frequency of less than 5.

	NATIONALITY OF FIRM[a]	
MARKET SELECTION	EUROPEAN	JAPANESE
The product marketed in all Triad regions	60.5%	82.1%
The product not marketed in all Triad regions	39.5%	17.9%
COLUMN TOTAL (%)	100.0%	100.0%

[a]χ^2=3.73 and significant at the .05 level.

This finding may be confirming the increasing similarity of consumer needs in Western Europe and Japan to those in the United States due to convergence of income levels, as long postulated by Linder (1961). Alternatively, it could well be because European and Japanese firms are increasingly seeking to develop a product to meet the greatest common denominator in consumer needs in Triad regions of the world (Ohmae 1985; Takeuchi and Porter 1986). Above all, no significant difference in the level of product adaptation is observed between European and Japanese firms. Therefore, no support is obtained for the hypothesis.

Hypothesis 4

This hypothesis explores how European and Japanese firms develop products to satisfy customer needs. It is hypothesized that Japanese firms pursue successive improvements in the product line to better satisfy the same customer needs, while European firms develop products to satisfy customer needs not met by their existing product line. As shown in Table 5–2, both approaches to satisfaction of customer needs were equally cited by European firms. On the other hand, the better satisfaction of existing needs is by far the principal approach Japanese firms adopt. The result is statistically significant ($\chi^2 = 7.98$, $p < .01$), and is consistent with the hypothesis.

Hypothesis 5

The crux of this hypothesis is the issue of global marketing. Japanese firms are hypothesized to be more oriented toward Triad marketing than European firms. As shown in Table 5–2, a majority of both European and Japanese firms market their products in all Triad regions of the world. In the relative sense, however, Japanese firms were more Triad market-oriented than European firms, thus confirming the hypothesis.

Hypothesis 6

Now that the differences in marketing strategies of European and Japanese firms have been examined, we are ready to investigate the impact of strategic differences on the firms' market performance. The overriding hypothesis here is that differences in marketing strategy, rather than the nationality of the firm, account for market performance differences between European and Japanese firms.

As there were categorical as well as quantitative explanatory variables, analysis of covariance (ANCOVA) was employed to explain the variation in market performance. The analysis was performed with and without nationality as an explanatory variable. If nationality accounts for market performance more than strategic differences do, then it should be expected that the impact of nationality will be not only statistically significant but also sufficiently large enough to suppress the impact of the other explanatory variables. The results of the analysis are presented in Table 5–3.

First, among the four explanatory variables that helped differentiate European firms from Japanese firms, future market growth rate is the only significant variable in explaining market performance in the model without nationality. It is found that the firm's emphasis on future market growth has a positive impact on market performance ($p < .01$), while the level of adaptation has a negative impact on market performance ($p < .01$).

Second, if the emphasis on future market growth rate is simply reflective of the nationality difference, then it should be expected that nationality sufficiently suppresses the impact of this variable on market performance. The inclusion of nationality in the model did not change the previous results in any measurable way. Rather, it increased the explanatory power

Table 5–3
Analysis-of-Covariance Results for Market Performance

VARIABLE		WITHOUT NATIONALITY[a]		WITH NATIONALITY[b]	
		ESTIMATED COEFFICIENT	t	ESTIMATED COEFFICIENT	t
Intercept		6.69	–	8.62	–
CURRENT PROFITABILITY		- .15	- .78	- .22	- 1.29
PROSPECT FOR (3--YEAR) FUTURE PROFIT		- .25	- .82	.10	.33
SALES VOLUME		.14	.81	- .02	- .09
FUTURE MARKET GROWTH RATE		.39	3.27[c]	.31	2.74[c]
PRODUCT ADAPTATION		- .77	- 3.37[c]	- .82	- 3.91[c]
MEANS OF CUSTOMER SATISFACTION	1	.08	.11	- .77	- 1.10
	2	- .12	- .25	- .40	- .90
	3	.00	–	.00	–
MARKET SELECTION	0	.51	1.03	.60	1.31
	1	.00	–	.00	–
PRODUCT TYPE	0	.10	.21	- .55	- 1.16
	1	.00	–	.00	–
NATIONALITY	0	n.a.	n.a.	- 1.65	- 3.10[c]
	1	n.a.	n.a.	.00	–

[a]R^2=36.1% and significant at the .01 level.
[b]R^2=46.8% and significant at the .001 level.
[c]Significant at the .01 level.

by 10.7 percent from 36.1 percent to 46.8 percent, without suppressing the impact of this explanatory variable. It implies that nationality accounts for some additional 10 percent of the performance difference between European and Japanese firms above and beyond the other explanatory variables including the emphasis on future market growth rate. It is to be stressed that the emphasis on future market growth rate and the level of product adaptation have a strong impact on market performance regardless of nationality. Therefore, it is concluded that marketing strategy counts to explain the performance of European and Japanese firms more than their nationality does. In fact, nationality as an explanatory variable could well be a blanket variable concealing some other strategic differences, including internal sourcing and innovative activities as explored in the earlier chapters.

CONCLUSIONS AND IMPLICATIONS

This chapter has compared the marketing strategies of Japanese and European firms in the U.S market. Similarities and differences in their relative emphasis of these marketing strategies provide some interesting corroborations and disagreements with previous research.

For European and Japanese multinational firms, their marketing goals in the United States mirror those of their respective headquarters managers. The short-term orientation of Western firms has been criticized as contributing to their lackluster performance in international markets. Emphasis on current profitability, particularly on near-future profits, continues to be a significant goal of European firms. Likewise, Japanese firms' emphasis on long-term market position (i.e., sales volume and future market growth) seems to be consistent in the U.S. market as well as in European markets. However, this chapter has found that European firms' short-term orientation does not necessarily have a negative impact on their market performance. On the other hand, regardless of nationality, those firms that emphasize the importance of future market growth rate have enjoyed a higher level of market performance than those that do not.

The Japanese approach to the satisfaction of customer needs (i.e., successive improvements via minor product adjustments) as contrasted to the European approach of developing major innovations (product alternatives) is consistent with the findings of other research (Doyle et al. 1986; Ward 1973a, 1973b). The European approach is probably due to their managers' long-held belief that U.S customers are very demanding and would expect frequent new product offerings (Ward 1973b), and also to the fact that European managers can receive high recognition and reward within their firms for successful new product development. In both cases, European and Japanese multinational firms' marketing strategies are consistent with those of their subsidiaries in the United Kingdom. Continual improvements on the product can be advantageous, since customers would believe that the firm would stand behind its product. On the other hand, periodic substitution that results in an existing product being made obsolete may signal the firm's lack of commitment to the existing product. The case of Sony Walkman illustrates this point vividly, as shown in Excerpt 5-1.

Japanese firms are more oriented toward marketing to the Triad markets

Excerpt 5-1

The Case of the Walkman

Sony's huge success with the Walkman line of portable stereo play-back headset units is well known. Since its first introduction in 1979, Sony has sold over 35 million units throughout the world in less than nine years, with 83 models in the lineup. This feat was made possible by Sony's incessant effort at continuous technical improvement and customer satisfaction. Sony has a strong corporate philosophy that customer satisfaction results from its continuously marketing newer, smaller, and higher performance products, and paying more attention to the fashion aspects as well. Mr. Kozo Ohsone, Senior General Manager at Sony, who was in charge of Walkman development, summarizes the company's effort as follows:

Our plan was to continuously develop the next model, and to complete preparation for the next generation of the Walkman, as we introduced the existing products to the market. To this day, we have enjoyed the luxury of marketing today's products with our successor releases for tomorrow already in mind. At any time, we are prepared to launch production and marketing of the future's follow-up models, since prototypes are developed, and preparations have already been made by the time we release today's new product.

Source: Kozo Ohsone, "Innovation in Management," a Speech Delivered at Harvard Business School, January 11, 1988.

than European firms, although Triad marketing does not have any significant impact on their market performance in the United States. It is also noteworthy that European firms are increasingly marketing their products in the Triad markets. In the case of Japanese firms, their overriding goal is to move down the experience curve faster. European firms may have initially marketed their products in other European markets and then in the United States because those markets were considered psychologically close. Now, they have started entering new and growth markets (such as Japan) since their initial markets (U.S. and European) got saturated.

The average levels of product adaptation necessary in European and Japanese firms' marketing strategy in the United States are relatively low and are not different by the nationality of firms. Interestingly, product adaptation is found to reduce market performance—dynamic aspects of market performance (i.e., the firm's ability to gain market share and sales growth rate). This finding is consistent with the findings reported in Chapter 2 in which we observed that product adaptation is negatively related to current market share and profitability—static aspects of market performance. This finding obviously signals to growth-oriented firms the strategic benefit of developing a product that appeals to various markets with no more than a cosmetic level of adaptation (Levitt 1983; Takeuchi and Porter 1986).

This chapter has shown that for European and Japanese firms, the differences in marketing strategies are uniquely related to market performance. It behooves those firms to continue to select marketing strategies (i.e., performance criteria, product adaptation/standardization, customer satisfaction, and market selection) carefully in the U.S. market. The Japanese model of marketing strategies appears to be one important determinant of the Japanese success in the U.S. market, and thus may as well be emulated by other competitors. Successful marketing strategies in the United States should emphasize products that better serve existing needs, and also sales and market share gains rather than short-term profitability.

The similarity of the marketing strategies of European and Japanese firms in the U.S. market is remarkable especially in light of Doyle, Saunders, and Wong's (1986) contention that a product is "marketed quite differently in Japan, Saudi Arabia, USA and the UK (p. 28)." No evidence was found to support their claim. Our finding is significant because it suggests that multinational firms could develop marketing strategies that are replicated across countries, or at least in countries with similar economic, social, and political characteristics. In other words, the notion of nationality as a blanket variable representing a set of marketing strategies developed and used by European and Japanese firms may conceal much of the importance of marketing strategies as determinants of market performance.

REFERENCES

Aaker, David (1988). *Developing Business Strategies*, 2nd ed. New York: John Wiley.

Abegglen, James C. and George Stalk, Jr. (1985). *Kaisha: The Japanese Corporation*. New York: Basic Books.

Ajami, Riad and David Ricks (1981). "Motives of Non-American Firms Investing in the United States." *Journal of International Business Studies*, 12 (Winter), 25–34.

Ayal, Igal and Jehiel Zif (1979). "Market Expansion Strategies in Multinational Marketing." *Journal of Marketing*, 43 (Spring), 84–94.

Banting, P. M. and R. E. Ross (1973). "The Marketing Mix: The Canadian Perspective." *Journal of the Academy of Marketing Science*, 1 (Spring), 1–11.

Boyer, Edward (1986). "Foreign Investors Still Love the U.S." *Fortune*, May 12, 93.

Brooks, Harvey (1983). "Japanese Technological Advances and Possible United States Responses Using Research Joint Ventures." Presented at House Subcommittee on Investigations and Oversight and the Subcommittee on Science, Research, and Technology of the Committee on Science and Technology, 98th Congress, 1st session, June 29–30.

Buffa, Elwood S. (1984). "Making American Manufacturing Competitive." *California Management Review*, 26 (Spring), 29–46.

Burke, Marian C. (1984). "Strategic Choice and Marketing Managers: An Examination of Business-Level Marketing Objectives." *Journal of Marketing Research,* 21 (November), 345–359.

Business Week (1988a). "The Global 1000—The Leaders," July 18.

———— (1988b). "How Companies Stack Up Globally," July 18.

Buzzell, Robert D. and Bradley T. Gale (1987). *The PIMS Principles.* New York: The Free Press.

Channon, Derek and Michael Jalland (1978). *Multinational Strategic Planning.* New York: AMACOM.

Craig, C. Samuel, Susan P. Douglas, and Srinivas K. Reddy (1987). "Market Structure, Performance and Strategy: A Comparison of U.S. and European Markets." In *Advances in International Marketing,* vol. 2, S. Tamer Cavusgil, ed. Greenwich, CT: JAI Press, 1–21.

Daniels, John (1970). "Recent Foreign Direct Manufacturing Investment in the United States." *Journal of International Business Studies,* 1 (Spring), 125–132.

Douglas, Susan P. and C. Samuel Craig (1983). "Examining Performance of U.S. Multinationals in Foreign Markets." *Journal of International Business Studies,* 14 (Winter), 51–62.

Doyle, P., J. Saunders, and V. Wong (1986). "Japanese Marketing Strategies in the U.K.: A Comparative Study." *Journal of International Business Studies,* 17 (Spring), 27–46.

Dunning, John H. and R. D. Pearse (1981). *The World's Largest Industrial Enterprises.* New York: St. Martin's Press.

———— (1985). *The World's Largest Industrial Enterprises 1962–1983.* New York: St. Martin's Press.

England, George (1983). "Japanese and American Management: Theory Z and Beyond." *Journal of International Business Studies,* 14 (Fall), 131–142.

Faith, Nicholas (1972). *The Infiltrators: The European Business Invasion of America,* London: Hamilton.

Flowers, Edward (1975). "Oligopolistic Reaction in European Direct Investment in the United States." Ph. D. Dissertation, Georgia State University.

Fortune (1990). "Are the Japanese Buying Too Much?" Pacific Rim 1990 Special Issue, 98–101.

Franko, Lawrence (1976). *The European Multinationals.* Stamford, CT: Greylock Press.

Furstenberg, F. (1974). *Why the Japanese Have Been So Successful in Business.* London: Leviathan House.

Graham, E. M. (1974). "Oligopolistic Imitation and European Direct Investment in the United States." Ph. D. Dissertation, Harvard University.

Harrell, Gilbert D. and Richard D. Keifer (1981). "Multinational Strategic Market Portfolio." *MSU Business Topics,* 29 (Winter), 5–15.

Hayes, Robert H. (1985). "Strategic Planning—Forward in Reverse?" *Harvard Business Review,* 63 (November–December), 111–119.

———— and William J. Abernathy (1980). "Managing Our Way to Economic Decline." *Harvard Business Review,* 58 (July–August), 67–77.

Herr, Ellen (1988). "U.S. Business Enterprises in 1987." *Survey of Current Business,* May, 50–59.

Houston, Franklin S. (1986). "The Marketing Concept: What It Is and What It Is Not." *Journal of Marketing*, 50 (April), 81–87.

Johansson, Jan and J. E. Vahlne (1977). "The Process of the Firm—A Model of Knowledge and Increasing Foreign Market Commitments." *Journal of International Business Studies*, 8 (Spring/Summer), 22–32.

Johansson, Johny K. and Ikujiro Nonaka (1983). "Japanese Export Marketing: Structures, Strategies, Counterstrategies." *International Marketing Review*, 1 (Winter), 12–24.

Johnson, Keith N. (1987). "The Growing Foreign Role in U.S. Policy: America Can No Longer Shape Its Economic Destiny without Paying Heed to Investors from Overseas." *Fortune*, July 6, 36.

Keegan, Warren J. (1969). "Multinational Product Planning: Strategic Alternatives." *Journal of Marketing*, 23 (January), 58–62.

———— (1989). *Global Marketing Management*, 4th ed. Englewood Cliffs, NJ: Prentice-Hall.

Kim, Wi Saeng and Esmeralda O. Lyn (1987). "Foreign Direct Investment Theories, Entry Barriers and Reverse Investments in U.S. Industries." *Journal of International Business Studies*, 18 (Summer), 53–66.

Knickerbocker, Frederick T. (1973). *Oligopolistic Reaction and Multinational Enterprise*. Boston: Harvard Business School Press.

Kogut, Bruce (1985). "Designing Global Strategies: Comparative and Competitive Value-Added Chains." *Sloan Management Review*, 26 (Summer), 15–28.

Kotabe, Masaaki and Glenn S. Omura (1989). "Sourcing Strategies of European and Japanese Multinationals: A Comparison." *Journal of International Business Studies*, 20 (Spring), 113–130.

Kotler, Philip and Gary Armstrong (1989). *Principles of Marketing*, 4th ed. Englewood Cliffs, NJ: Prentice-Hall.

Kotler, Philip, Liam Fahey, and Somkid Jatusripitak (1985). *The New Competition*. Englewood Cliffs, NJ: Prentice-Hall.

Leroy, Georges (1976). *Multinational Product Strategy: A Typology for Analysis of Worldwide Product Innovation and Diffusion*. New York: Praeger.

Levitt, Theodore (1983). "The Globalization of Markets." *Harvard Business Review*, 61 (May–June), 92–102.

Linder, Staffan B. (1961). *An Essay on Trade and Transformation*. New York: John Wiley.

Ohmae, Kenichi (1985). *Triad Power*. New York: The Free Press.

Porter, Michael E. (1980). *Competitive Strategy*. New York: The Free Press.

————, ed. (1986). *Competition in Global Industries*. Boston: Harvard Business School Press.

Robinson, Richard D., ed. (1987). *Direct Foreign Investment: Costs and Benefits*. New York: Praeger.

Samiee, S. (1982). "Elements of Marketing Strategy: A Comparative Study of U.S. and Non-U.S. Based Companies." *Journal of International Marketing*, 1, 119–126.

Sims, J. Taylor (1986). "Japanese Market Entry Strategy at Work: Komatsu vs. Caterpillar." *International Marketing Review*, 3 (Autumn), 21–32.

Skrzycki, Cindy (1987). "America on the Auction Block: The Cheap Dollar Makes

U.S. Assets Bargains for Foreigners but Our National Security May Be at Stake." *US News and World Report*, March 30, 56.

Sorenson, Ralph Z. and Ulrich E. Wiechmann (1975). "How Multinationals View Marketing Standardization." *Harvard Business Review*, 53 (May–June), 38–56.

Stopford, John M. and Louis T. Wells, Jr. (1972). *Managing the Multinational Enterprise*. New York: Basic Books.

Takeuchi, Hirotaka and Michael E. Porter (1986). "Three Roles of International Marketing in Global Strategy." In *Competition in Global Industries*, Michael E. Porter, ed. Boston: Harvard Business School Press, 111–146.

Takitani, Kenji (1973). "A Prototype for Japanese Investment in the United States?" *Columbia Journal of World Business*, 8 (Summer), 31–33.

Terpstra, Vern (1987). *International Marketing*, 4th ed. New York: The Dryden Press.

United Nations Center on Transnational Corporations (1983). *Transnational Corporations in World Development, Third Survey*. New York: United Nations.

Ward, James J. (1973a). "Product and Promotion Adaptation by European Firms in the U.S." *Journal of International Business Studies*, 4 (Spring), 79–85.

——— (1973b). "How European Firms View Their U.S. Customers." *Columbia Journal of World Business*, 8 (Summer), 79–82.

Wind, Yoram and Susan Douglas (1981). "International Portfolio Analysis and Strategy: The Challenge of the 80's." *Journal of International Business Studies*, 12 (Fall), 69–82.

Chapter 6 ————————————————

New Product Development: The Japanese Model

The previous chapters have demonstrated the tremendous stride of Japanese multinational firms that are progressively adopting global strategy. The ascendance of Japanese firms has presented a number of strategic thrusts of great significance: (1) proactive product standardization, (2) simultaneous emphasis on both product and manufacturing innovative activities, (3) integrated sourcing of major components, and (4) marketing in all Triad regions of the world.

It is clear that the competitive strengths of Japanese firms stem from the extent to which they can proactively standardize their product offerings. Such product standardization subsequently makes it possible for the Japanese firms to pursue economies of scale and experience effects by way of emphasizing both product and manufacturing process innovations with integrated components sourcing and marketing finished products on a global scale. A sequence of strategic thrusts that have led to Japanese firms' competitive strengths is summarized in Figure 6–1.

The strategic thrust paradigm illustrated in Figure 6–1 should equally be applicable to all multinational firms that opt to pursue global markets and global strategy. In this chapter, we will explore the approach that Japanese multinational firms employ to developing globally marketable products—a *sine qua non* for their successful implementation of these strategic thrusts. To make a strong case for the superior corporate strategy implementation by Japanese firms, some myths surrounding the sources of Japanese competitiveness will be examined in the next section.

Figure 6–1
Sources of the Competitive Strengths of Japanese Firms

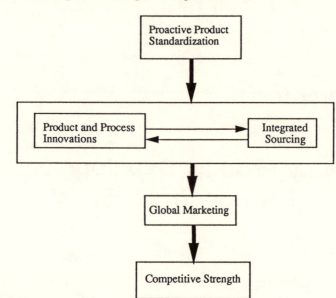

SOURCES OF JAPANESE COMPETITIVENESS

The decade of the 1980s saw a great surge in the global market success of many Japanese firms. Increasingly, there has been talk about the beginning of the Japanese century and the emergence of an overpowering Japanese economy. U.S. policymakers, in particular, have responded to these visions by expressing concern about the trade competitiveness of the United States and taking actions designed to break down Japan's trade "barriers" and reduce the U.S. massive trade deficits vis-a-vis Japan. In other words, U.S. policymakers allegedly have found the root of the Japanese competitiveness in its trade barriers.

The U.S. trade deficit with Japan had reached an all-time high of a staggering $59.8 billion in 1987 (U.S. Department of Commerce 1987, 1988). The U.S. trade deficit with Japan alone accounts for almost 40 percent of its total deficit with the world and over 60 percent of U.S. deficit with the Triad market, which consumes almost 80 percent of the world production (Ohmae 1985). Thus, various solutions to the trade deficit problem have been proposed.

Depreciation of the U.S. dollar is one solution that is often suggested (e.g., Brownstein 1990; Johnson 1987). The dollar depreciated against the Japanese yen from 239 yen/dollar in 1985 to 130 yen/dollar in 1990, or by about 50 percent over the past five years. The dollar depreciated similarly against other key currencies of the world. In fact, that depreciation has allowed the U.S. trade deficits with many countries around the world to decline. While this has been true particularly with Western Europe, the trade deficit still remains a sticky problem with Japan that has not been sufficiently corrected despite the dramatic depreciation of the U.S. dollar against the Japanese yen (Stout 1990).

Another solution that is often proposed is the removal of Japanese import restrictions (e.g., *Business America* 1990; Norton 1989). While many formal trade restrictions existed in Japan into the 1970s (Kotabe 1985), U.S. trade deficits with Japan over the past ten years do not appear to be due strictly to various trade barriers in Japan. Data from the General Agreement on Tarrifs and Trade (GATT) and other sources strongly suggest that the United States has as many tariff and nontariff barriers as does Japan (see, for example, Bergsten and Cline 1985; Onkvisit and Shaw 1988).

Thus, it seems clear that real answers to Japan's (and Japanese firms') competitiveness in the past two decades cannot be found completely in its macroeconomic structural differences, but rather in the superior corporate strategies and technological prowess of Japanese firms. The aggressive "global reach" of Japanese firms can be found in the rapid expansion of their foreign direct investment and patent holdings. As shown in Chapter 5, Japanese direct investment has increased substantially over the past five years with a cumulative total investment position of $190 billion worldwide in 1990, of which over $70 billion have been plowed into the United States, making Japan the second largest investor nation after Britain in the United States. On the technological front, a Japanese company became the top-ranked patent receiver in the United States in 1986, and by 1987 the top three companies were all Japanese (Canon, Hitachi, and Toshiba) (Shapiro 1989).

There is no doubt that Japanese firms' current global competitiveness is not of the Japanese government's making, to say the least. Competitiveness is driven and maintained to a large degree by individual firms and their marketing efforts. As demonstrated in the previous chapters, a review of the market performance achieved by Japanese products confirms this perspective.

Japanese firms have been successful in established industries where U.S. firms were once thought invincible, as well as in newly developing industries. They have been able to capture not only third-country market share from the U.S. competition, but have also obtained major footholds in the U.S. domestic market. They supplied almost 20 percent of the U.S. imports in 1989 and achieved their surplus in manufacturers trade based on both high-technology as well as non-high-technology products.

As a result, U.S. producers' domestic market share for color televisions has dropped from 90 percent in 1970 to less than 10 percent in 1990, and the U.S. domestic share of semiconductor production has declined from 89 percent to 60 percent (Port 1989). Even more startling are the developments in the newly emerging high definition television technology, which harbors the promise of a new electronic age. Several Japanese electronics giants have developed HDTV technology commercially. U.S. producers in turn balked at the idea of such technology long ago as they did not see a ready market for it and are now seeking shelter behind standard-setting rules by the U.S. government.

In spite of the expenditure of vast funds on research and development, a number of U.S. products do not seem to be able to perform sufficiently well in the marketplace. The strong sense of Yankee ingenuity, which long supported U.S. firms' technological and manufacturing prowess, seems to have become either dormant or withered away. Yankee ingenuity once referred to Americans successfully imitating and improving upon foreign technology (Brooks 1983; Starr and Ullman 1988). For example, the British had discovered and developed penicillin, but it was a small American company, Pfizer, which improved on the fermentation process, and, as a result, became the world's foremost manufacturer of penicillin. The Germans had developed the first jet engine, but it was again American companies, Boeing and Douglas, that improved on the technology and eventually dominated the jet plane market (Drucker 1985).

Yankee ingenuity has indeed reemerged in the form of Japanese marketing techniques, which appear to see what many others do not recognize and often are right on target in identifying market needs around the world. Perhaps it is time that U.S. firms rediscover their own talents of old in order to compete with renewed vigor in the global market.

NEW PRODUCT DEVELOPMENT

Incrementalism versus the Giant Leap

Technology researchers argue that the natural sequence of industrial development comprises imitation (manufacturing process learning), followed by more innovative adaptation, which leads to pioneering product innovations. Figure 6–2 illustrates this point. In other words, continual improvement in manufacturing processes can enable a firm not only to maintain product-innovation-based competitiveness, but also improve its innovative abilities in the future. Failed innovators in turn lack the continual improvement of their products subject to a market-oriented focus.

Table 6–1 summarizes the advantages and disadvantages of incrementalist and giant leap approaches to new product development. Japanese firms have pursued and accomplished a successful incrementalist approach. In this chapter, what constitutes the incrementalist approach will be examined in light of the Japanese experience.

Figure 6–2
Sequence of Industrial Development

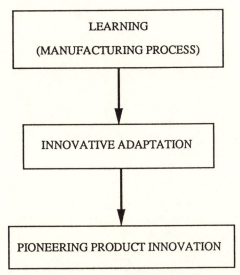

During the postwar period, Japanese firms relied heavily on licensed U.S. and European technology for product development. Product quality was improved through heavy investment in manufacturing processes with the goal of garnering differential advantage over foreign competitors. Continued major investment in R&D earmarked for product innovation heralded the technological maturation within Japanese firms, where the quality and productivity levels began to match or even surpass those of the original licensors.

U.S.-style product innovation has placed major emphasis on pure research, which would allegedly result in "giant leap" product innovations as the source of competitive advantage. By comparison, incremental improvements on products and manufacturing processes were neglected and relegated to applied research. As Drucker (1989) argues, however, research success may very well require the end of the nineteenth-century demarcation between pure and applied research. Increasingly, a minor change in machining may require pure research into the structure of matter (e.g., Honda's Formula 1 engine), while creating a totally new product may involve only careful reevaluation of a problem so that already well-known concepts can be applied to its solution (e.g., Sony's Walkman).

By contrast, the Japanese incrementalist view of product development emphasizes continual technological improvement aiming at making an already successful product better for customers. Take the case of Japanese VLSI (very large-scale integration) technology. The origin of VLSI technology was the transistor. Recognizing consumers' unsatisfied need to

Table 6–1
Incrementalist versus Giant Leap View of New Product Development

	INCREMENTALIST	GIANT LEAP
Technological Emphasis	• Incremental Improvement on Products • Manufacturing Process	• Pure Research
Rate and Speed of Product Innovation	• Fast and Easily Accepted by Customer • Continually "Newer" Products	• Slow but Create New Lifestyle • Sometimes Disruptive
Competitive Benefit	• Gain Experience • Debug Technological Glitches • Reduce Costs • Adaptive Designs	• Dominant Position • Monopoly Profit
Marketing Research	• Context-Specific • Designers', Engineers', and Marketing Personnel's Job	• Context-Free Generalizations • Marketing Research Specialist's Job

```
         _____
        /           \

  ┌─────────────────────────────┐
  │  MARKETPLACE AS A VIRTUAL    │
  │  R&D LABORATORY              │
  └─────────────────────────────┘
```

tune in on their favorite music anywhere, any time, Sony introduced small portable solid-state transistor radios in 1955. Other Japanese companies quickly followed suit. There was quick market acceptance of the product worldwide.

Mass production made it possible to lower cost and improve quality of the product. In a short time, Japan reached a technological level at par with, and soon surpassed, the United States in transistor technology. As the age of ICs (integrated circuits) began, compact electronic calculators using this emerging technology boosted the growth of Japan's IC industry. Subsequently, the IC evolved into LSI (large-scale integration) and now into VLSI.

These emerging technologies are used in consumer products, including personal computers, Japanese-language word processors, VCRs, CD players, and HDTVs. Many electronics products have been sold in extremely large volumes, which has subsequently made ongoing investment in production and further technological development possible. Incremental improvements in IC technology have enabled Japanese firms to continually improve on a variety of products. In the end, as a result of continual improvements, products such as HDTVs have emerged and are truly different from what they used to be both in form and in concept. Thus, Japanese firms have amply demonstrated that "giant leap" innovations could also originate de facto from continual forward-looking improvements after improvements on existing products.

This incremental technological improvement is not limited to high-tech or electronics industries, however. Steel making is considered a mature or declining industry in most developed countries having relinquished their competitive positions to emerging NICs like South Korea. However, Japanese steel makers are still moving toward higher levels of technological sophistication, for example, by developing vibration-damping steel sheet (two steel sheets sandwiching a very thin plastic film as a sound absorber).

Indeed, it is little more than a small technological improvement. But this innovation has a wide range of possible applications. Because of the growing popularity of quiet washing machines in Japan, this steel sheet has been successfully used as the outer panels of washing machines, and it is increasingly finding its way into other noise-reducing applications such as roofing, flooring, and automotive parts.

The Marketplace as R&D Lab

Owing to the incrementalist product development approach, Japanese firms have also been able to increase the speed of new product introductions, meet the competitive demands of a rapidly changing marketplace, and capture market share. As documented in Chapter 5, Japanese firms adopt emerging technologies initially in existing products to satisfy customer needs better than their competitors. This affords them an opportunity to gain experience, debug technological glitches, reduce costs, boost performance, and adapt designs for worldwide customer use.

In other words, *the marketplace becomes a virtual R&D laboratory for Japanese firms to gain production and marketing experience as well as to perfect technology.* This requires close contact with customers, whose inputs help Japanese firms improve upon their products on an ongoing basis.

In the process, they introduce newer products one after another. Year after year, Japanese firms unveil not-entirely-new products that keep getting better in design, more reliable, and less expensive. For example, Philips marketed the first practical VCR in 1972, three years before Japanese competitors entered the market. However, Philips took seven years to replace the first-generation VCR with the all-new V2000, while the late-coming Japanese manufacturers launched an onslaught of no fewer than three generations of improved VCRs in this five-year period.

Another recent example worth noting is the exploitation of the so-called fuzzy logic by Hitachi and others. Ever since fuzzy logic was conceived in the mid-1960s by Lotfi A. Zadeh, a computer science professor at the University of California at Berkeley, nobody other than several Japanese firms has paid serious heed to it for its potential application in ordinary products. Fuzzy logic allows computers to deal with shades of gray or something vague between 0 and 1—no small feat in a world of binary computers that exist today. Today, Hitachi, Matsushita, Mitsubishi, Sony, and Nissan Motors, among others, use fuzzy logic in their products. For example, Hitachi introduced a fuzzy train that automatically accelerates and brakes so smoothly that no one uses the hanging straps. Matsushita, the maker of Panasonics, began marketing a fuzzy washing machine with only one start button that automatically judges the size and dirtiness of the load and decides the optimum cycle times, amount of detergent needed, and water level. Sony introduced a palm-size computer capable of recognizing written Japanese, with a fuzzy circuit to iron out the inconsistencies in different writing styles. Now fuzzy circuits are put into the autofocus mechanisms of video cameras to get constantly clear pictures. By the beginning of 1990, fuzzy chips were appearing at a fast pace in a wide range of consumer products.

This is not limited to the electronics industry, however, The incrementalist philosophy can also be found in Japan's beer industry. Once dormant and stable, and dominated by Kirin Breweries, the beer industry has been shaken by dry beer introduced by Asahi Breweries in the 1980s. Since then, the four major breweries—Kirin, Asahi, Sapporo, and Suntory—have manufactured more than 40 brands of beer among themselves at any time, let alone foreign brands of beer brewed under license. As one executive puts it, "some beers are good for blue sky and hot weather. Others are good for fish, others for Western food. Japanese consumers are very demanding and we must be ready to meet their needs" (Rhodes 1990).

The continual introduction of newer and better designed products also brings a greater likelihood of market success. Ideal products often require a giant leap in technology and product development, and naturally are subject to a much higher risk of consumer rejection. Not only does the Japanese approach of incrementalism allow for continual improvement and a stream of new products, but it also permits quicker consumer adoption. Consumers are likely to accept improved products more quickly than very different products, since the former are more compatible with the existing patterns of product use and lifestyles (Fefer et al. 1990).

Product Design

Design is the process of seeking to optimize consumer satisfaction and company profitability through the creative use of major design elements (i.e., performance, quality, durability, appearance, and cost) in connection with the products, environments, information, and corporate identities (Kotler and Rath 1984). Japanese firms view design not simply as the product designers' domain of responsibility but rather as that across various functional areas including designers, engineers, production, and marketing people. This is primarily accomplished by the use of a tightly knit integrated project team. Japanese use a longer initial design phase followed by a second phase run in parallel with much of the advanced product development phase. As a result, few design decisions have to be reworked, and the whole design process is shorter than the conventional design and development process (Lorenz 1986).

Industrial design is increasingly considered to be a strategically important function. Design directors are on the executive committees at Sony and Sharp, while design is a separate business unit at Canon and Ricoh. Many European firms, including Braun and Olivetti, also have top-level design executives. The United States, an early leader in industrial design, lost its focus but is returning to its ranks of followers through such corporations as Ford, IBM, and Xerox.

All large Japanese auto makers now have design studios in Southern California, following Ohmae's (1985) observation that it is necessary to become a true insider in the Triad regions, of which the United States is a major part. The Japanese are particular masters at design for global markets; they live in the target country, establish local partnerships, use product probes to test the market, and have designers do qualitative work.

Particularly in markets where proprietary know-how may be circumvented and new technologies easily developed, companies can no longer rely on technology alone to sustain competitive advantage. Therefore, the appropriate design of products, image, and branding with continual incremental improvements that add value to the customer is required (Schneider 1989). This is where many Japanese firms have outperformed their competitors around the world.

Willingness for Systematic Redesign

Japanese firms also display a willingness to take the progress achieved through incrementalism and develop a new market approach around it. An excellent example is provided by the strategies used by different Japanese automobile manufacturers. After decades of honing refinements in their products, these firms, within a very short period of time, developed their Infiniti, Lexus, and Acura brands, which were substantially different in the consumer's mind from the existing cars.

Each of these new brands was introduced to the market through an entirely new distribution system. Even though pundits had argued that in the automotive sector the time for new brands was over, let alone the likelihood of success for new channels, the approach chosen seems to be crowned by more success than the more traditional acquisition route taken by Ford (Jaguar) or GM (Saab).

The Role of Market Research

Market research is a key ingredient for successful ongoing development of newer products. The goal is to provide customers with more "value" in the products they purchase. Product value is determined by cost and quality factors. In the United States, cost reduction and quality improvement are too often thought to be contradictory objectives, particularly when quality is perceived to be mainly measured by choice of materials or engineering tolerances.

Japanese firms, by contrast, see cost reduction and quality improvements as parallel objectives that go in tandem. The Japanese word *Keihakutansho* epitomizes Japanese firms bent on creating value by simultaneously lowering cost and increasing quality. Keihakutansho literally means "lighter, slimmer, shorter, and smaller," and thus implies less expensive and more useful products that are economical in purchase, use, and maintenance.

Furthermore, Japanese perceptions consider quality in a product to be generated by the contextual usage of the product. If a product "fits" better for a given usage or usage condition, it delivers better quality. That is why Japanese firms always try to emphasize both the "high-tech" as well as the "high-touch" dimension in their product innovations, as illustrated in Excerpt 6–1. Indeed, industrial designers are the only ones who are trained in human interface with products. Japanese firms' goal is to delight the customer—a higher standard and a deeper quest than a goal of customer satisfaction—and may well be their secret weapon (Rose 1991).

Another recent market success is Sony's Watchman, a liquid crystal hand-held TV set, illustrating the point. Conventional market research failed to show that a market existed for such products in the United States. Studying the contextual usage of TV sets, however, Sony found that in addition to the main family color TV sets, Americans wanted a small portable TV to take with them to the backyard or on weekends.

Excerpt 6–1

Changing Concept of Japanese Quality

Uh oh, Detroit, watch out. Once again, something extraordinary is happening in Japan. Just as U.S carmakers are getting their quality up to par, the Japanese are redefining and expanding the term. The new concept is called *miryokuteki hinshitsu*—making cars that are more than reliable, that fascinate, bewitch, and delight. In plain English, it translates into "things gone right." . . . [It] signals a campaign by the Japanese to engineer unprecedented measuress of look, sound, and "feel" into everything from family sedans to luxury models, at the same time that they continue to improve reliability.

Source: Excerpted from "A New Era for Auto Quality," *Business Week*, October 22, 1990, p. 83, with permission from the publisher.

How Does Japanese Market Research Differ?

U.S. market researchers, after developing an insulated staff function of their own, have grown enamored mainly with hard data. By processing information from many people and applying sophisticated data manipulations, statistical significance is sought and, more often than not, found. Japanese executives have said that they do not believe in marketing research in the traditional sense because it does not help them develop new products.

Nishikawa (1989), marketing manager at Hitachi, summarizes the general Japanese attitude toward such so-called scientific market research. He cautions against the danger of relying too much on a general survey of consumers for new product development for five reasons:

1. Indifference—careless random sampling causes mistaken judgment, since some people are indifferent toward the product in question.
2. Absence of responsibility—the consumer is most sincere when spending, but not when talking.
3. Conservative attitudes—ordinary consumers are conservative and tend to react negatively to a new product.
4. Vanity—it is human nature to exaggerate and put on a good appearance.
5. Insufficient information—the research results depend on the information of product characteristics given to survey participants.

Japanese firms prefer more down-to-earth methods of information-gathering such as fact-finding and social forecasting gathered through informal observation and intuition. Johansson and Nonaka (1987) illustrate the benefit of using context-specific market information on a mix of soft data (brand and product managers' visits to dealers and other members of the distribution channels) and hard data (shipments, inventory levels, and retail sales). Such context-specific market information is directly relevant to consumer attitudes about the product or to the manner in which buyers have used or will use specific products.

Several things stand out in Japanese new product development (or better called, continual product and design improvements). First, Japanese new product development involves context-specific market research as well as ongoing sales research. Second, some of the widely observed idiosyncrasies of the Japanese distribution system serve as major research input factors. For example, when a manufacturer dispatches his own sales personnel to leading department stores, not only are business relationships strengthened, but a direct mechanism for observation and feedback is developed as well. Third, significant effort is expended on developing data, be it through point-of-sales computer scanners, or the customer discount cards that also carry electronically embedded consumer profiles. Fourth, engineers and product designers carry out much of the context-specific research.

Toyota recently sent a group of its engineers and designers to Southern California to nonchalantly "observe" how women get in and operate their cars. They found that women with long fingernails had trouble opening the doors of their cars and operating various knobs on the dashboard. Naturally, Toyota engineers and designers were able to "understand" the women's plight and redraw some of their automobile exterior and interior designs.

City, another highly acclaimed small Honda car, was conceived in a similar manner. Honda dispatched several engineers and designers of the City project team to Europe to "look around" for a suitable product concept for City. Based on the Mini-Cooper, a small British car developed decades ago, the Honda project team designed a "short and tall" car, which defied the prevailing idea that a car should be long and low.

Hands-on market research by the very people who design and engineer a prototype model is not necessarily unique to Japanese firms, however. Successful companies also have a history of doing so, regardless of nationality. As discussed in Chapter 4, the best-performing German machine toolmaking companies make continual, incremental product and design improvement, with new developments passed rapidly on to customers. According to a McKinsey study reported in *The Economist* (1991), new products developed by these companies tend to "start their lives with 'fuzzy' specifications, allowing for significant design changes before they reach the customer," indicating a great deal of customer input in the design process.

Another example is Boeing, an American aircraft maker. The Boeing

737 was introduced about 20 years ago to compete with the McDonnell-Douglas DC-9. However, DC-9s were a somewhat superior plane as they had been introduced three years before the 737 and were faster. Witnessing a growing market potential in Third World countries, Boeing sent a group of engineers to those countries to "observe" the idiosyncrasies of Third World aviation. These engineers found that many runways were too short to accommodate jet planes. Boeing subsequently redesigned the wings along with low-pressure tires for shorter landings without bouncing and engines for quicker takeoff. As a result, the Boeing 737 has become the best-selling commercial jet in history.

A new development is also taking place at traditional companies to embrace success formulas. Indeed, General Motors' adoption of a decentralized organizational structure at the Buick-Olds-Cadillac operation is a promising move. In its traditional matrix system, personnel involved in designing new cars were divided along functional lines (i.e., car body engineers under one vice-president, and manufacturing and purchasing personnel under another). In order to stave off the onslaught of nimble Japanese competitors, the world's largest car maker formed an integrated marketing, manufacturing, and design operation managed by one vice-president. The product-oriented system at GM has proved to be more successful in developing higher quality new models on a shorter schedule than its traditional matrix system. It is epitomized by GM's Cadillac, which recently won a Malcolm Baldrige Award for its quality.

Hands-on market research does not negate the importance of conventional market research emphasizing quantity of data and statistical significance. In developing the ProMavica professional still video system, which, unlike conventional 35mm still cameras, records images on a 2-inch-square floppy disk, Sony did extensive market research involving a mail survey, personal and phone interviews, and on-site tests to elicit user response to the product during its development. What was unique was that the ProMavica task force included both engineers and sales/marketing representatives from Sony's medical systems and broadcast units. Sony's engineers learned from talking with prospects and incorporated user comments into product modifications as much as did their marketing peers.

It is clear by now that engineers and designers, usually detached from market research, can and should indeed engage in context-specific market research side-by-side with professional market researchers. After all, engineers and designers are the ones who convert market information into products.

SOME RECOMMENDATIONS

Clearly, U.S. new product development and market research are sophisticated and successful. Yet, in order to further improve on the competitiveness dimension, several aspects of Japanese activities could be considered by U.S. firms.

First, the incrementalist approach to product development appears to offer advantages in the areas of costs, speed, learning, and consumer acceptance. Second, such an approach does require a continuous understanding of current and changing customer needs and of the shortcomings of one's own products and those of the competition. In order to achieve such understanding, market research is of the essence.

In order for such research to be successful, the contextual usage and usage conditions of products need to be investigated and, once found, acted upon. While extremely useful in their own right, hard data alone often provide only limited insights into these contextual conditions.

It is therefore important to include soft information based on down-to earth market observation. Since the ability to recognize dimensions of context is not uniquely confined to market researchers, it is important to fully include product managers, designers, and engineers in the research process.

Marketing research should not be a "staff" function performed only by professional market researchers, but rather a "line" function executed by all participants in the product development process. Not only will such an approach allow for the discovery of more knowledge, but it will immediately also achieve the transformation of gleaned market data into information that is disseminated and applied throughout the firm.

One caveat should be in order, however. Although Japanese firms have amply demonstrated the importance of the incrementalist approach to product development, it is also true that they are beginning to have to look for more great technological leaps as they have now caught up with the technological prowess of U.S. and European firms they once were imitating and improving upon. Nonetheless, U.S. and European firms should emphasize continual product and process improvement more than they have done in the past.

REFERENCES

Bergsten, C. Fred and William R. Cline (1985). *The United States-Japan Economics Problem.* Washington DC: Institute for International Economics, October.

Brooks, Harvey (1983). "Japanese Technological Advances and Possible United States Responses Using Research Joint Ventures." Presented at House Subcommittee on Investigations and Oversight and the Subcommittee on Science, Research, and Technology of the Committee on Science and Technology, 98th Congress, 1st session, June 29–30.

Brownstein, Vivien (1990). "A Weaker Dollar Will Help Keep the Deficit Shrinking." *Fortune,* April 23, 23ff.

Business America (1990). "Statement of President Bush, Secretary Mosbacher on Super 301 Decisions." March 7, 6.

Drucker, Peter F. (1985). *Innovation and Entrepreneurship: Practice and Principles*. New York: Harper & Row.

——— (1989). "The 10 Rules of Effective Research." *Wall Street Journal*, May 30, A18.

The Economist (1991). "Less is More." May 25, 75–76.

Fefer, Mark D., Rick Tetzeli, Tricia Welsh, and Wilton Woods (1990). "Why Toyota Keeps Getting Better and Better and Better." *Fortune*, November 19, 66–79.

Johansson, Johny K. and Ikujiro Nonaka (1987). "Marketing Research the Japanese Way." *Harvard Business Review*, 65 (May–June), 16–22.

Johnson, Omotunde E.G. (1987). "Currency Depreciation and Export Expansion." *Finance and Development*, 24 (March), 23–26.

Kotabe, Masaaki (1985). "The Roles of Japanese Industrial Policy for Export Success: A Theoretical Perspective." *Columbia Journal of World Business*, 20 (Fall), 59–64.

Kotler, Philip and G. Alexander Rath (1984). "Design: A Powerful but Neglected Strategic Tool." *Journal of Business Strategy*, 5 (Fall), 16–21.

Lorenz, Christopher (1986). *The Design Dimension: The New Competitive Weapon for Business*. New York: Basil Blackwell.

Nishikawa, Toru (1989). "New Product Planning at Hitachi." *Long Range Planning*, 22 (4), 20–24.

Norton, Robert E. (1989). "Unfair Traders: A Passing Storm." *Fortune*, (June 19), 16.

Ohmae, Kenichi (1985). *Triad Power*. New York: The Free Press.

Onkvisit, Sak, and John J. Shaw (1988). "Marketing Barriers in International Trade." *Business Horizons*, 31 (May–June), 64–72.

Port, Otis (1989). "Back to Basics." *Business Week*, Special 1989 Bonus Issue, 14–18.

Rhodes, Joe (1990). "Suds for All Seasons." *American Way*, October 1, 36–39.

Rose, Frank (1991). "Now Quality Means Service Too." *Fortune*, April 22, 97ff.

Schneider, Eric (1989). "Unchaining the Value of Design." *European Management Journal*, 7 (3), 320–31.

Shapiro, Amran R. (1989). "A Rush to the Patent Office." *Across the Board*, 26 (June), 7–9.

Starr, Martin K. and John E. Ullman (1988). "The Myth of Industrial Supremacy." In *Global Competitiveness*, Martin K. Starr, ed. New York: W. W. Norton.

Stout, Hilary (1990). "In a Major Turnaround, U.S. is Posting Surplus in Trade with Europe." *Wall Street Journal*, July 10, pp. A1, A4.

U.S. Department of Commerce (1987). *Survey of Current Business*, 67 (March).

——— (1988). *Business America*, 109 (April 25).

Part II

The Case of U.S. Multinational Firms

Chapter 7

Hollowing-Out

As the earlier chapters have amply shown, U.S. multinational firms are faced with competition from European and Japanese multinational firms not only in the U.S. market but also in foreign markets around the world. The rapid rise of European and Japanese multinational firms has created a tremendous competitive pressure on U.S. multinational firms. European and Japanese multinational firms have been increasingly exploiting strategic advantages gained from the coordination and integration of operations across national boundaries (Kogut 1985; Porter 1986; Prahalad and Doz 1987). This globalization of competition has prompted U.S. multinational firms to act accordingly, or face unpalatable consequences that are already plaguing many industries including steel, automobiles, and consumer electronics, to name but a few.

Global strategy suggests the complex nature of trade and foreign production *managed* by multinational firms. The development of sourcing and marketing across countries on a global scale has become a central issue for many U.S. multinational firms. So far, European and Japanese multinational firms have been highlighted in this book. In the next two chapters, we will explore U.S. multinational firms' sourcing strategies and their market performance implications.

Sourcing of components and finished products from abroad by U.S. multinational firms, often referred to as "offshoring," "outsourcing," or "production sharing," has received an increasing amount of attention, since it affects the domestic employment and economic structure in the United States as well as a multinational's global strategy. *Business Week* (1986) recently debated the issue of hollowing-out of U.S. firms such that U.S. firms either have shifted their production to other countries or have

Excerpt 7–1

The Hollow Corporation

In 1986, *Business Week* issued a scathing warning to U.S. multinational manufacturers. This is the strongest indictment ever of their global sourcing strategy. It argues:

U.S. manufacturers are pursuing a strategy of outsourcing—buying parts or whole products from other producers, both at home and abroad—with a vengeance. Outsourcing breaks down manufacturers' traditional vertical structure, in which they make virtually all critical parts, and replaces it with networks of small suppliers. Even such product giants as International Business Machines Corp. and General Electric Co. are doing it to varying degrees. In the short run, the new system may be amazingly flexible and efficient. In the long run, however, some experts fear that such fragmented manufacturing operations will merely hasten the hollowing process.

The article goes on to argue that hollowed-out firms will eventually bring dire consequences to U.S. competiveness and standard of living.

The U.S. will continue to lose markets and see its industrial base shrink if business persists in the process of hollowing its own manufactuting capability and focusing only on short-run returns. *This is an economics of instant gratification, an abdication of responsibility to future investors, workers, and consumers* ... U.S. manufacturers will wind up simply licking the labels and sticking them on products that are made abroad (emphasis added).

Source: Excerpted from "The Hollow Corporation: The Decline of Manufacturing Threatens the Entire U.S. Economy," *Business Week*, March 3, 1986, pp. 58 and 84, with permission from the publisher.

come to buy components and assembled products from countries that can make quality products at low prices. It criticized the hollowing-out strategy by U.S. firms as "an economics of instant gratification, an abdication of responsibility to future (American) investors, workers, and consumers" (see Excerpt 7–1). If this criticism were true, then the question, "Is hollowing-out a symptom of declining competitiveness of U.S. firms?" would be an appropriate research issue to be raised.

A related issue was explored in Chapter 3. Based on the data provided by European and Japanese multinational firms, the answer to the above question appears to be in the affirmative. This chapter addresses the same issue using the available data on U.S. multinational firms.

HOLLOWING-OUT

In an increasingly competitive world with a shortened innovational lead time, U.S. firms can no longer enjoy the long-term monopolistic advantages they enjoyed years ago (Thurow 1985). Outsourcing has been increasingly used by U.S. multinational firms to maintain cost and quality competitiveness. Numerous examples have been cited frequently in the popular business press. For example, Caterpillar Tractor Company has shopped overseas for more than 15 percent of components it buys for its tractors in recent years, and the outsourcing percentage has been on the increase. General Electric spent some $1.5 billion to import foreign-made products for resale in the United States under the GE brand. Similarly, to diversify from its stagnant film business, Kodak is sourcing video camera recorders and videotapes from Japanese firms. Honeywell, Inc. markets in the United States the products manufactured in its European plants.

However, such examples alone fail to provide any indication as to how sensible those strategies are. We take the viewpoint that such strategy is sensible as long as it can permit those U.S. multinational firms to maintain and/or improve their global competitiveness in an increasingly competitive world *in the long run*. As *Business Week* criticized, are they sensible only in the short run, but not so in the long run? In this chapter, we will look into the long-term performance implications of such hollowing-out phenomena.

It has been shown in earlier chapters that when we study the relationship between hollowing-out and the market performance of U.S. firms, it is crucial to distinguish between outsourcing on a "contractual" basis and outsourcing on an "intra-firm" basis, since these two types of outsourcing will have a different impact on U.S. multinational firms' market performance.

It is criticized that by outsourcing from independent foreign suppliers on a contractual basis, U.S. multinational firms are increasingly adopting a designer role of offering innovations in product design without being able to manufacture the product as efficiently as foreign producers, thereby relinquishing their R&D-directed competitive lead in the long run (Teece 1987). This type of outsourcing will likely make U.S. firms lose sight of emerging technologies and know-how, less adept at understanding how new technology can be exploited, and eventually lose the ability to design. As Hayes and Wheelwright (1984) emphasize, proprietary manufacturing processes are just as formidable weapons to maintain competitiveness as are proprietary products.

While outsourcing from independent suppliers appears to give almost instant rewards, continued outsourcing is likely to forebode U.S. firms' long-term loss of market performance. A frequently cited anecdote is the recent development of high definition television technology perfected by several Japanese electronics giants (closely followed by European competitors) (*Business Week* 1988). As mentioned in earlier chapters, video cassette recorders preceded, and were the harbinger of, HDTV technology. Although U.S. firms are rapidly catching up, they have not been able to meet this competition easily. It is primarily because they had outsourced color TVs and VCRs from Japanese manufacturers for so long that they had not foreseen the next generation of commercial development of emerging technology and lagged in design capability.

In this very context, *Business Week*'s criticism of hollowing-out seems plausible. However, if technology and know-how developed by a multinational firm are kept as trade secrets and proprietary knowledge and are exploited within its multinational corporate system (i.e., by its foreign affiliates and by the parent firm itself), the firm can retain its technological superiority within itself for a longer period without unduly disseminating it to competitors as if it were a "public" good (Buckley and Casson 1976; Dunning 1977; Rugman 1982). Technology will eventually diffuse to competitors in a variety of ways, including inventing around the original innovation, reverse engineering, exchange of technical reports, licensing of related technology, industrial espionage, and so on.

In addition, by getting involved in design and production on its own, the multinational firm can keep abreast of emerging technologies and innovations originating anywhere in the world for potential use in the future. This is known as the learning (or experience) curve effect. As a result, intra-firm trade, or sourcing of major components and finished products between the parent firm and its affiliates abroad and between its foreign affiliates themselves, has been increasing dramatically (Business International 1982; Dunning and Pearse 1981; UN Center on Transnational Corporations 1988). It is estimated that up to 60 percent of the U.S. trade deficit in 1985 was attributed to imports from U.S. majority-owned affiliates (Shepherd and Hutchins 1988).

As part of my continuing research on competitiveness issues, this chapter focuses on, and is limited to, intra-firm sourcing and its market performance implications. Indeed, intra-firm sourcing constitutes a significant portion of total U.S. imports. According to Helleiner's (1981) estimate, intra-firm sourcing as managed by U.S. multinational firms accounted for at least 32 percent of total U.S. imports. The latest survey by the United Nations Center on Transnational Corporations (1988) reports that about 40 percent of U.S. imports is accounted for by foreign affiliates exporting to their U.S. parent firms. According to Shepherd and Hutchins' (1988) recent estimate, the intra-firm sourcing ratio is as high as 60 percent of total U.S. imports. While estimates vary depending on the methods used, the extensive nature of U.S. firms' intra-firm imports is evident.

It does not, by any means, negate the importance of other types of sourcing. For the purposes of this chapter, "hollowness" is defined as the percentage of U.S. multinational firms' total domestic sales originating from their foreign affiliates. One assumption behind this definition is that these manufactured imports could have been manufactured in the United States. This assumption is comparable to the concept of competitive import replacements popularized by Leontief (1956). Due to a variety of imperfections in the marketplace caused by such factors as tariffs and nontariff barriers across national borders and risk and uncertainty in market transactions, comparative advantage alone cannot explain all aspects of international trade of manufactured products between independent parties.

Multinational firms are known to reduce some imperfections in the marketplace by conducting trade within the multinational corporate system (i.e., intra-firm sourcing), and to benefit from economies of scale in production and marketing (Buckley and Casson 1976; Casson 1979; Dunning 1977). Increased intra-firm sourcing of major components reflects increased efficiency in international trade managed by U.S. multinational firms and thus in the use of resources on a global scale. U.S. imports from the foreign affiliates of U.S. multinational firms, rather than from independent suppliers abroad, should reflect the competitive efficiency of U.S. multinational firms over foreign competition.

Much of the published work on global sourcing has been descriptive in nature, usually focusing on the extent of intra-firm trade involving parent companies and/or parent countries (usually the United States) (Dunning and Pearse 1981; Moxon 1974; UN Center on Transnational Corporations 1988). However, there has been no empirical investigation into the effect of global sourcing on U.S. multinational firms' market performance.

GLOBAL SOURCING AND MARKET PERFORMANCE OF U.S. MULTINATIONAL FIRMS

Before the relationship between global sourcing and market performance of U.S. multinational firms is explored, it is necessary to examine the shift in their market performance on a global basis. In other words, in order to study the impact of sourcing strategies on their market performance, other factors that might have bearing on their market performance should be accounted for. U.S. multinational firms' consolidated global market share is employed as a proxy measure of their market performance on a global basis. The market performance shift is explored in detail in the Appendix to this chapter. Overall, the results show that U.S. multinational firms have maintained their global market share over the years.

Throughout the book, sourcing strategy is defined as those decisions determining which production units will serve which particular markets and how components will be supplied for production. A high level of internal exports by the U.S. multinational firm of key equipment and components to its "internal" members (majority- to wholly owned foreign affiliates; foreign affiliates, thereafter) signifies the firm's motivation to maximize the benefit of its R&D effort. A high level of internal exports of key equipment and components is motivated by the U.S. firm's commitment to maintain and/or improve its competitiveness on a global basis. Although the U.S. parent's internal exports of equipment and components may be simultaneously employed in the manufacturing activities of its foreign affiliates, there also appear to be different reasons at work. The U.S. parent exports its own equipment to its foreign affiliates for three different reasons. First, because of high transfer costs (i.e., transportation costs, import tariffs, and other governmental restrictions on imports of finished products in foreign countries), the U.S. parent may be compelled to shift production to its affiliates abroad. Second, foreign production may be preferred particularly when a high level of modification of the product is necessary for the firm to better cater to local tastes and requirements. Third, the foreign affiliates may be deployed to take advantage of inexpensive but skilled labor abroad for manufacture of the product that could otherwise be produced in the United States, if not as economically and efficiently.

The hollowness of U.S. multinational firms becomes obvious when the third reason outweighs the first two in a significant way. This is because foreign production induced by labor economies augurs the importation of the products back to the United States, while foreign production induced by transfer costs or by product adaptation does not. The data limitation we face in this chapter does not allow us to differentiate among the reasons for the U.S. parent's internal equipment export to its foreign affiliates. It is anticipated that internal equipment exports motivated by transfer costs and product adaptation outweigh those motivated by labor economies (Caves 1974). Therefore, the net impact of internal equipment exports on the hollowness of the U.S. multinational is relatively small. On the other hand, the U.S. parent's internal exports of components to its foreign affiliates are obviously motivated by the use of inexpensive labor, particularly in newly industrialized countries such as Taiwan, Singapore, and Mexico, to be used for export of finished products to other countries including the United States (Moxon 1974).

These two types of internal exports signify the strategic thrust of the U.S. multinational firm. A high level of internalization through internal exports would ensure an efficient transaction of R&D-intensive equipment and components within the multinational corporate system, thereby contributing positively to its global market performance. Of course, R&D spending by the U.S. firm is not simply earmarked for production of equipment and components for internal exports, but it makes the U.S. firm globally competitive through increased domestic sales and exports of finished products from the United States (Hufbauer 1970). Given the size of the U.S. market, increased domestic sales will definitely mitigate the importation of finished products from foreign affiliates of the U.S. firm.

Similarly, R&D activities by foreign affiliates of the U.S. firm can be seen as part of the U.S. firm's global strategy. R&D activities by the U.S. parent firm and those by its affiliates tend to be highly integrated if the product modifications required for different markets are minimal. Even if technical advantage consists of market-related product developments, the U.S. parent's R&D activities and those of its affiliates are closely related because of their complex communication needs that affect the organization of R&D itself and the interface between R&D and production establishments (Hirschey and Caves 1981). Whichever case it may be, the U.S. multinational firm behaves as a global maximizer of private profits in locating its R&D activities and transferring technology internationally.

As Mansfield and Romeo (1984) have corroborated elsewhere, foreign R&D activities are no longer devoted merely to the servicing and adaptation of U.S. technology, but have begun to produce technology with worldwide application intended. Given the increasing tendency for U.S. firms to integrate their R&D activities on a global basis and to take a global view of their operations, it is expected that the U.S. parent's internal exports of equipment and components to its foreign affiliates are closely tied to the R&D activities of these affiliates. It should be further expected that a high level of R&D spending by the foreign affiliates will promote not only their local sales and exports to other foreign markets but also their exports back to the United States.

What is to be expected as a result of the globalization of U.S. multinational firms should be clear by now. The hollowing-out of U.S. firms manifested by increased U.S. imports from their foreign affiliates appears to represent a logical evolutionary process by which U.S. firms could maintain their competitive strength not only in their domestic markets but, more importantly, on a global basis. As pointed out earlier, the United States may have lost its attractiveness as a production location. All the more, the extent of hollowness of U.S. firms may be indicative of their global strategy in maintaining and/or enhancing their competitiveness at home as well as abroad.

THE MODEL

This chapter aims to generate insight into the hollowing-out of U.S. multinational firms *from an intra-firm sourcing perspective*. The questions that need to be asked are what gives rise to hollower firms, and whether

Figure 7–1
**Expected Relationships among the Variables Linking Hollowness of U.S. Firms
and Their Global Competitiveness**

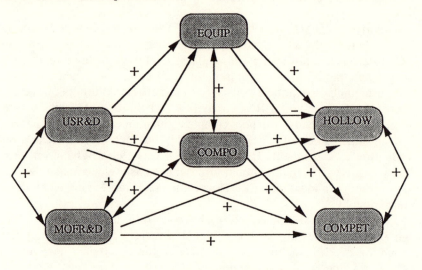

LEGEND

USR&D	=	The R&D intensity of U.S. parent firm
MOFR&D	=	The R&D intensity of majority owned foreign affiliates
EQUIP	=	The extent of equipment exports by U.S. parent to its foreign affiliates
COMPO	=	The extent of components exports by U.S. parent to its foreign affiliates
HOLLOW	=	The extent of "hollowness" of U.S. parent firm
COMPET	=	The global competitiveness of U.S. multinational firm (U.S. parent and its foreign affiliates combined)

hollowness is indicative of, if not causally related to, U.S. firms' global competitiveness.

The model describing the above discussion relating the hollowness of the U.S. multinational firms to their global competitiveness is presented in Figure 7–1. A direct arrow indicates a presumed causal link, while a line with arrowheads at both ends shows a correlation with no causal link implied or established. Plus and minus signs indicate positive and negative relationships, respectively.

RESEARCH METHODOLOGY

The Procedure

Path analysis was employed in this chapter for two reasons. First, the hypothesized relationships involve both direct causal chains (e.g.,

USR&D → HOLLOW) and indirect causal chains (e.g., USR&D → COMPO → HOLLOW). Second, multicollinearity exists among independent variables (e.g., between USR&D and MOFR&D in explaining COMPET), rendering the estimated coefficients of a regression analysis unstable. Path analysis is primarily the analysis of a correlation into its components called path coefficients. Within a given structural model, path analysis, unlike multiple regression, determines what part of a correlation is due to the direct effect of a cause and what part is due to indirect effects (Kerlinger and Pedhazur 1973).

The Data

The 1977 and 1982 benchmark surveys of U.S. direct investment abroad were used in this chapter (Bureau of Economic Analysis 1981, 1985). The 1982 benchmark survey results, published in 1985, are the most recent comprehensive data base available today (at the time of this writing). A next round of benchmark survey results is overdue and expected to be published in 1992 by the Bureau of Economic Analysis (BEA) of the U.S. Department of Commerce. Since reporting in the survey of all business transactions is mandatory under the International Investment Survey Act of 1976, data collected in these benchmark surveys constitute a population of U.S. multinational firms. Data are classified by industry, as the act mandates that they should not be published in such a manner that firms can be identified. Because of this limitation in the data, the unit of analysis is at the industry level, rather than at the enterprise level.

Using the benchmark surveys, this chapter investigated a total population of more than 2,000 U.S. parent firms and approximately 18,500 affiliates abroad representing 29 manufacturing industries with the average of 8.2 affiliates abroad per parent firm. The BEA's benchmark survey employed its Enterprise Standard Industrial Classification (ESIC) for classification of U.S. industries. In order to estimate the global competitiveness of U.S. multinational firms at the industry level, the industrial production of foreign countries was required. *U.N. Industrial Statistics Yearbook* (United Nations 1983, 1985), the foreign production data base used in this chapter, was classified by United Nations International Standard Industrial Classification (ISIC). Therefore, in order to establish the concordance of the ESIC data with the ISIC, it was necessary to regroup some of the 29 ESIC industries into 26 industries. Although there is no one-to-one concordance between the two classification schemes, similar attempts have been made elsewhere (Blades and Simpson 1985; Hufbauer 1970). Table 7–1 shows the concordance between ESIC and ISIC employed in this chapter.

Table 7-1

Concordance between United States Enterprise Standard Industrial Classification (ESIC) and United Nations International Standard Industrial Classification (ISIC)

Industry	ESIC	ISIC
	Classification	
Food and Kindred Products		
1. Beverages	20.8	313
2. Other	20.3 to 20.7, 20.9	311,312
Chemicals and Allied Products		
3. Industrial Chemicals and Synthetics	28.1	3511, 3513
4. Drugs	28.3	3522
5. Agricultural Chemicals	28.7	351-(3511+3513)
6. Other	28.4, 28.5, 28.9	352-3522
Primary and Fabricated Metals		
7. Ferrous (Primary Metal)	33.1	371
8. Nonferrous (Primary Metal)	33.5	372
9. Fabricated Metal Products	34	381
Machinery, except Electrical		
10. Office and Computing Machines	35.7	3825
11. Other	35.1 to 35.6, 35.8 to 35.9	382-3825
Electric and Electronic Equipment		
12. Radio, Television, and Communication Equipment	36.6	3832
13. Other	36.3, 36.7, 36.9	383-3832
Transportation Equipment		
14. Motor Vehicles and Equipment	37.1	3843
15. Other	37.3, 37.7, 37.9	384-3843
Other Manufacturing		
16. Tobacco Manufactures	21	314
17. Textile Products and Apparel	22,23	321,322
18. Lumber, Wood, and Furniture Fixtures	24,25	331,332
19. Paper and Allied Products	26	341
20. Printing and Publishing	27	342
21. Rubber Products	30.5	50% of 324, 355
22. Miscellaneous Plastic Products	30.7	356
23. Glass Products	32.1	362
24. Stone, Clay, and Other Non-metallic Products	32.5, 32.7, 32.9	361, 369
25. Instruments and Related Products	38	385
26. Other	31, 39	323, 50% of 324, 390

Sources: *Enterprise Standard Industrial Classification Manual 1974*. Washington, DC: U.S Government Printing Office, 1974; and *U.N. Indexes to the ISIC of All Economic Activities*, Statistical Papers, Series M, no. 4, Rev. 2, Add. 1. New York: United Nations, 1971.

The Variables

Hollowness (HOLLOW). Hollowness is defined as the ratio of U.S. manufactured imports from foreign affiliates of U.S. multinational firms to their total U.S. sales as a system (U.S. parents and their foreign affiliates combined) for each industry. This definition implicitly assumes that U.S. manufactured imports from the U.S. firms' foreign affiliates could otherwise be produced domestically by their U.S. parents. This assumption of "import substitutability" is in line with other econometric studies of international trade.

Global Market Performance (PERFORM). The global market performance of U.S. multinational firms is defined as their relative global market share; more specifically, the ratio of their consolidated global sales to the total production of ten major Organization for Economic Cooperation and Development (OECD) member countries and five leading newly industrialized countries combined for each industry. U.S. multinational firms' consolidated sales were calculated in such a way as to eliminate double counting of internal sales between the parent and its foreign affiliates by the method described by Lupo (1973). This method has been used with the 1977 benchmark survey data in another study (Sleuwaegen 1985).

The use of world production as a point of reference to analyze U.S. competitiveness in the global market was first suggested by Mullor-Sebastian (1983). This posed an insurmountable task in this chapter. And, worse yet, a great deal of estimation and conversion errors could have occurred. Since the 24 OECD member nations produced some 80 percent of the world GNP (excluding Soviet Bloc nations) in recent years according to various estimates (Central Intelligence Agency 1986; OECD 1985; World Bank 1984), and since ten of the more industrialized OECD nations account for some 90 percent of the OECD's total manufacturing output (Blades and Simpson 1985), total industrial production by these ten OECD member countries was used to represent industrialized countries. These countries are Australia, Canada, France, West Germany, Italy, Japan, Netherlands, Sweden, United Kingdom, and the United States. In addition, since five leading NICs have become increasingly inportant players in international commerce, they are also considered in developing a proxy for world production. These NICs are Brazil and the Four Asian Tigers (Hong Kong, South Korea, Singapore, and Taiwan).

In UN production data bases, most countries define "production" as the value of sales or deliveries, but France, Italy, Sweden, and Germany use the concept of "gross output" as defined in the national accounts. Gross output includes own-account construction of fixed assets and changes in stocks of finished goods in addition to the value of goods sold to third parties (Blades and Simpson 1985). For these countries, therefore, production (read "sales") is slightly higher than for other countries. Therefore, global share estimates used in this chapter are computed *on a sales basis* (i.e., U.S. multinational firms' consolidated sales to total sales by the countries in question) and are likely to be consistently underestimated to a small extent.

R&D Intensity of U.S. Parents and of their Foreign Affiliates (USR&D and MOFR&D, respectively). U.S. parents' R&D intensity has commonly been defined as R&D expenditures as a share of total sales by U.S. parents and is also used here so that comparison can be made across different industries (e.g., Baldwin 1971; Gruber, Mehta, and Vernon 1967; Hufbauer 1970; Sleuwaegen 1985). Similarly, foreign affiliates' R&D intensity is defined as a share of total sales by foreign affiliates.

Extent of U.S. Parents' Internal Exports of Equipment (EQUIP), and Components (COMPO). As in the case of R&D intensity measures, EQUIP and COMPO are measured as a share of total sales by U.S. parents.

Nature of the Study

This study is cross-sectional in nature. A separate path analysis was employed on the 1977 and 1982 benchmark survey data bases. Some of the changes that took place between 1977 and 1982 are highlighted. It should be stressed that the BEA's benchmark surveys mandated by the International Investment Survey Act of 1976 capture the population of U.S. multinational firms. All the path coefficients reported in this chapter are, therefore, true parameters of the population and do not contain any significant sampling error. Errors resulting from coding and measurement process are assumed to be minimal according to the BEA and, of course, are beyond control of statistical analysis.

RESULTS

The findings for 1977 and 1982 are shown in Figure 7–2. As expected, high R&D intensity by U.S. parents (USR&D) appears to have strongly influenced the extent of internal exports of equipment (EQUIP) and of components (COMPO), indicating a high level of technological content in U.S. parent-made equipment and components. While the U.S. parents' internal exports of components increased their foreign affiliates' exports of finished products back to the United States (observed as a positive path coefficient between COMPO and HOLLOW), their internal exports of equipment show almost no impact in 1977 and a very small impact in 1982 on the hollowness of U.S. firms (HOLLOW). The direct effect of

Figure 7–2
Observed Relationships among the Variables Linking Hollowness of U.S. Firms and Their Global Competitiveness for 1977 and 1982

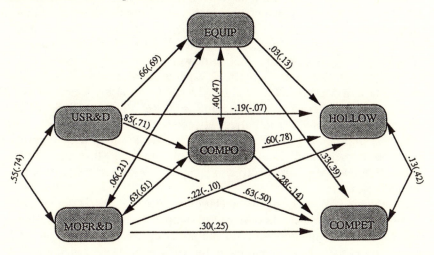

Note: Path coefficients in parentheses are for 1982.

LEGEND

USR&D	=	The R&D intensity of U.S. parent firm
MOFR&D	=	The R&D intensity of majority owned foreign affiliates
EQUIP	=	The extent of equipment exports by U.S. parent to its foreign affiliates
COMPO	=	The extent of components exports by U.S. parent to its foreign affiliates
HOLLOW	=	The extent of "hollowness" of U.S. parent firm
COMPET	=	The global competitiveness of U.S. multinational firm (U.S. parent and its foreign affiliates combined)

U.S. parents' R&D intensity on the extent of hollowness is weak but negative, as expected. All in all, U.S. parents' internal exports of components appear to have contributed most significantly to the extent of hollowness of U.S. firms.

The internal exports of technologically sophisticated equipment and components to foreign affiliates were expected to contribute positively to the global market performance of U.S. multinational firms (PERFORM). However, the negative path coefficient between COMPO and PERFORM, which was unexpected, indicates that the higher the level of internal exports of sophisticated components, the lower would be the global market performance of U.S. multinational firms. However, this line of reasoning could be misleading because components exported by U.S. parents to their foreign affiliates may have been incorporated into the affiliates' R&D-based technology, which positively contributed to the global market performance of U.S. firms. Therefore, the net effect of internal exports of U.S. parent-made components on the global market performance of U.S. firms is far from clear. This point will be discussed below.

As expected, R&D intensities of U.S. parents and their foreign affiliates (USR&D and MOFR&D) are closely related. As argued previously, a high correlation between USR&D and MOFR&D may not indicate the integrated nature of R&D activities between U.S. parents and their foreign affiliates. In order to examine this, it is important to see how U.S. parent-made equipment and components shipped to their foreign affiliates (EQUIP and COMPO, respectively) were used with R&D activities conducted abroad.

As indicated by a very small correlation between MOFR&D and EQUIP in 1977, U.S. parent-made equipment shipped to their foreign affiliates was used almost independently of the affiliates' R&D activities in 1977. However, the increased coefficient for 1982 appears to reflect that by 1982, U.S. parent-made equipment shipped to foreign affiliates was gradually, but increasingly, accommodating their local R&D activities. This R&D interaction between U.S. parents and their foreign affiliates may serve as one tangible proof of gradual globalization of U.S. multinational strategy.

On the other hand, a large correlation between MOFR&D and COMPO for 1977 and 1982 suggests that U.S. parent-made components have been incorporated into the affiliates' R&D-based technology during this period. This finding is further confirming of the notion that U.S. multinational firms are increasingly integrating R&D activities on a global scale.

Once this synergistic relationship between U.S. parent-made components shipped to foreign affiliates and their R&D activities is considered, the net effect of the internal exports of components on global market performance of U.S. multinational firms is the sum of the direct effect of internal exports of components and their indirect effect via foreign affiliates' R&D activities, and is measured to be $(-.28) + (.63 \times .30) = -.091$ in 1977 and $(-.14) + (.61 \times .25) = .013$ in 1982. That is, the net effect of internal exports of U.S. parent-made components on global market performance was extremely small and virtually non-existent during this period. This finding is interesting for the following reason. Increased exports of components by U.S. parents may alone be related to the decline in global market performance of U.S. multinational firms. But, once R&D activities by their foreign affiliates requiring U.S. parent-made components are considered, U.S. multinational firms as a whole appear to have successfully nullified the decreased attractiveness of the United States as a production location as conjectured by Lipsey and Kravis (1985).

As expected, the R&D intensity of foreign affiliates (MOFR&D) also contributed positively to the market performance of U.S. multinational firms on a global basis, if not as strongly as did the R&D intensity of the U.S. parents (USR&D). A negative path coefficient between MOFR&D and HOLLOW was not anticipated. It was originally hypothesized that a high level of R&D spending by the foreign affiliates could promote not only their local sales and exports to other foreign markets, but also their exports back to the United States, thereby further contributing to the hollowness of U.S. firms.

This was not the case, however. This unanticipated finding rather indicates that R&D activities by foreign affiliates were geared toward expanding local sales and exports to other foreign markets in a way that would reduce their exports back to the United States. In this sense, the role of their foreign affiliates' R&D activities generally appears to enhance U.S. multinational parent networks' competitiveness in *foreign* markets where exports from the United States would not serve the local needs as efficiently as could local competitors, due to excessive transfer costs (including transportation costs, tariffs, and nontariff barriers) and/or due to the necessity of product adaptation.

Finally, the correlation between the extent of hollowness of U.S. firms (HOLLOW) and their global market performance (PERFORM) was positive, as anticipated, both in 1977 and in 1982. Interestingly, the correlation strengthened dramatically from .11 in 1977 to .42 in 1982. In fact, the average global market performance of U.S. multinational firms at the industry level had been stable at 31 percent of the total manufacturing output of leading ten OECD member countries and five NICs combined during the period. On the other hand, the average hollowness of U.S. multinational firms had increased from 2.3 to 3.4 percent (or, by 48 percent from the 1977 base year) during the same period.

Since several industries (i.e., nonferrous metals, office and computing machines, motor vehicles and equipment, and instruments and related products) posted a much higher degree of hollowness than the remaining group, an outlier effect was initially suspected. Removal of these industries from analysis did not alter any of the findings, however. In addition, the average hollowness, which appears relatively low, represented a significant portion of U.S. trade and should be understood in the context of this nation's trade statistics. In 1977, intra-firm imports constituted around 40 percent of the total imports of the United States in 1977 and have since been increasing (UN Center on Transnational Corporations 1983).

During the 1977–82 period, the U.S. dollar had appreciated against a basket of major currencies by 10 percent (International Monetary Fund

Table 7–2
Correlation Coefficients between Hollowness of U.S. Firms and Their Domestic Employment Relative to Global Employment, 1977 and 1982

	HOLLOW	RDJOB	NRDJOB
HOLLOW	1.000	-.009 (-.147)	-.152 (-.375)
RDJOB		1.000	.756 (.648)
NRDJOB			1.000

Note: Correlation coefficients represent the parameters, or true values, of the population. Correlation coefficients for 1982 are in parentheses.

[1]R&D-related (Non-R&D-related) relative employment is the ratio of domestic R&D-related (non-R&D-related) employment by U.S. parents to global R&D-related (non-R&D-related) employment by U.S. multinationals as a system (i.e., parents and their foreign affiliates combined).

1978, 1983). The appreciation of the dollar would weaken the domestic production base as the cost of domestic production increases relative to foreign locations, thereby inducing U.S. firms to establish offshore production facilities for export back to the United States. If the exchange rate were the only cause of offshore production, then one could conclude that the elasticity of the effect of the exchange rate fluctuation on the extent of offshore production was a whopping 4.8 during the 1977–82 period.

However, a high offshore production elasticity by no means guarantees strong global market performance. The point that needs to be stressed here is not about the strength of this elasticity per se, but rather about what really makes it possible for U.S. multinational firms to hollow out as much as they did during this period. One could argue that it is the strategic readiness of U.S. multinational firms to exploit locational as well as corporate resources on a global basis that has led to this hollowness. This strategic readiness is manifested by the changes in hollowness and global market performance that are highly and positively correlated (correlation coefficient = .41). Although the causal direction is neither apparent nor implied, it may be said that globally competitive U.S. multinational firms have become "hollower" in their domestic operations.

Tables 7–2 and 7–3 show the correlation between the extent of hollowness and two types of relative domestic employment ratios. As Table 7–2 shows, the negative impact of hollowness (HOLLOW) on relative domestic employment for R&D-related employment (RDJOB) and for non-R&D-related employment (NRDJOB) was minimal in 1977, but became

Table 7–3
Correlation Coefficients for the Changes from 1977 to 1982 in Hollowness of U.S. Firms and in Their Domestic Employment Relative to Global Employment

	ΔHOLLOW	ΔRDJOB	ΔNRDJOB
ΔHOLLOW	1.000	-.259	-.212
ΔRDJOB		1.000	-.046
ΔNRDJOB			1.000

Note: Correlation coefficients represent the parameters, or true values, of the population.

[1]R&D-related (Non-R&D-related) relative employment is the ratio of domestic R&D-related (non-R&D-related) employment by U.S. parents to global R&D-related (non-R&D-related) employment by U.S. multinationals as a system (i.e., parents and their foreign affiliates combined).

Table 7–4
Absolute Domestic Employment by U.S. Parent Firms (in 1,000s)

Year	1977	1982	Change
Total Employment	11,010	10,254	-756
R&D-Related	332	504	172
Non-R&D-Related	10,678	9,750	-928

more apparent in 1982. Table 7–3 also confirms this gradual longitudinal shift (in terms of the change that took place from 1977 to 1982).

These findings show that U.S. multinational firms were increasing foreign employment relative to domestic employment during this period. As shown in Table 7–4, in absolute terms total employment in the United States by U.S. parent firms in 26 industries decreased from 11.0 million in 1977 to 10.3 million. However, total R&D employment by U.S. parents dramatically increased from 0.3 million in 1977 to 0.5 million in 1982, almost by 67 percent. Not surprisingly, this finding is consistent with U.S. multinational firms' strategic shift toward high-technology, R&D-intensive businesses.

CONCLUSIONS AND IMPLICATIONS

The highly criticized hollowing-out phenomenon appears to represent the progressive adaptation of U.S. multinational firms to the state of global competition and opportunities, unbound by political boundaries. One important implication of this chapter is that the prevailing method of analyzing an industry's strength based on its balance-of-trade position may indeed give an erroneous conclusion as to the true market performance of U.S. industries. This chapter has shown the significance of evaluating multinational firms on a consolidated basis transcending boundaries of national trade accounts in an attempt to assess their true competitive strength in the global market.

The hollowing-out of U.S. multinational firms studied here partially allows one to answer the question raised by *Business Week* (1986): "Is hollowing-out an abdication of U.S. firms' responsibility to future American investors, workers, and consumers?" U.S. multinational firms with a competitive, and therefore efficient, operation will likely serve their investors with higher profitability, and their consumers with better products than will domestic firms. As evidenced by relative employment figures, U.S. multinational firms are becoming increasingly "hollow" with respect to their domestic employment in pursuit of global market performance. In absolute terms, however, U.S. parent firms increased R&D-related employment while cutting down on non-R&D-related employment at home. There appear to be few reasons to believe that hollowing out of U.S. multinational firms *on an intra-firm basis* is detrimental to the U.S. economy.

The U.S. economy, as a whole, has gradually shifted from a manufacturing-oriented economy to a more service-oriented economy. This is aptly called deindustrialization, or hollowing-out. From the perspective of U.S. multinational firms, hollowing-out has been the result of their strategic readiness in maintaining and enhancing their market performance by exploiting comparative advantages in various locations as well as their corporate resources on a global scale. While hollowing-out can help maintain and improve U.S. multinational firms' global performance, there is no guarantee that hollower firms will automatically yield superior performance. This chapter has empirically confirmed that global competitive advantage can be gained by incorporating foreign resources into global sourcing, provided that managers can skillfully execute strategies. In this sense, hollowing-out on an intra-firm basis has, in fact, represented a reindustrialization of U.S. multinational firms on a global scale, a very welcome industrial development.

LIMITATIONS

First of all, this study was both cross-sectional and longitudinal, but limited to the 1977–82 period. Unfortunately, the 1982 benchmark survey is still the most recent comprehensive data base available today. Since this period was characterized as a worldwide recessionary period with drastic fluctuations in the foreign exchange market, the observations made in this study may not have captured a long-term trend of U.S. multinational strategy. Next, due to data limitations, foreign licensing and other contractual arrangements that U.S. multinational firms entered into to develop a global strategy were excluded from this study. Therefore, the increasingly important issue of hollowing-out, or outsourcing of components and finished products from independent suppliers on a contractual basis, was not examined with respect to its impact on long-term market performance of U.S. multinational firms, although some implications have been offered. Third, partly because of the aggregate nature of the data, issues of fine-tuning a global strategy for local governmental requirement and product adaptation were not considered. Fourth, this study is limited to market share strategies of mature U.S. multinational firms, and therefore did not consider smaller multinational firms that tend to employ other strategies, including product differentiation and niche strategy.

Finally, U.S. multinational firms' consolidated global market share was assumed to represent their global competitiveness. However, global market share essentially reflects the result, rather than the source, of multinational firms' current competitiveness. Numerous studies have shown the importance of firms' innovative ability as a major source of its competitiveness in international commerce. In an era of global competition, U.S. multinational firms' innovative ability has become increasingly important as it determines the quality and features of products and the efficiency with which they are produced. Thus, U.S. multinational firms' innovative ability portrays not only their current competitiveness but also presages their future competitiveness. In Chapter 8, we will explore how international sourcing strategies of U.S. multinational firms are related to their product innovative ability.

APPENDIX: THE SHIFT IN GLOBAL MARKET SHARE OF U.S. MULTINATIONAL FIRMS

Primarily, there are three alternative, if not mutually independent or sequentially related, strategic orientations for U.S. multinational firms to take to achieve their global market share.[1] First, U.S. parent companies may increase their exports to enhance their market share abroad. Second, U.S. multinational firms may improve their competitive position in the United States where they compete both with domestic firms and with foreign firms marketing their products. Finally, the foreign subsidiaries of U.S. multinational firms may increase their sales in local foreign markets or their exports to other countries as well as back to the United States.

In order to show how U.S. multinational firms fared in global competition, this study traces what portion of the shift in their global market share has resulted from each of those strategic orientations over the years. For this phase of the investigation, the 1977 benchmark survey results and 1985 preliminary survey results by U.S. Department of Commerce of U.S. direct investment abroad were used in this study (Bureau of Economic Analysis 1981 and 1987). At the time this study was conducted, the 1985 survey data (published in 1987) were the most recent that could be used to measure U.S. multinational firms' global market shares.

Three Strategic Thrusts

This investigation adopts the perspective that U.S. multinational firms' global strategy consists of three strategic orientations in pursuit of global market share: (1) export orientation, (2) home market orientation, and (3) foreign production orientation (or multinationality).

Export orientation is measured as U.S. parents' export share relative to world production, as used in Mullor-Sebastian (1983). Home market orientation is the inverse of U.S. parents' export intensity, or a share of U.S. parents' exports relative to their total sales (domestic sales and exports from the United States combined). Finally, foreign production orientation, or multinationality, is computed as a ratio of U.S. multinational firms' consolidated sales to total sales by U.S. parents. The latter two measures are adopted from Dunning and Pearse (1981). By multiplying these three strategic orientation ratios the U.S. multinational firms' global market share can be reconstructed:

$$\text{(Global Market Share)} = \text{(Export Orientation)} \times \text{(Home Market Orientation)} \times \text{(Multinationality)}$$

A total differential of this equation will be used to estimate the change that took place between 1977 and 1985.

RESULTS

Global Market Share of U.S. Multinational Firms. Table 7–5 shows the change in global market share position of U.S. multinational firms for each of the 26 industries brought about by three strategic thrusts. U.S. multinational firms, all combined, enjoyed an overall global market share of 28.0 percent in 1977, and 28.4 percent in 1985. As a whole, there occurred a small net increase in U.S. multinational firms' global market share of 0.4 percent. This global market share gain translates into a gain of $13.3 billion in 1985 (or $8.1 billion in 1977 dollar value) over the U.S. multinational firms' global consolidated sales measured at $870.3 billion in 1977. It is therefore concluded that despite the decline in the U.S. share of total world trade and its increased trade deficits over the years, the U.S. multinational firms on the average had maintained and even slightly improved their global market share during this period.

As shown in Table 7–5, three strategic thrusts affected the performance of U.S. multinational firms in a variety of ways. First, it is to be pointed out that U.S. multinational firms representing 14 industries out of a total of 26 posted a relative decline in domestic sales, with the two largest declines observed in "agricultural chemicals" and "miscellaneous chemicals (e.g., toiletries)" industries. [In Table 7–5, "miscellaneous" is referred to as "other."] The overall relative decline in domestic sales by U.S. parent companies is attributable to the 24 percent appreciation of the U.S. dollar vis-a-vis a basket of major foreign currencies over the 1977–85 period which accelerated U.S. imports from abroad (International Monetary Fund 1987).

Second, in order to compensate for the relative loss of sales at home, U.S. parent companies in many industries increased exports abroad despite the dollar appreciation. Significant gains in U.S. parents' exports were observed in "office & computing machines," "miscellaneous chemicals," "food and kindred products," and "miscellaneous transportation equipment (e.g., aircraft)" industries, with an export-pushed global market share increase by 24 percent, 18 percent, 14 percent, and 12 percent, respectively.

Third, another strategic thrust by which to maintain global market share is to increase foreign production (i.e., multinationality). Fifteen of the 26 industries recorded a varying degree of decline in foreign production relative to U.S. parent companies' sales. Only the "office & computing machines" industry experienced a drastic relative decline in foreign production, accounting for 18 percent global market share points due chiefly to rapidly emerging foreign competition cutting into U.S. multinational firms' share abroad, as revealed in the table. On the other hand, "agricultural chemicals," "miscellaneous plastic products," and "miscellaneous chemicals" industries posted a relatively strong gain in foreign production resulting in an increase in global market share by 3 percent, 3 percent and 4 percent, respectively.

Further analysis indicates that the change in net foreign direct investment position of U.S. multinational firms in this study is correlated highly and positively to the change in multinationality ($\rho = 0.83$) and correlated very weakly and negatively to the change in U.S. parents' export share ($\rho = -0.17$). Although the share of U.S. foreign direct investment has been declining, the *absolute* foreign direct investment position increased until 1980 and has since stayed relatively the same (Bureau of Economic Analysis 1986). In this foreign direct investment environment, U.S. multinational firms that increased direct investment abroad generally gained foreign production without significantly losing their export share. This

Table 7–5
Change in the Effect of Three Strategic Thrusts on the U.S. Multinationals'
Global Market Share Relative to World Production, 1977–85[a,b]

Industry	Change in Relative Global Market Share due to:			
	US Parent's Export Share	US Parent's Home Market Orientation	Extent of Multinationality	Change in Global Share
	(A)	(B)	(C)	(A + B + C)[c]
Food and Kindred Products				
(1) Beverages	14.0	-2.5	-1.3	10.2
(2) Other	14.7	-10.0	-1.3	3.3
Chemicals and Allied Products				
(3) Industrial chemicals and synthetics	-3.5	-5.9	1.0	-8.4
(4) Drugs	-0.1	6.7	-5.8	0.8
(5) Agricultural chemicals	-5.7	-14.5	3.1	-17.1
(6) Other	18.3	-38.3	4.1	-15.9
Primary and Fabricated Metals				
(7) Ferrous (primary metal)	0.4	-11.3	0.2	-10.6
(8) Non-ferrous (primary metal)	0.6	-0.1	-2.4	-2.0
(9) Fabricated metal products	-1.6	2.4	0.3	1.2
Machinery, except Electrical				
(10) Office and computing machines	24.3	-5.1	-18.2	0.9
(11) Other	-7.5	3.4	-0.3	-4.4
Electric and Electronic Equipment				
(12) Radio, television, and communication equipment	2.3	0.6	-0.4	2.5
(13) Other	7.1	6.4	-2.5	11.1
Transportation Equipment				
(14) Motor vehicles and equipment	9.8	-5.8	-4.7	-0.7
(15) Other	12.0	-2.7	-3.9	5.4
Other Manufacturing				
(16) Tobacco manufactures	-1.3	-5.5	-1.2	-8.0
(17) Textile products and apparel	-1.9	0.8	-0.3	-1.4
(18) Lumber, wood and furniture fixtures	-1.4	1.9	-0.2	0.3
(19) Paper and allied products	-7.4	5.9	0.0	-1.4
(20) Printing and publishing	-3.9	7.4	-1.0	2.5
(21) Rubber products	7.4	-9.0	-3.0	-4.6
(22) Miscellaneous plastic products	-5.2	2.0	3.0	-0.2
(23) Glass products	0.9	-0.9	-1.1	-1.1

Table 7–5 (continued)

Industry	Change in Relative Global Market Share due to:			
	US Parent's Export Share	US Parent's Home Market Orientation	Extent of Multinationality	Change in Global Share
	(A)	(B)	(C)	(A+B+C)[c]
Other Manufacturing				
(24) Stone, clay and other non-metallic products	-5.4	6.1	-0.9	-0.1
(25) Instruments and related products	-4.8	8.4	-3.4	0.2
(26) Other	2.7	-4.8	1.0	-1.1
Weighted mean[d]	2.1	-1.5	-0.2	0.4

[a]All values are expressed in percentages.

[b]World production is represented by total industrial production of ten leading OECD member countries (Australia, Canada, France, West Germany, Italy, Japan, the Netherlands, Sweden, the United Kingdom, and the United States) and four Asian newly industrialized countries (Hong Kong, Singapore, South Korea, and Taiwan).

[c]The total may be different from the sum of individual items due to rounding.

[d]Average industrial production by ten OECD nations and four Asian NICs for the 1977–85 period is used as a weight.

Sources: Compiled from *US Direct Investment Abroad: 1977 Benchmark Survey Data*. Washington, DC: U.S. Department of Commerce, 1981; *US Direct Investment Abroad: Preliminary 1985 Estimates*. Washington, DC: U.S. Department of Commerce, 1987; and various annual issues of *UN Industrial Yearbook*. Vol. 1. New York: United Nations.

indicates that the increase in foreign production by U.S. multinational firms is not necessarily a substitute for their exports from the United States as generally argued (e.g., Grosse 1981).

Once all changes in global market share due to three strategic thrusts are added together, the overall shift in global market share during the 1977–85 period is observed for each industry. None of the industries represented by U.S. multinational firms gained in all strategic thrusts, indicating a complex nature of maneuvering global competition. A very drastic adjustment in global strategy occurred in "miscellaneous chemicals," and "office & computing machines" industries. U.S. multinational firms in the "miscellaneous chemicals" industry lost 38.3 percent share points from their home market orientation, while gaining a total of 22.4 percent by shifting their strategic focus to foreign markets through increased exports and foreign production, but with a resulting net global share loss of 15.9 percent. On the other hand, U.S. multinational firms in the "office & computing machines" industry appear to have faced an interesting strategic dilemma. They lost 18.2 percent share points in foreign production due to the increased local competition in Europe and Japan, but dramatically increased exports abroad from U.S. home bases by 24.3 percent, more than offsetting their loss in foreign production. It appears that despite the appreciation of the U.S. dollar during this period, U.S. multinational firms in this industry had strengthened their domestic operations and increased consolidation of their production at home.

It is widely accepted that U.S. multinational firms' R&D intensity is positively related to their competitive strengths (see, for example, excellent classic treatises by Hufbauer 1970 and Caves 1971). It is also argued that U.S. firms with high R&D intensity have increased their market share, while those with medium to low R&D intensity have gradually lost ground in global competition (Kaplan 1988). However, findings of this study suggest that the changes in global share of U.S. multinational firms are not necessarily unidimensionally determined.

Table 7–6 reveals such a complex relationship between U.S. multinational firms' R&D intensity and the changes in their export orientation, home market orientation, and multinationality that took place during the 1977–85 period. R&D intensity has a positive impact on the relative change in exports, in domestic production, and in multinationality. However, its impact is much smaller than is commonly thought, since foreign multinational firms have stepped up their R&D activities in their respective industries at a faster rate than have U.S. multinational firms (Ferdows and Rosenbloom 1981; *Fortune* 1986), and therefore crowded out some of U.S. multinational firms' competitive advantages.

On the other hand, what is truly surprising is a strongly negative correlation between R&D intensity and the change in multinationality ($\rho = -0.69$), further confirming that R&D-intensive U.S. multinational

Table 7–6
The Relationship among Changes in Export Orientation, Home Market
Orientation, Multinationality, and Global Market Share, 1977–85[1]

	R&D Intensity[2]	Export Orientation	Home Market Orientation	Multinationality	Global Market Share
R&D intensity	1.00	0.34	0.13	−0.69	0.20
Export orientation		1.00	−0.52	−0.51	0.21
Home market orientation			1.00	−0.22	0.65
Multinationality				1.00	−0.37
Global market share					1.00

[1] Correlation coefficients represent the parameters, or true values of the population.

[2] The R&D intensity of US multinational firms is computed as a ratio of total R&D expenditure to their consolidated global sales for each industry.

firms had reduced the role of their foreign production relative to domestic production and increased consolidation of production in the United States at a faster rate than had less R&D-intensive multinational firms. This point is made all the more apparent by correlations among changes in three strategic orientations. A relatively large negative correlation between changes in export orientation and multinationality ($\rho = -0.51$) implies that an increasing portion of foreign production had been replaced by exports from U.S. bases. Similarly, a negative correlation between changes in home market orientation and export orientation ($\rho = -0.52$) suggests that U.S. multinational firms had stepped up exports from U.S. home bases so as to compensate for the lackluster sales growth at home.

All in all, the change in export orientation is somewhat positively related, while the change in multinationality is somewhat negatively related, to the change in global market share. Given the fact that the United States consistently produced a little over one-quarter of world GNP during the 1977–85 period (Central Intelligence Agency 1985), it is not surprising to observe that the change in home market orientation is strongly correlated positively with the change in global market share.

Conclusions and Implications

The measure of the shift in overall global market share of U.S. multinational firms over the 1977–1985 period showed a small market share gain of 0.4 percent, amounting to an increase in dollar consolidated sales of $13.3 billion in 1985. This small gain at the aggregate level meant that the relative decline in global sales of some U.S. multinational firms had been more than offset by the relative gain in global sales of other U.S. multinational firms during this period.

Because of the large *absolute* sizes of U.S. multinational firms in "electric & electronic equipment," and "office & computing machines" industries, they accounted for some 55 percent of the gain in aggregate global share. For the same reason, U.S. multinational firms in "ferrous metal (e.g., steel)" and "miscellaneous machinery (e.g., farm equipment)" industries, which experienced a decline in global market share, almost wiped out the absolute gain made by those in the former industries.

Furthermore, despite the super dollar period in the first half of the 1980s, R&D-intensive U.S. multinational firms reduced the relative role of foreign production and moved to consolidate their production at home. The appreciation of the dollar would have made it difficult to increase exports from the United States. Paradoxically, however, they relied more on exports from their U.S. bases to increase their global market share.

Although the U.S. balance of trade position cannot be directly associated with the competitive strength of U.S. multinational firms representing various industries, it is at least safe to conclude that the U.S. balance of trade (deficit of $31 billion in 1977, and deficit of $125 billion in 1985) does not reflect the performance of U.S. multinational firms on a global basis. Without U.S. firms representing steel and farm equipment industries, the overall global performance of U.S. multinational firms would have been much more favorable. All in all, U.S. multinational firms maintained their competitive strengths on a global basis.

These findings offer a number of managerial implications. First, U.S. multinational firms have more growth alternatives than domestic firms, unbound by the evolutionary path (i.e., domestic market first, followed by export from home, then finally foreign production) described in the international product cycle model. Thus, in times of decline in domestic demand, multinational firms may increase exports abroad or increase foreign production as observed in this study, whereas domestic firms have to live with a direct impact of domestic economic fluctuations and foreign competition on the U.S. market. Ohmae (1985) is correct in stressing the importance of U.S. multinational firms being global players, implying that they have to maintain competitive strengths in all Triad regions of the world so as to keep foreign competitors at bay and from making further inroads into the U.S. market. During the 1977–85 period, however, there was not a single industry in which U.S. multinational firms gained in all strategic thrusts. Strategically sound as the Triad power paradigm may be, reality indicates how difficult it is, at least for now, to put Ohmae's normative guideline into actual use in global competition.

Second, the United States as a production site may not be as unattractive as is commonly argued. Based on the same U.S. Department of Commerce's data base as used in our study—albeit older (1957–1977)—Lipsey and Kravis (1985) concluded that as a result of the decline in attractiveness of the United States as a production location due to high wages, U.S. multinational firms were prompted to increase foreign production not only for local sales but also for export back to the United States to maintain their global market performance. Our study rather shows R&D-intensive U.S. multinational firms consolidating production at home to maintain their global share by increasing exports, while relatively reducing the role of foreign production as a means to serve foreign markets. Two plausible arguments may be made. Facing rapidly emerging competition abroad, R&D-intensive U.S. multinational firms might have realized the disadvantages of spreading R&D activities around the world and have decided to consolidate them at home for the benefit of economies of scale. It could also be that they had come to realize the difficulties involved in the spatial separation of the conception of the product and the production process (design and engineering) from actual production (Schoenberger 1987).

Third, the second point raises an interesting question on U.S. multinational firms' hollowing-out or outsourcing of high-technology components and even finished products to their specification from independent suppliers abroad. This strategy is increasingly employed by U.S. firms to maintain cost competitiveness. If the increased consolidation of production at home by R&D-intensive U.S. multinational firms has been necessitated by economies of scale and difficulties associated with spatial separation for new product development as discussed above, outsourcing from independent foreign suppliers may portend long-term deterioration in their inability to keep abreast of emerging technologies and production know-how. If this trend continues unabated, as Teece (1987) has emphatically cautioned, U.S. firms may eventually become a designer of new innovations in product design without being able to manufacture the product as efficiently as foreign competitors, thereby relinquishing their R&D-directed competitive lead.

So far, on the average, U.S. multinational firms appear to have enjoyed an untattered competitive stature, enjoying an ingrained set of advantages not shared by domestic firms. It has yet to be seen, however, whether they can maintain their competitive position in global competition, and how long.

NOTE

1. Due to data limitations, licensing, and other contractual arrangements, which U.S. multinational firms may enter into with foreign partners as an alternative to direct foreign production, are excluded from the study.

REFERENCES

Blades, Derek and Wendy Simpson (1985). *The OECD Compatible Trade and Production Data Base*. Paris: OECD Economics and Statistics Department Working Papers, no. 18 (January).

Baldwin, Robert E. (1971). "Determinants of the Commodity Structure of U.S.Trade." *American Economic Review,* 61 (March), 126–146.

Buckley, Peter J. and Mark Casson (1976). *The Future of the Multinational Enterprise*. London: Macmillan.

Bureau of Economic Analysis (1981). *U.S. Direct Investment Abroad: 1976 Benchmark Survey Data*. Washington, DC: U.S. Department of Commerce.

—— (1985). *U.S. Direct Investment Abroad: 1982 Benchmark Survey Data*. Washington, DC: U.S. Department of Commerce.

—— (1986). *United States Trade Performance in 1985 and Outlook*. Washington, DC: International Trade Administration, October.

—— (1987). *U.S. Direct Investment Abroad: Preliminary 1985 Estimates*. Washington, DC: Bureau of Economic Analysis, June.

Business International (1982). *The Effects of U.S. Corporate Foreign Investment 1970–1980*. New York: Business International Corporation.

Business Week (1986). "Special Report: The Hollow Corporation." March 3, 56–85.

—— (1988). "The Television of the Future." April 4, 62–63.

Casson, Mark (1979). *Alternatives to Multinational Enterprise*. New York: Holmes & Meier.

Caves, Richard E. (1971). "International Corporations: The Industrial Economics of Foreign Investment." *Economica,* 38 (February), 1–27.

—— (1974). "Multinational Firms, Competition, and Productivity in Host Country Markets." *Economica,* 41, 176–193.

Central Intelligence Agency (1985, 1986). *Handbook of Economic Statistics 1985 and 1986*. Washington, DC, p. 4.

Dunning, John H. (1977). "Trade, Location of Economic Activity and the MNE: A Search for an Eclectic Approach." In *The International Allocation of Economic Activity,* Bertil Ohlin, Per-Ove Hesselborn, and Per Magnus Wijkman, eds. New York: Holmes and Meier, pp. 395–418.

—— and R. D. Pearse (1981). *The World's Largest Industrial Enterprises*. New York: St. Martin's Press.

Ferdows, Kasra and Richard S. Rosenbloom (1981). "Technology Policy and Economic Development: Perspectives for Asia in the 1980s." *Columbia Journal of World Business,* 16 (Summer), 36–46.

Fortune (1986). "Where U.S. Stands," October 13, 28–40.

Grosse, Robert (1981). "The Theory of Foreign Direct Investment." *Essays in International Business*. University of South Carolina, No. 3 (December).

Gruber W., D. Mehta, and R. Vernon (1967). "The R & D Factor in International Trade and International Investment of United States Industries." *Journal of Political Economy,* 75 (February), 20–37.

Hayes, Robert H. and Steven C. Wheelwright (1984). "The New Competitive Challenge for Manufacturing." In *Restoring Our Competitive Edge: Com-*

peting Through Manufacturing, Robert H. Hayes and Steven C. Wheelwright, eds. New York: John Wiley.

Helleiner, Gerald K. (1981). *Intra-Firm Trade and the Developing Countries.* New York: St. Martin's Press.

Hirschey, Robert C. and Richard E. Caves (1981). "Research and Transfer of Technology by Multinational Enterprises." *Oxford Bulletin of Economics and Statistics,* 43 (May), 115–130.

Hufbauer, G. C. (1970). "The Impact of National Characteristics and Technology on the Commodity Composition of Trade in Manufactured Goods." In *The Technology Factor in International Trade,* Raymond Vernon, ed. New York: Columbia University Press, 145–231.

International Monetary Fund (1978). *International Financial Statistics,* February. Weashington, DC.

—— (1983). *International Financial Statistics,* February. Washington, DC.

—— (1987). *International Financial Statistics,* February. Washington, DC, p. 16.

Kaplan, Daniel P. (1988). *Using Federal R&D to Promote Commercial Innovation.* Washington, DC: Congress of the United States, Congressional Budget Office, April.

Kerlinger, Fred N. and Elazar J. Pedhazur (1973). *Multiple Regression in Behavioral Research.* New York: Holt, Rinehart and Winston.

Kogut, Bruce (1985). "Designing Global Strategies: Comparative and Competitive Value-Added Chains." *Sloan Management Review,* 26 (Summer), 15–28.

Leontief, Wassily (1956). "Factor Proportions and the Structure of American Trade: Further Theoretical and Empirical Analysis." *Review of Economics and Statistics,* 38 (November), 386–407.

Lipsey, Robert E., and Irvin Kravis (1985). "The Competitive Position of U.S. Manufacturing Firms." *Banca Nazionale de Lavoro Quarterly Review,* 153 (June), 127–154.

Lupo, Leonard A. (1973). "Worldwide Sales by U.S. Multinational Companies." *Survey of Current Business,* January, 33–39.

Mansfield, Edwin, and Anthony Romeo (1984). " 'Reverse' Transfers of Technology from Overseas Subsidiaries to American Firms." *IEEE Transactions on Engineering Management,* EM–31(3) (August), 122–127.

Moxon, Richard W. (1974). *Offshore Production in the Less Developed Countries—A Case Study of Multinationality in the Electronics Industry,* Bulletin No. 98–99. New York University Institute of Finance.

Mullor-Sebastian, Alicia (1983). "The Product Life Cycle Theory: Empirical Evidence." *Journal of International Business Studies,* 14 (Winter), 95–105.

Ohmae, Kenichi (1985). *Triad Power.* New York: The Free Press.

Organization for Economic Cooperation and Development (1985). *Quarterly National Accounts,* no. 4, Paris, p. 11.

Porter, Michael E. (1986). *Competition in Global Industries.* Boston: Harvard Business School Press.

Prahalad, C. K. and Yves L. Doz (1987). *The Multinational Mission.* New York: The Free Press.

Rugman, Alan M. (1982). "Internalization and Non-Equity Forms of International

Involvement." In *New Theories of the Multinational Enterprise*, Alan M. Rugman, ed. London: Croom Helm.

Schoenberger, Erica (1987). "Technological & Organizational Change in Automobile Production: Spatial Implications." *Regional Studies*, 21, 199–214.

Shepherd, William G. and Dexter Hutchins (1988). "There's No Trade Deficit, Sam!" *Financial World*, February 23, 28–32.

Sleuwaegen, Leo (1985). "Monopolistic Advantages and the International Operations of Firms: Disaggregated Evidence from U.S.-Based Multinationals." *Journal of International Business Studies*, 16 (Fall), 125–133.

Teece, David J. (1987). "Capturing Value from Technological Innovation: Integration, Strategic Partnering, and Licensing Decisions." In *Technology and Global Industry: Companies and Nations in the World Economy*, Bruce R. Guile and Harvey Brooks, eds. Washington, DC: National Academy Press.

Thurow, Lester C., ed. (1985). *The Management Challenge*. Cambridge, MA: MIT Press.

United Nations (1983). *Yearbook of Industrial Statistics 1981*, vol. 1. New York.

———— (1985). *Industrial Statistics Yearbook 1982*, vol. 1. New York.

United Nations Center on Transnational Corporations (1988). *Transnational Corporations in World Development: Trends and Perspectives*. New York: United Nations.

World Bank (1984). *World Tables*, 3rd ed. vol. 1. "Series 3. Economic Data." Washington, DC, p. 8.

Chapter 8 ─────────────

Offshore Sourcing and Innovativeness

Since World War II, many U.S. firms from textiles to electronics to semiconductors have moved part or all of manufacturing to developing countries in order to take advantage of inexpensive labor supply there and for managerial flexibility. Firms generally retained R&D work and automated production at home and moved labor-intensive processes over-seas. However, in recent years, these distinctive roles of home and offshore manufacturing have become increasingly tenuous. U.S. multi-national firms are manufacturing more sophisticated components and products with advanced technologies in offshore locations. For example, sophisticated automobile engines are being manufactured in high volume in Mexico for a U.S. auto manufacturer. The plant manager described the Mexican factory as truly international, combining "U.S. managers, European technology, Japanese manufacturing, and Mexican workers," to compete with the most successful engine plants anywhere in the world (Shaiken 1987).

In response to global competition, the integration and coordination of production and marketing on a consolidated basis (i.e., international sourcing) has become one of the most critical issues for U.S. multinational firms (Kotler, Fahey, and Jatusripitak 1985; Ohmae 1985; Porter 1986). Faced with competition from European and Japanese firms in the United States, U.S. multinational firms have come to learn the advantages of creating and integrating sourcing operations across national boundaries. Thus, they have stepped up offshore production to reexport subassemblies and finished products to the home market or other export markets (Grun-wald and Flamm 1985).

Thus, U.S. imports under Items 9802.00.60 and 9802.00.80 of the U.S.

Harmonized Tariff Schedule (formerly known as 806.30 and 807.00 of the U.S. Tariff Schedules until 1989) (the provision 9802 imports, hereafter) have dramatically increased over the past 20 years. The 9802 tariff provisions permit the duty-free importation by U.S. firms of their components previously sent abroad for further processing or assembly. More specifically, item 9802.00.60 applies to reimportation for further processing in the United States of any metal initially processed or manufactured in the United States that was shipped abroad for processing. Item 9802.00.80 permits reimportation for sale in the United States of finished products assembled abroad in whole or in part made up of U.S.-made components.

According to the most recently published data (U.S. International Trade Commission 1990), 17 percent of total U.S. imports came under these tariff items in 1988, and the extent of provision 9802 imports has been on the increase. At a glance, this percentage figure does not appear significant. It is to be noted that 30 to 60 percent of total U.S. imports are attributed to U.S. firms' foreign affiliates exporting back to the United States (Helleiner 1981; Shepherd and Hutchins 1988; United Nations Center on Transnational Corporations 1988). This phenomenon is also called intra-firm sourcing or intra-firm trade. A good portion of the provision 9802 imports is of intra-firm nature, thus representing a significant portion of intra-firm trade managed by U.S. multinational firms.

During 1985–88, for example, U.S. imports under 9802 provisions increased by 142 percent to $74 billion, at a faster pace than total U.S. imports, which rose by 27 percent to $437 billion. Of the total imports under the 9802 provisions, almost 99 percent are imports that fall under item 9802.00.80. Canada, Japan, Malaysia, and Mexico are major supplying countries, accounting for more than half of the provision 9802 imports. The trend for provision 9802 imports over the past 18 years is presented in Figure 8–1.

The 9802 tariff provisions have a pivotal role in U.S. multinational firms' offshore sourcing strategy for the domestic market. Sourcing strategy generally refers to those decisions determining how components will be supplied for production and which production units will serve which particular markets (Davidson 1982). U.S. multinational firms have been pursuing integrated sourcing strategy to a greater extent than before, because an integrated operation allows them to exploit not only their competitive advantages but also the comparative advantages of various locations (Kogut 1985).

However, increased offshore sourcing by U.S. firms for the domestic market affects the domestic employment and economic structure in the United States. As discussed earlier, the hollowing-out of U.S. firms has been criticized as being "an economics of instant gratification, an abdication of responsibility to future (American) investors, workers, and consumers" (*Business Week* 1986). In a study of U.S. multinational firms'

Figure 8–1
Trends of Total U.S. Imports and Imports under 9802.00.60 and 9802.00.80,
1970–88

Billion dollars

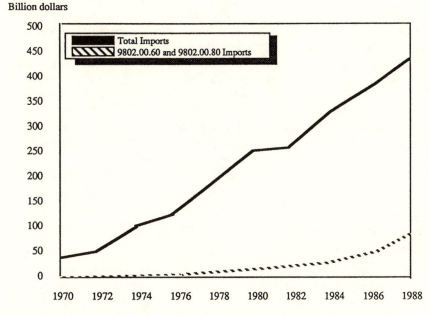

Source: Based on official statistics of the U.S. Department of Commerce.

sourcing practice presented in Chapter 7, it is found that U.S. firms that were extensively engaged in international sourcing within the corporate system enjoyed a higher global market share than those that were not. Relative global market share may be indicative of U.S. multinational firms' current competitive strength (Channon and Jalland 1978). But it does not necessarily imply their future growth and profit potential. Rather, U.S. firms' future competitive viability relies heavily on new product innovations (Booz, Allen & Hamilton 1982).

Little is empirically known, however, about the relationship between offshore sourcing by way of provision 9802 imports and U.S. firms' innovative ability. The purpose of this chapter, therefore, is to examine the extent to which the provision 9802 importation of components and finished products practiced by U.S. firms is related to their innovative ability. Since other factors, such as R&D intensity and human skills, are also known to affect innovative ability, these variables are also incorporated into our analysis. However, our primary interest is in estimating the impact of provision 9802 offshore sourcing on innovative ability after the impact of such frequently used explanatory factors is accounted for.

AN OVERVIEW

The current literature is in a state of flux as to whether or not U.S. firms' offshore sourcing stifles their innovative ability. Indeed, innovation is a multifaceted concept. Generally, three components, or sources, of innovation can be identified: product innovation (the set of ideas embodied in the product), process innovation (the set of ideas involved in the manufacture of the product or the steps necessary to combine raw materials for the manufacture), and management innovation (the set of management procedures in marketing the product and administering the business unit) (Capon and Glazer 1987). As continual product innovations play a pivotal role in determining future growth and profit potential, supported by both manufacturing and marketing skills (Booz, Allen & Hamilton 1982), this chapter focuses primarily on product innovations.

In this section, two opposing perspectives will be reviewed, thus leading to two opposing hypotheses.

Necessity of Continual Involvement in R&D and Manufacturing

It was not until the mid-1970s that the provision 9802 imports by U.S. firms for sale in the United States received any serious research inquiry. In a seminal study of provision 9802 imports by U.S. electronics industry, Moxon (1975) showed that offshore production occurred most often in response to competitive pressure, both foreign and domestic, and less frequently as an aggressive strategic move in response to opportunities for opening new markets for a new product. His findings concurred with Vernon's (1974, p. 106) international product cycle argument regarding the senescent stage of competition in which U.S. multinational firms farmed out the manufacture of all sorts of components to their foreign subsidiaries, components that eventually would find their way into assembled electric razors, toys, automobiles, radios, and many other products in which costs and price were of primary importance.

The international product cycle argument represents the multinational firm's defensive strategy in international competition. Thus, offshore sourcing does not become part of the multinational firm's corporate strategy until its innovational lead that created entry barriers to competition has been eroded.

U.S. firms using such practice are also criticized for increasingly adopting a "designer role" of offering innovations in product and product design without investing in manufacturing process technology at home (Teece 1987). It is argued that the provision 9802 imports are essentially a way of substituting inexpensive labor abroad for capital. It may provide some temporary respite from price competition for the multinational firm, but it will cost the firm an opportunity to improve on manufacturing technology at home in a rapidly changing technological environment (Hayes and Wheelwright 1984; Teece 1987; Markides and Berg 1988). The importance of keeping abreast of emerging technology through continual improvement in R&D and manufacturing should be recognized as it allows the multinational firm to keep abreast of emerging technologies and innovations originating anywhere in the world for potential use in the future (Snow 1981; Imai 1986). It is argued that offshore sourcing will have deleterious impact on the ability of U.S. firms to maintain their innovativeness in the long run (Hayes and Abernathy 1980; Markides and Berg 1988). Therefore, *the extent of U.S. firms' provision 9802 offshore sourcing is negatively related to their innovative ability* (Hypothesis 1).

Strategic Mobility Along the Value Chain

In contrast with the above perspective, two related theses, under the general rubric of strategic mobility, have been offered. They stress a more proactive role of provision 9802 offshore sourcing strategy by U.S. firms.

First of all, strategic mobilization—configuration and coordination—of resources on a global basis, popularized by Porter (1986), has increasingly become a key determinant of corporate success for many multinational firms, irrespective of their nationality. Thanks to emerging CAD/CAM technology, it has become possible for many multinational firms to develop a dynamic organizational network through increased use of subsidiaries, joint ventures, subcontracting, and licensing activities across international borders (Miles and Snow 1986). This mobile network system allows each component participant to pursue its particular competence. Because of the complementary nature of network participants, a dynamic network can accommodate a vast amount of complexity while maximizing specialized competence, and it provides much more effective use of resources in various locations that would otherwise have to be accumulated, allocated, and maintained by a single organization at a single location. The provision 9802 imports represent such a dynamic approach to global configuration and coordination between U.S. parent firms and their affiliates abroad for product development, manufacturing, and sourcing activities around the world.

Second, rapid technological change is indeed the most salient factor constantly prompting today's multinational firms, whether U.S. or foreign, to act proactively (Schuller 1988). The introduction of new products alone does not seem to guarantee any measurable immunity from competitive threat in an environment of rapid technological turnover (Davidson and Harrigan 1977; Davidson 1980; Mansfield and Romeo 1984). It is further argued that the life cycle of a product has become so short that the international product cycle concept may have lost much of its meaning for managerial purposes (Thurow 1985). Today, new product innovations are reverse-engineered, improved upon, and invented around with relative ease by competition (Levin et al. 1987). Contrary to the expectation of the IPC model, management of U.S. multinational firms no longer has this luxury of time to observe product innovations trickle down from the most to the least technologically advanced countries (Ohmae 1985). U.S. multinational firms spin off manufacture of increasingly high-technology components and even finished products to offshore locations to improve on cost competitiveness at an early stage of the product life cycle (Drucker 1979; Business International 1982; UN Center on Transnational Corporations 1983; Kotabe and Omura 1989). Therefore, these arguments lead to a counter hypothesis that *the extent of U.S. firms' provision 9802 offshore sourcing is not negatively related to their innovative ability* (Hypothesis 2).

One consensus in these two opposing arguments is that innovation is a critical determinant of U.S. multinational firms' long-term competitive viability. However, at the current level of knowledge, mostly conceptual or anecdotal, the literature fails to present any empirical evidence as to whether or not increased provision 9802 offshore sourcing by U.S. multinational firms will indeed stifle their innovativeness.

METHODOLOGY

The Sample

To investigate this issue, data were collected chiefly from various U.S. government sources, among others. All data were classified by 4-digit SIC except for provision 9802 imports. When this study was under way, provision 9802 imports were still measured and categorized (until 1989) by industry classification used in the Tariff Schedules of the United States (TSUS Classification). Therefore, for subsequent analysis, TSUS classification of imports under items 806.30 and 807.00 (806/807 imports) was employed. A classification concordance needed to be established between SIC and TSUS. Due to the economic significance of certain industries represented in provision 9802 imports (or 806/807 imports) as well as to the limited availability of published data on provision 9802 imports, industries selected for this chapter were mostly from machinery, electrical/ electronic equipment, transportation equipment, and measuring instrument (SIC 35, 36, 37, and 38) industries. Since available TSUS data were classified at a higher level of aggregation, it was necessary to aggregate 4-digit SIC industries into 30 TSUS industries. Table 8–1 shows the classification concordance used in this chapter. Although there is no one-to-one concordance between the two classification schemes, similar attempts have been made elsewhere (Hufbauer 1970; Blades and Simpson 1985;

Table 8–1

Concordance between Tariff Schedules of the United States Classification (TSUS) and Standard Industrial Classification (SIC)

TSUS Industry	SIC Industry
Ceramic and Glass Products	3211, 3221, 3229, 3231, 3261
Internal Combustion Engines, Non-Piston Type and Parts	3519
Compressors and Parts	3563
Air Conditioning Machines, Industrial Heating and Refrigeration Machinery	3585
Earth-moving and Mining Machinery	3523, 3531-3533
Sewing Machines and Parts	3636
Office Machines and Parts, (excl. Typewriters) and Cash Registers	3573, 3574, 3576, 3579
Hand Tools with Self-Contained Electric Motors	3544-3546
Television Receivers/Apparatus and Parts; Radio Apparatus and Parts	3651
Semiconductors and Parts/Electronic Memories	3674
Motor Vehicles	3711
Tractors and Parts, Non-Agricultural Type	3524, 3537
Aircraft, Nonmilitary	3721, 3724, 3728
Scientific Instrument	3811
Photographic Equipment	3861
Baseballs, Softballs, Tennis Rackets, and Other Sporting Goods; Toys, Dolls, and Models	3944, 3949
Steam Turbines and Boilers; Gas Generators and Parts	3511
Pumps for Liquid and Parts	3561, 3586
Fans, Blowers, and Parts	3564
Elevators, Conveyors, Winches, and Hoists	3534-3536
Machines for Working Metal, Stone, and Other Materials	3541, 3542, 3549
Wrapping, Packing, Canning, Bottling, Aerating, Dish-Washing Machines and Parts; Automatic Vending Machines	3589
Miscellaneous Machinery and Mechanical Equipment	3599
Gear Boxes and Other Speed Changers	3566, 3568
Transformers	3612
Electric Motors, Generators, Rectifiers, and Inductors	3643-3645
Electric Household Appliances and Parts	3631-3635
Equipment for Making, Breaking, or Connecting Electric Circuits, and Voltage Regulators	3675-3678
Radio, Telegraphic, Telephonic, Radio-Navigational, Radar Apparatus	3661, 3662
Motor Vehicle Parts, Motor Cycles, Tractors and Off-Highway Type Work Vehicles	3713, 3714, 3751

Table 8–2
The Variables

VARIABLE		DEFINITION
Innovation Propensity	=	Number of Innovations / Total Employment (in 1,000's)
Provision 9802 Import Propensity	=	Provision 9802 Imports / Total Value of Shipments
R&D Intensity	=	Company R&D Expenditures / Total Sales
Skill Intensity	=	Value Added By Manufacture / Number of Production Workers
Four-Firm Concentration Ratio	=	As reported
Unionization Ratio	=	As reported
Advertising Intensity	=	Advertising Expenditures / Total Sales
Capital Intensity	=	Gross Assets / Value-of-Shipments

Kotabe 1989). Therefore, the variables used in this chapter follow the
TSUS classification scheme.

The Measures

This section explains how each of the variables was developed for this
chapter. The definitions of the variables are presented in Table 8–2, and
data sources for them are listed in Table 8–3.

Criterion Variable: Innovation Propensity

Innovation begins with an invention, proceeds with the development
of the invention, and results in the introduction of a new product, process,
or service to the marketplace (Acs and Audretsch 1988). However, there
is empirical difficulty identifying meaningful measures of innovation. One
frequently used variable is the number of patents issued. However, patents are not necessarily a good measure of innovation for two reasons.
First, patents do not offer the innovator a high level of appropriability or
protection, since they are increasingly easily invented around by competition without infringing upon the innovator's patent (von Hippel 1988).
Appropriability refers to the extent to which an innovating firm is able to
capture economic rents or value associated with innovation before competitors can overcome their initial competitive disadvantage. Second, not
all innovations are patented in order to keep them secret from competition
(Pakes and Griliches 1980).

To overcome these limitations, a more direct measure of innovative

Table 8–3
Data Sources of Items Used for Development of the Variables

Item	Source
Innovations	Keith L. Edwards and Theodore J. Gordon, "Characterization of Innovations Introduced on the U.S. Market in 1982: A Final Report," The Futures Group, Inc., U.S. Small Business Administration, Contract No. SBA-6050-OA-82, 1984.
Total Employment (in 1,000s)	U.S. Bureau of Census, *1977 Census of Manufacturers*, vol. 1, U.S. Government Printing Office, 1981.
Total Value of Shipments (in millions of dollars)	Same as above
Value Added by Manufacture (in millions of dollars)	Same as above
Number of Production Workers (in 1,000s)	Same as above
Four-Firm Concentration Ratio (%)	Same as above
Gross Assets (in millions of dollars)	Same as above
Provision 9802 Imports[a] (in 1,000s of dollars)	U.S. International Trade Commission, *Imports Under Items 806.30 and 807.00 of the Tariff Schedules of the United States, 1977-80*, Washington, D.C., July 1981.
Company R&D Expenditures (in 1,000s of dollars)	U.S. Federal Trade Commission, *Statistical Report: Annual Line of Business Report 1976*, U.S. Government Printing Office, May 1982.
Total Sales (in 1,000s of dollars)	Same as above
Advertising Expenditures (in 1,000s of dollars)	Same as above
Unionization Ratio (%)	Richard B. Freeman and James L. Medoff, "New Estimates of Private Sector Unionism in the United States," *Industrial and Labor Relations Review*, vol. 32, January 1979, 143-174.

[a]Formerly known as 806/807 Imports.

activity has recently become available. The measure used in this chapter is innovative output, or the *number of product innovations* (classified by 4-digit SIC industry) identified by the U.S. Small Business Administration (SBA). It is assumed that innovative output is naturally the result of a firm's innovative ability. This data base is reported in Edwards and Gordon (1984). The SBA developed this data base by examining a total of 108 technology, engineering, and trade journals published in 1982. It is reported that on the average, inventions occurred 4.2 years earlier for innovations introduced in 1982. Since most of the provision 9802 imports are executed by relatively large firms (Grunwald and Flamm 1985), innovations by firms (mostly in SIC 35, 36, 37, and 38 industries) with at least 500 employees were selected.

In order to remove the impact of different industry sizes on the number of product innovations, innovation propensity was computed as a ratio of the number of product innovations to total employment (in 1,000s) in each TSUS industry in 1982.

Explanatory Variables

An explanatory variable of primary interest is provision 9802 imports. Following Moxon (1975), a provision 9802 import propensity index was computed to compare the extent of provision 9802 imports for different industries (provision 9802 imports divided by total value of shipments in 1980). Similarly, following the tradition of Mansfield (1981), among others, it is assumed that innovations result from innovation-inducing inputs in the previous period (4–5 years). In addition to the provision 9802 import propensity, the other explanatory variables expected to be important were derived from Acs and Audretsch (1988) and used as control variables: R&D intensity (company R&D expenditures/total sales in 1976); skill intensity (value added by manufacture, divided by the number of production workers in 1977); the four-firm concentration ratio in 1977; the mean percentage of unionization by production workers between 1973 and 1975; advertising intensity (advertising expenditures divided by total sales in 1976); capital intensity (gross assets divided by value-of-shipments in 1977).

In Acs and Audretsch's (1988) work, concentration ratio, advertising intensity, and capital intensity are hypothesized to facilitate appropriability and therefore encourage innovation (see, for example, Kamien and Schwartz 1975; Teece 1987). On the other hand, unionization is considered to stifle appropriability and corporate performance (Connolly, Hirsch, and Hirschey 1986; Buzzell and Gale 1987).

Table 8–4
Correlation Matrix of the Variables

	Y	X1	X2	X3	X4	X5	X6	X7
Innovation Propensity (Y)	1.000	.409[b]	.569[a]	.419[a]	.145	-.380[b]	.047	.034
Provision 9802 Import Propensity (X1)		1.000	.202	-.034	.187	-.182	.220	.147
R&D Intensity (X2)			1.000	.757[a]	.248	-.507[a]	-.157	.318[c]
Skill Intensity (X3)				1.000	.360[b]	-.195	-.207	.104
Four-Firm Concentration Ratio (X4)					1.000	.269	.272	.073
Unionization Ratio (X5)						1.000	.095	-.343[c]
Advertising Intensity (X6)							1.000	.021
Capital Intensity (X7)								1.000

[a] $p<.01$
[b] $p<.05$
[c] $p<.10$

ANALYSIS AND RESULTS

Before employing regression analysis, preliminary correlation analysis was performed to check for multicollinearity. Table 8–4 shows the correlation matrix. It indicates that R&D intensity and skill intensity are highly correlated ($r = .76, p < .01$), resulting in a multicollinearity problem in regression analysis.

Therefore, these two variables were used one at a time in two separate regression analyses. Results are shown in Table 8–5. Since R&D intensity and unionization were also correlated ($r = -.51, p < .01$), an additional multicollinearity problem was suspected in Model 1. A condition index (i.e., the square root of the ratio of the largest eigenvalue to each individual eigenvalue) was computed to check for multicollinearity. The condition index of 14.1 was well within the acceptable range, indicating that multicollinearity would not significantly bias the results in this model (Belsley, Kuh, and Welsch 1980).

Consistent results have been obtained in both regression models. The only significant variables (at least $p < .10$) are provision 9802 import

Table 8–5
Multiple Regression Analysis for Innovation Propensity (N = 30)

Variables	Model 1[a]			Model 2[b]		
	Beta Coefficient	t-Value	Significance Level	Beta Coefficient	t-Value	Significance Level
Provision 9802 Import Propensity	.29	1.78	.09	.38	2.23	.04
R&D Intensity	.53	2.50	.02	-	-	-
Skill Intensity	-	-	-	.43	2.15	.04
Four-Firm Concentration Ratio	-.02	-0.09	.93	-.02	-0.11	.91
Unionization Ratio	-.13	-0.62	.54	-.27	-1.42	.17
Advertising Intensity	.09	0.53	.60	.09	0.51	.62
Capital Intensity	-.23	-1.37	.18	-.17	-0.97	.34

[a]R^2=46.6%, significant at the .02 level
[b]R^2=43.5%, significant at the .03 level

propensity and R&D intensity in both models, respectively explaining over 40 percent of the variation in innovation propensity across industries.

Undoubtedly, both R&D intensity (p = .02) and skill intensity (p = .04) are significant in explaining innovation propensity. As stated earlier, our primary interest is in estimating the impact of provision 9802 import propensity on innovation propensity after the impact of the other variables is accounted for.

The existing literature has offered two opposing arguments on a relationship between provision 9802 import propensity and innovation propensity. The provision 9802 import propensity is found to have a positive relationship to innovation propensity in both models, although it appears somewhat marginal in the first model (p = .09 in the first model as opposed to p = .04 in the second model). This result is not inconsistent with the hypothesis that U.S. firms' international sourcing by way of provision 9802 imports reflects their strategic mobility in exploiting their competitive strengths and comparative advantages of various locations. A statistically significant positive relationship was not expected. However, it is premature to conclude, based on this strategic mobility hypothesis, that increased offshore sourcing improves the firm's innovative ability. At least, no evidence has been found that U.S. firms' provision 9802 import propensity impedes their innovative prowess. This unexpected finding goes beyond the hypothesized relationships and will be addressed later.

Interestingly, the variables, previously found to be significant in Acs and Audretsch's (1988) work, are not significant in our study. Three possible reasons may be offered to reconcile this contradictory finding. First, Acs and Audretsch were concerned about the absolute number of innovations rather than the relative scale of innovation propensity as used in our study. Second, our study is limited mostly to SIC 35, 36, 37, and 38 industries whose provision 9802 import propensity is higher than that of the other industries, and did not capture a wider range of industries. The variance in those variables could have been smaller, thus making it difficult to find a significant result. Third, the higher aggregation of the data imposed by data concordance could have also reduced the variance.

It is to be noted further that as expected, unionization ratio is negatively correlated to innovation propensity ($r = -.38$, $p < .05$) although it was not significant in the regression analysis. The impact of unionization was attenuated by other explanatory variables in the models (particularly by R&D intensity in the first model). Due to the cross-sectional nature of the sample in this study, a strongly negative correlation between unionization and R&D intensity may be reflective of the fact that newer industries (e.g., semiconductors) tend to be more R&D-intensive and less unionized than older ones. As argued by Connolly, Hirsch, and Hirschey (1986) and Acs and Audretsch (1988), among others, it is also conceivable that a high level of unionization stifles the corporate R&D activities, thereby reducing the firm's innovative ability.

CONCLUSIONS AND SUGGESTIONS FOR RESEARCH DIRECTIONS

Moxon (1975) stated in his earlier study of provision 9802 imports (in the electronics industry) that for most products, foreign competitors were already entrenched in the U.S. market before offshore plants were established by U.S. firms to lower the cost of production. Without offshore plants, many U.S. firms would have had to drop the product completely, subcontract their manufacture to a foreign company, or automate their production process in the United States. Therefore, provision 9802 imports were perceived to be a defensive strategy for products that lost much of their innovative value.

In our study, however, a different picture has emerged. The extent of provision 9802 imports by U.S. firms is positively related to the level of their innovative ability. This finding appears to contradict the predictions of Hayes and Wheelwright (1984) and Teece (1987), among others, who essentially argue that continual improvement in manufacturing process is necessary to maintain the firm's long-term competitiveness and its ability to learn the future direction of technology and bring about product innovations. It is conceivable that their logic may not apply to U.S. firms that are capable of transferring technology between foreign affiliates and themselves across national borders. Industries in our sample are the ones in which firms extensively engage in provision 9802 offshore sourcing and for which official data are available. Therefore, firms in these industries may be systematically different from those that are more domestically oriented and do little of offshore sourcing.

At least in those industries represented in our sample (mostly machinery, electrical/electronic equipment, transportation equipment, and measuring instruments), a positive relationship between U.S. firms' provision 9802 imports and their innovative ability is not inconsistent with the strategic mobility argument. There does not appear to be any empirical basis to argue that such offshore production will deteriorate U.S. firms' innovative ability, at least, in the intermediate run (4–5 years).

Such a positive relationship does not necessarily imply that provision 9802 offshore sourcing directly improves the firm's innovative ability, however. Rather, it may be concluded that since the firms' innovative ability is a prerequisite for their sustained competitiveness in an increasingly competitive world, their provision 9802 imports indicate nothing less than their strategic readiness to exploit comparative advantages in various locations along with their corporate resources on a global scale. Although causal linkages are not clear at the current stage of knowledge on this issue, the findings of this chapter may well suggest that U.S. multinational firms with a higher level of integration and coordination of production and marketing on a consolidated basis tend to retain innovative ability more efficiently and effectively than would otherwise be the case.

It is worthwhile here to pursue this strategic mobility thesis a little further to cast some insight into possible reasons for the positive relationship between provision 9802 imports and innovative ability. Some future research directions will also be offered for this important issue.

First of all, now that many U.S. multinational firms have affiliates established in many parts of the world, they have become capable of tapping various resources on a global scale, if they are strategically ready to do so (Davidson 1980). Porter (1986) has further argued that the global competitor can locate activities wherever comparative advantage lies, decoupling comparative advantage from the firm's home base or country of ownership. Today, these investments represent important resources that can be simultaneously utilized to promote further expansion domestically as well as abroad. Increased offshore sourcing represents one such strategic move. This argument may be strengthened if today's rapidly changing technological environment is taken into consideration. Quick technological obsolescence makes it economically difficult to invest in capital-intensive operations at home as they take a longer period to break even than would technological obsolescence to occur (Livingstone 1975). However, the more extensive the sourcing operations become, the more difficult it will likely be to coordinate various activities along the value chain around the world. As Monczka and Giunipero (1984) reported, logistics/inventory/distance, nationalism, and lack of working knowledge about foreign business practices, among others, tend to thwart effective coordination. Studies are needed to see what level of strategic readiness manifested by provision 9802 imports will be optimal, given these logistical constraints.

Second, if one can extend the intertwined role of product innovations and manufacturing process innovations as joint determinants of competitiveness (e.g., Abernathy and Utterback 1978 for conceptual argument; Kotabe and Murray 1990 for empirical finding), then it may be argued that the U.S. firms' product development capability is complemented by manufacturing innovative abilities of their offshore affiliates. Mansfield and Romeo (1984) documented the increased significance of complementary R&D activities by foreign affiliates of the U.S. firms and their reverse technology transfer back to the U.S. parents. They argue that technology developed overseas by U.S.-based firms tends to be introduced about as rapidly in the United States as in the country where it is developed. As a result, the U.S. firms' competitiveness depends as much on overseas R&D as on domestic R&D. Furthermore, findings in Chapter 7 have added empirical evidence to support the importance of parent-affiliates' joint R&D activities to determine the firm's global competitiveness. Therefore, U.S. parents' provision 9802 imports are considered not only to help improve their cost competitiveness, but also to help prevent their innovative ability-led competitive edge from getting easily neutralized by competition. However, no study is available that shows to what extent manufacturing process innovations do actually occur at offshore locations, let alone how geographically spread out product and manufacturing process innovations are managed.

Third, U.S. firms' provision 9802 imports are increasingly partaking of an intra-firm transaction offering internalization advantages. Provision 9802 imports originate mostly from newly industrialized countries capable of manufacturing high-technology complementary products (Helleiner 1981; Grunwald and Flamm 1985). As long as key technology and expertise developed by the U.S. multinational firm are used globally within its corporate system, it may be argued that the firm will likely retain its key technological base to itself without unduly disseminating them to competitors as if it were a "public" good (Buckley and Casson 1976; Dunning 1977; Rugman 1982). Innovation is represented in components and finished products, in blueprints and other proprietary documents, or in R&D personnel. U.S. parent firms' provision 9802 importation of components and finished products from their affiliates abroad can be considered to provide a means of internalizing its technological base within its corporate system. Given the relative ease of reverse engineering and inventing around by competition, however, the question still remains as to how tight the "appropriability regime" of such multinational operations might be (Teece 1986). Further research is desired to identify what internalization advantage, other than the cost advantage, provision 9802 offshore sourcing might provide the firm that domestic sourcing (including procurement of components and production) cannot.

LIMITATIONS

Two groups of limitations exist in this study. The first group deals with the findings of the study, while the second group is a result of research methodology.

The findings of this study are limited in two ways. While increased offshore production is positively related to U.S. firms' innovative ability, it does not guarantee the firm's market success or innovative ability. Skillful execution of integrated strategies is necessary. Also, not all industries are conducive to offshore production. As Grunwald and Flamm (1985) argued, the propensity to produce offshore depends heavily on transportation costs and the separability of labor-intensive operations, among other factors. Thus, as shown in our data set, industries such as machinery, electrical/electronic equipment, transportation equipment, and measuring instruments are the most conducive.

Methodologically, data availability placed a number of limitations. First, the time period represented by the data was late 1970s to early 1980s. Although data were the latest available for this particular study, the situation could have changed since. In particular, a dramatic increase in provision 9802 imports has been observed in the 1980s. Second, because of the need for establishing data concordance between two industry classification schemes (TSUS and SIC), many of the 4-digit SIC industries needed to be aggregated, resulting in an approximate equivalent of 3-digit SIC classification on the average. Third, the assumption of innovations resulting from innovation-inducing inputs in the previous period (the average of 4–5 years) does not hold true across all industries, although it is a traditional assumption in innovation studies at an aggregate level (e.g., Mansfield 1981). Fourth, the 500 employee cutoff for large firms in the SBA study could have eliminated product innovations by smaller firms that extensively engaged in provision 9802 offshore sourcing, although such cases are reportedly relatively few (Grunwald and Flamm 1985). Finally, the possible impact of R&D activities by U.S. firms' foreign affiliates on provision 9802 offshore sourcing was not considered. As pointed out earlier, some circumstantial evidence indicates that the increased internationalization of R&D activities coordinated jointly by U.S. parents and their affiliates abroad has a bearing on their global competitiveness (Mansfield and Romeo 1984; Kotabe 1989).

All in all, this study was cross-sectional in nature and presented the results based on a snapshot of innovational relationships observed across various industries. Although the innovation lag period was considered, a cross-sectional study may not capture all the implications of a dynamic system that could change over time. Therefore, longitudinal studies and firm-level studies are strongly desired to better cast the relationship between offshore sourcing and innovative activities before a better conceptual logic can be developed.

REFERENCES

Abernathy, William J. and James M. Utterback (1978). "Patterns of Industrial Innovation." *Technology Review,* 80 (June-July), 40–47.

Acs, Zoltan J. and David B. Audretsch (1988). "Innovation in Large and Small Firms: An Empirical Analysis." *American Economic Review,* 78 (September), 678–690.

Belsley, David A., Edwin Kuh, and Roy E. Welsch (1980). *Regression Diagnostics: Identifying Influential Data and Sources of Collinearity.* New York: John Wiley.

Blades, Derek, and Wendy Simpson (1985). *The OECD Compatible Trade and Production Data Base.* Paris: OECD Economics and Statistics Department Working Papers, No. 18, (January).

Booz, Allen & Hamilton (1982). *New Products Management for the 1980s.* New York: Booz, Allen & Hamilton.

Buckley, Peter J. and Mark Casson (1976). *The Future of the Multinational Enterprise.* London: MacMillan.

Business International (1982). *The Effects of U.S. Corporate Foreign Investment 1970–1980.* New York: Business International Corporation.

Business Week (1986). "Special Report: The Hollow Corporation." March 3, 56–59.

Buzzell, Robert D. and Bradley T. Gale (1987). *The PIMS Principles.* New York: The Free Press.

Capon, Noel and Rashi Glazer (1987). "Marketing and Technology: A Strategic Coalignment." *Journal of Marketing,* 51 (July), 1–14.

Channon, Derek and Michael Jalland (1978). *Multinational Strategic Planning.* New York: AMACOM.

Connolly, Robert A., Barry T. Hirsch, and Mark Hirschey (1986). "Union Rent Seeking, Intangible Capital, and the Market Value of the Firm." *Review of Economics and Statistics,* 68 (November), 567–577.

Davidson, William H. (1980). *Experience Effects in International Investment and Technology Transfer.* Ann Arbor, MI: UMI Research Press.

——— (1982). *Global Strategic Management.* New York: John Wiley.

——— and Richard Harrigan (1977). "Key Decisions in International Marketing:

Introducing New Products Abroad." *Columbia Journal of World Business,* 12 (Winter), 15–23.

Drucker, Peter F. (1979). "Production Sharing, Concepts and Definitions." *Journal of the Flagstaff Institute,* 3 (January), 2–9.

Dunning, John H. (1977). "Trade, Location of Economic Activity and the MNE: A Search for an Eclectic Approach." In *The International Allocation of Economic Activity,* Bertil Ohlin, Per-Ove Hesselborn, and Per Magnus Wijkman, eds. New York: Holmes and Meier, 395–418.

Edwards, Keith L. and Theodore J. Gordon (1984). *Characterization of Innovations Introduced on the U.S. Market in 1982: A Final Report.* The Futures Group, Inc., U.S. Small Business Administration, Contract No. SBA-6050–0A-82.

Freeman, Richard B. and James L. Medoff (1979). "New Estimates of Private Sector Unionism in the United States." *Industrial and Labor Relations Review,* 32 (January), 143–174.

Grunwald, Joseph and Kenneth Flamm (1985). *The Global Factory: Foreign Assembly in International Trade.* Washington, DC: The Brookings Institution.

Hayes, Robert H. and William J. Abernathy (1980). "Managing Our Way to Economic Decline." *Harvard Business Review,* 58 (July–August), 67–77.

Hayes, Robert H. and Steven C. Wheelwright (1984). *Restoring Our Competitive Edge: Competing through Manufacturing.* New York: John Wiley.

Helleiner, Gerald K. (1981). *Intra-Firm Trade and the Developing Countries.* New York: St. Martin's Press.

Hufbauer, G. C. (1970). "The Impact of National Characteristics and Technology on the Commodity Composition of Trade in Manufactured Goods." In *The Technology Factor in International Trade,* Raymond Vernon, ed. New York: Columbia University Press, 145–231.

Imai, Masaaki (1986). *Kaizen.* New York: Random House Business Division.

Kamien, Morton I. and Nancy L. Schwartz (1975). "Market Structure and Innovation: A Survey." *Journal of Economic Literature,* 13 (March), 1–37.

Kogut, Bruce (1985). "Designing Global Strategies: Comparative and Competitive Value-Added Chains." *Sloan Management Review,* 26 (Summer), 15–28.

Kotabe, Masaaki (1989). " 'Hollowing-out' of U.S. Multinationals and Their Global Competitiveness: An Intrafirm Perspective." *Journal of Business Research,* 19 (August), 1–15.

Kotabe, Masaaki and Glenn S. Omura (1989). "Sourcing Strategies of European and Japanese Multinationals: A Comparison." *Journal of International Business Studies,* 20 (Spring), 113–130.

Kotabe, Masaaki and Janet Y. Murray (1990). "Linking Product and Process Innovations and Modes of International Sourcing in Global Competition: A Case of Foreign Multinational Firms." *Journal of International Business Studies,* 21 (Third Quarter), 383–408.

Kotler, Philip, Liam Fahey and S. Jatusripitak (1985). *The New Competition.* Englewood Cliffs, NJ: Prentice-Hall.

Levin, Richard C., Alvin K. Klevorick, Richard R. Nelson, and Sidney G. Winter (1987). "Appropriating the Returns from Industrial Research and Development." *Brookings Papers on Economic Activity,* Issue 3, 783–831.

Livingstone, James M. (1975). *The International Enterprise*. New York: Halsted Press.

Mansfield, Edwin (1981). "Composition of R&D Expenditures: Relationship to Size of Firm, Concentration, and Innovative Output. *Review of Economics and Statistics,* 63 (November), 610–615.

———— and Anthony Romeo (1984). " 'Reverse' Transfers of Technology From Overseas Subsidiaries to American Firms." *IEEE Transactions on Engineering Management,* EM-31(3) (August), 122–127.

Markides, Constantinos C. and Norman Berg (1988). "Manufacturing Offshore Is Bad Business." *Harvard Business Review,* 66 (September–October), 113–120.

Miles, Raymond E. and Charles C. Snow (1986). "Organizations: New Concepts for New Forms." *California Management Review,* 28 (Spring), 62–73.

Monczka, Robert M. and Larry C. Giunipero (1984). "International Purchasing: Characteristics and Implementation." *Journal of Purchasing and Materials Management,* 20 (Fall), 2–9.

Moxon, Richard W. (1975). "The Motivation for Investment in Offshore Plants: The Case of the U.S. Electronics Industry." *Journal of International Business Studies,* 6 (Fall), 51–66.

Ohmae, Kenichi (1985). *Triad Power*. New York: The Free Press.

Pakes, Ariel and Zvi Griliches (1980). "Patents and R&D at the Firm Level: A First Report." *Economic Indicators,* 5, 377–381.

Porter, Michael E. (1986). *Competition in Global Industries*. Boston: Harvard Business School.

Rugman, Alan M. (1982). "Internalization and Non-Equity Forms of International Involvement." In *New Theories of the Multinational Enterprise*. Alan M. Rugman, ed. London: Croom Helm.

Schuller, Frank C. (1988). *Venturing Abroad: Innovation by U.S. Multinationals*. Westport, CT: Quorum Books.

Shaiken, Harley (1987). *Automation and Global Production: Automobile Engine Production in Mexico, the United States, and Canada*. San Diego: Center for U.S.-Mexican Studies, University of California, San Diego.

Shepherd William G., and Dexter Hutchins (1985). "There's No Trade Deficit, Sam!" *Financial World,* February 23, 28–32.

Snow, C. P. (1981). *The Physicists*. London: Macmillan.

Teece, David J. (1986). "Firm Boundaries, Technological Innovation, and Strategic Management." In *The Economics of Strategic Planning,* Lacy G. Thomas, III, ed. Lexington, MA: Lexington Books, 187–199.

———— (1987). "Capturing Value from Technological Innovation: Integration, Strategic Partnering, and Licensing Decisions." In *Technology and Global Industry: Companies and Nations in the World Economy,* Bruce R. Guile and Harvey Brooks, eds., Washington, DC: National Academy Press, 65–95.

Thurow, Lester C. (1985). *The Management Challenge*. Cambridge, MA: MIT Press.

United Nations Center on Transnational Corporations (1983). *Transnational Corporations in World Development, Third Survey*. New York: United Nations.

——— (1988). *Transnational Corporations in World Development: Trends and Perspectives*. New York: United Nations.

U.S. Bureau of the Census (1981). *1977 Census of Manufacturers,* vol. 1. Washington, DC: U.S. Government Printing Office.

U.S. Federal Trade Commission (1982). *Statistical Report: Annual Line of Business Report 1976*. Wasington, DC: U.S. Government Printing Office, May.

U.S. International Trade Commission (1981). *Imports under Items 806.30 and 807.00 of the Tariff Schedules of the United States, 1977–80*. Washington, DC, July.

——— (1990). *Imports under Items 9802.00.60 and 9802.00.80 of the Tariff Schedules of the United States*. Washington, DC.

Vernon, Raymond (1974). ''The Location of Economic Activity.'' In *Economic Analysis and the Multinational Enterprise,* John H. Dunning, ed. London: George Allen and Unwin, 89–114.

von Hippel, Eric (1988). *The Sources of Innovation*. Oxford: Oxford University Press.

Chapter 9 ———————

New Trends

We have come a long way in understanding the sources of competitive advantage for successful multinational firms around the world. Our competitive world is evolving continuously and at a faster rate than ever before, and it is shaping and reshaping the future that no pundits can dare to predict with accuracy. Nonetheless, one thing is certain—that is, findings of the various empirical studies reported in this book are, by definition, a thing of the present that may change as the climate of the time changes. None of us is confident enough to write about either what the business environment will be like 20 or 30 years from now or how corporate strategy will change as a result. It is simply too far off into the future. However, we may be able to forecast with some certainty how corporate strategy will likely change in the near future based on the changes taking place in today's competitive environment.

Our purpose will be best served if we highlight our findings reported in the book. Many successful multinational firms have adopted four strategic thrusts: (1) proactive product standardization, (2) simultaneous emphasis on both product and manufacturing innovative activities, (3) integrated sourcing of major components, and (4) marketing in all Triad regions of the world for growth. In other words, those firms strive to develop an innovative product with customers from around the world in mind such that the product can meet different segments of the world with as few modifications in the product and components as possible, stress manufacturing efficiency and flexibility for production, are capable of procuring in-house key components for the product, and are willing to take the challenge of marketing it in all Triad regions. In essence, those firms take advantage of economies of both scale and scope, proprietary learning, and differentiation by integrating the three key value-adding activities of R&D, manufacturing, and marketing on a global basis (Chandler 1990; Kumpe and Bolwijn 1988; Prahalad and Hamel 1990).

Such strategic thrusts have been a necessary response to the current business climate in which consumer tastes and the scope of competition are becoming truly global and even "borderless" (Ohmae 1990). Add to it recent developments around the world, including the European Integration by the end of 1992, a pending U.S.-Mexico free-trade area, the dismantling of the Soviet command society and its ex-satellite countries in Eastern Europe into market economies, and the opening of Third World economies such as Mexico, Chile, and Thailand into the world economy. It is easily conceivable to envision in the near future a global *market* economy comprising Triad regions and emerging market economies around them. Indeed, the emergence of global markets and global competition has led Chandler (1990), a reputed business historian, to the conclusion that firms have to be large and integrated in closely related industries to compete globally.

Indeed, the above argument allegedly borders on a theory that global competitors, to be successful, should be Jacks-of-all-trades and masters of everything in industry. Indeed, it had long been the primary mode of operation for many multinational firms to achieve a high level of market performance around the world. In recent years, however, we have seen a growing number of strategic alliances. The emergence of strategic alliances is an admission to the fact that not all firms can be fully integrated such that they could perform all important value-adding activities in-house.

Strategic alliances are a collaborative agreement between (or among) competitors in which they contribute their respective superior technology and know-how to make synergistically possible what could not otherwise be achieved by each individual firm (Buckley and Casson 1988; Hamel, Doz, and Prahalad 1989; Jain 1987). The payoffs and pitfalls of strategic alliances have been discussed as though they were manageable if acted proactively (Hamel et al. 1989; Harrigan 1987; Lei and Slocum 1991). However, a fundamental issue still remains: Can strategic alliances be equitable such that all partners will gain without hurting others in the long run? Some doubt has been cast on the equity issue (Doz et al. 1990; Reich and Mankin 1986). This fundamental built-in inequity in strategic alliances will be a focal point in this chapter.

First, the sources of competitive advantage are further elaborated upon. So far, we have emphasized the normative issues of *what needs to be done* to succeed in the global marketplace, and we have not explicitly discussed the sources of competitive advantage. Second, benefits of strategic alliances are reviewed briefly. Third, based on our understanding of global sourcing strategy and its implications presented in this book, we will explore how strategic alliances could affect multinational firms' market performance in the long run.

SOURCES OF COMPETITIVE ADVANTAGE

Consistent with the transaction cost stream of research, Teece (1986, 1987, 1988) has identified three primary sources of competitive advantage: (1) appropriability regime, (2) dominant design, and (3) complementary assets. They are used here as they provide a useful conceptual foundation for our argument in which to discuss the dynamics of competition.

Appropriability regime refers to aspects of the commercial environment that govern a firm's ability to retain its technological advantage. It depends on the efficacy of legal mechanisms of protection such as patents, copyrights, and trade secrets. Levin et al. (1987) reported, however, that in today's highly competitive market, legal means of protecting proprietary technology have become ineffective as new product innovations are relatively easily reverse-engineered, improved upon, and invented around by competitors without violating patents and other proprietary protections bestowed on them. They found that the most effective ways of securing maximum returns from a new product innovation are through lead time and moving fast down the experience curve (i.e., quickly resorting to mass production). Furthermore, strategic alliances facilitate such technology diffusion through official and unofficial channels among competitors sharing technology. Obviously, the value of owning technology has lessened drastically in recent years as the inventing firm's temporary monopoly over its technology has shortened.

Dominant design is a narrow class of product designs that begins to emerge as a "standard" design. A firm that has won a dominant design status has an absolute competitive advantage over its competition. In an early stage of product development, many competing product designs exist. After considerable trial and error in the marketplace, a product standard tends to emerge. A good case example is Sony's Betamax format and Matsushita's VHS format for VCRs. The Betamax format was technologically superior with better picture quality than the VHS format but could not play as long to record movies as the VHS. Although the Sony system was introduced slightly earlier than the Matsushita system, the tape's capability to record movies turned out to be fatal to Sony as the VHS tape was increasingly used for rental home movies and home recording of movies. Thus, the VHS has emerged as the worldwide standard for video cassette recording.

Was it simply the act of the "invisible hand" in the marketplace? The answer is clearly no. Matsushita actively licensed its VHS technology to Sanyo, Sharp, and Toshiba for production and supplied VHS format video cassette recorders to RCA, Magnavox, and GTE Sylvania for resale under their respective brand names (Rosenbloom and Cusumano 1987). When Philips introduced a cassette tape recorder, a similar active licensing strategy had been employed for a quick adoption as a dominant standard around the world. Despite various government hurdles to stall the Japanese domination of emerging HDTV technology, Sony is currently trying to make its format a standard by working its way into Hollywood movie studios. It is clear that a wide adoption of a new product around the world, whether autonomous or deliberated, seems to guarantee it a dominant design status.

Complementary assets are manufacturing process and marketing-related assets (both hardware and software) that are in almost all cases required for successful commercialization of a product innovation. The importance of manufacturing innovations has already been amply shown throughout the book. The issue here is to what extent those assets are specialized to the development and commercialization of a new product. Indeed, many successful companies have highly committed their productive assets to closely related areas without diversifying into unrelated businesses (Rumelt 1986; Chandler 1990). This commitment is crucial. Take semiconductor production for example. A director at SEMATECH (a U.S. government-industry semiconductor manufacturing technology consortium established in Austin, Texas, to regain U.S. competitive edge in semiconductor manufacturing equipment from Japanese competition) admits that despite and because of a rapid technological turnover, any serious firm wishing to compete on a state-of-the-art computer chip with the Japanese will have to invest a minimum of half a billion dollars in a semiconductor manufacturing equipment and facility. As we all know, General Motors has already invested upward of $5 billion for its Saturn Project to compete with the Japanese in small car production and marketing. A massive retooling is also necessary for any significant upgrade in both industries. Furthermore, the software side of complementary assets may be even more difficult to match as it involves such specialized operational aspects as JIT (just-in-time) manufacturing management, quality control, and components sourcing relationships. It has been found that irrespective of nationality, those multinational firms that are successful in global markets tend to excel not only in product innovative ability but also in manufacturing and marketing competences. It is clear that innovative firms committed to manufacturing and marketing excellence will likely remain strong competitors in industry.

These three sources of competitive advantage are not independent of each other. Given the relative ease of learning about competitors' proprietary technology without violating patents and other legal protections, many firms resort to mass production and mass marketing to drive down the cost along the experience curve. To do so requires enormous investment in manufacturing capacity. As a result, the efficacy of appropriability regime is highly dependent on investment in complementary assets. Similarly, a wide acceptance of a product is most likely necessary for the product to become a dominant design in the world for a next generation of the product. Thus, mass production and marketing on a global scale is likely to be a necessary, if not sufficient, condition for a firm to attain a dominant design status for its product. The argument comes back full circle to Chandler's (1990) conclusion that firms have to be large and integrated in closely related industries to compete globally.

It is apparent that patents, copyrights, and trade secrets are not necessarily optimal means of garnering competitive advantage unless they are strongly backed by strengths in innovative manufacturing on a global basis. Likewise, as shown in earlier chapters, firms strong in manufacturing without innovative products also suffer from competitive disadvantage. In other words, it takes such an enormous investment to develop new products and to penetrate new markets that few firms can go it alone any more. Thus, to compete with integrated global competitors, an increasing number of firms have entered into strategic alliances so as to complement their competitive weaknesses with their partner's competitive strengths. In the next section, strategic alliances of complementary nature are discussed.

STRATEGIC ALLIANCES

Market globalization is not the only challenge facing multinational firms today. Today's competitive environment is also characterized by rapid technological change and intensity, shrinking product life cycle to recoup R&D investment, fragmentation of technology, and enormous investment requirement. These environmental and technological changes are forcing firms to reconsider their global strategy. A high-ranking marketing executive at Sony, the most innovative consumer electronics company in the world today, has told me with a sigh that its technological lead time over competition is no more than six months at best. As a result, many multinational firms have come to realize that they can no longer be Jacks-of-all-trades and masters of everything. Or worse yet, if they try to be Jacks-of-all-trades, then they are afraid that they will end up being masters of none. Enormous fixed investment has to be recouped in a relatively short time period. Ohmae (1990) argues convincingly that strategic alliances are a solution to maximize profit contribution to the firm's huge fixed costs as well as to maintain technological viability and flexibility.

Many firms have started experimenting with strategic alliances to compensate for what they are weak at. Strategic alliances are a form of business agreement between companies to exchange their respective strengths in pursuit of mutual benefits. They may or may not involve equity participation. A Toyota-GM joint venture in Fremont, California, involved equity investment in which Toyota could learn about management of American labor and GM could learn Toyota's JIT production know-how. Similarly, IBM and Apple Computer, threatened by Microsoft's encroaching domination of operating standards and software applications, have agreed to enter into a joint-venture alliance in order to develop a dominant operating system that will work on both systems. Without equity participation, Volkswagen distributes Nissan four-wheel-drive cars in Europe, and Nissan distributes Volkswagen cars in Japan, so that neither company has had to invest in a distribution system abroad. Recently, Apple Computer has also announced an agreement with Sony that the Japanese company will be providing lap-top computers to Apple. Apple can cover its weak spot in its product line, while Sony can learn about the technological and manufacturing aspects of the personal computer business in which the company has lagged behind its rival companies such as NEC and Sanyo. Such examples abound.

LONG-TERM PROSPECTS

Now the impending question is whether strategic alliances are a correct response to the limitations being felt by global competitors that came to realize they could no longer be masters of everything. Benefits of strategic alliances are clear, but risks associated with them are not as clear, particularly in the long run.

From the earlier discussion of the three sources of competitive advantage, appropriability regime is clearly the weakest as its efficacy tends to depend on investment in complementary assets. It means that product technology is more easily transferred than a manufacturing process competence in a strategic alliance arrangement between competitors. Firms with strong manufacturing competences are more likely to gain from their partners with strong product technology in a strategic alliance than the other way around. For example, Hamel, Doz, and Prahalad (1989) report that NEC has used numerous collaborative ventures—most notably with Honeywell and French Bull—to enhance its product technology and innovative competences, backed by its strong manufacturing capability. As a result, NEC has become the only company in the world with a leading position in telecommunications, computers, and semiconductors despite its lower R&D intensity than that of Texas Instruments, Northern Telecom, and L. M. Ericsson.

In a similar vein, achieving a dominant design hinges on strong manufacturing and marketing competences as it requires a wide adoption of a new product around the world. As indicated earlier, a VCR battle between Matsushita's VHS format and Sony's Betamax format was a prominent case example in the 1980s. A new battle is again brewing over digital recording technology between Matsushita and Sony. Matsushita has decided to ally with Philips to develop and produce Philips-designed digital compact cassettes (*Wall Street Journal* 1991). Digital cassette players play like existing analog cassette players and can also play existing analog tapes, but require the fast forwarding and rewinding of tapes to access a particular song. Sony has more innovative technology known as Mini Disc and DAT (digital audio tape). Sony's digital players make existing analog cassette tapes unusable but allow users to access any song quickly just like a compact disc player. While Sony is considered more innovative than Matsushita, it does not have the same manufacturing and marketing clout to set product standards. Similarly, product-innovative Philips could not set product standards if it were not for Matsushita's manufacturing and marketing competences.

What is worrisome for Philips, however, is its dependence on Matsushita's global manufacturing and marketing ability that it does not have. An alliance with Matsushita may solve for Philips a short- to intermediate-term problem of marketing Philips-designed digital cassettes and players and making its format a dominant design in the world. Matsushita is likely to drive down the manufacturing and marketing cost along the experience curve by way of marketing the product on a global scale much faster than Philips. Philips may eventually find it extremely difficult to compete with Matsushita on the basis of price, global penetration, product differentiation, and ease of manufacture.

History has shown many times over that many higher cost producers will also begin to outsource finished products from the lower cost producer on an OEM (original equipment manufacture) basis. Our studies have amply shown that the ability to procure major components in-house for product development on a global basis is a strong determinant of firms' market performance. While outsourcing may be an easy way out from a short-term perspective of cost efficiency, it will prevent outsourcing firms from keeping abreast of emerging product and manufacturing technologies that might be employed for further product and design improvement and, as a result, portend a long-term decline in their manufacturing competences and product innovative ability.

Therefore, as Hamel, Doz, and Prahalad (1989) have correctly argued, firms such as Philips must take steps to prolong the shelf life of their technology base. They suggest two strategies. First, Philips may limit the scope of the formal alliance agreement so as not to disclose an entire range of technologies to Matsushita. Second, Philips could take an incremental, incentive-based approach to technology transfer to its partner, such as an agreement to disclose its technology incrementally for an increased penetration of the market or a further improvement of the product by Matsushita. However, these strategies would only work *provided* that Philips had a long technological lead over Matsushita. Unfortunately such favorable situations have become rarer in today's highly competitive environment.

A NEW DIRECTION

The above argument is partially conjectural. Nonetheless, dynamics of global competition have been vividly demonstrated. Where should we go from here? At least it is certain that a company can no longer enjoy the luxury of time to pursue its technological strengths on a country-by-country basis. If it does, then competitors will simply pass it by. Similarly, strategic alliances may turn out to be a short-term Band-Aid that shrouds various weaknesses of participating companies but does not cure their problems.

In markets where patents may be easily circumvented and new technologies easily developed, firms cannot rely on technology alone to sustain competitive advantage. In such environments, the appropriate design of products, image, and branding with continual incremental improvements that add value to the customer is all the more necessary to differentiate the firm's product offerings. As a result, in recent years, the importance of design has been advanced as a core competence of the firm (Lorenz 1986; Schneider 1989). For example, Procter & Gamble believes that if the company does not think through the concept of a new product on a global basis from the very beginning, it will not be able to enter additional markets until it sees the results from its initial country introduction. Global development from the beginning has almost certainly saved years in their global product introductions.

Kotler and Rath (1984) rightfully pointed out that industrial design was a powerful but neglected strategic tool. Today, design directors serve on the executive committees at an increasing number of innovative companies such as Sony and Sharp. Many European firms, including Braun and Olivetti, also have top-level design executives. Similarly, such U.S. firms as Ford, IBM, and Xerox are increasing the roles of design executives to regain their earlier leadership in industrial design.

Furthermore, design's roles in assisting product and manufacturing process innovation should also be recognized. They include speed to market, innovation promotion, global penetration, reducing product costs, improved performance and styling for differentiation, ease of manufacture (i.e., design for manufacturability), ease of service (i.e., design for maintainability), new market application, and safety, among others. These all support the interdependency of product and process innovative activities.

It is not to negate the importance of earlier sources of competitive advantage. Rather, it is to indicate that what we are seeing is a gradual "power shift" in sources of competitive advantage from proprietary technology to manufacturing and marketing competences, and now to industrial design. Proprietary technology is essentially a *raw* muscle power to obtain initial competitive advantage, and it is easy to imitate by inventing around, by reverse engineering, or even by industrial espionage. Manufacturing and marketing competences revolve around the "sweat and tears" of skilled human inputs, which take years to accomplish by continual improvement after improvement and, as a result, are much harder to copy.

Now, industrial design is emerging as a third generation of competitive advantage that has yet to be fully exploited. Industrial designers are the only ones who are trained in human interface with products. It is the requirement of coupling high-tech and high-touch dimensions for which designers are specifically suited. It is in this interface that we see a strong bond between a manufacturer and consumers. Again, Japanese competition has taken the lead in design and brought the concept of customer orientation to a higher dimension. The ultimate goal of industrial design is to delight the customer. My colleague, Bob Peterson, calls it the "L" word—a customer's love affair with the product.

As explored earlier in Chapter 6, Japanese firms view design not simply as the product designers' domain of responsibility but rather as that across various functional areas including designers, engineers, production, and marketing people. This is primarily accomplished by the use of a tightly knit integrated project team. It suggests the importance of the firm's proprietary technology and manufacturing/marketing ability as jointly supportive of industrial design efforts. As such, industrial design advantage is an outgrowth of the other sources of competitive advantage.

The pitfall of this strategic power shift to industrial design is to assume erroneously that product design ability would be a sufficient condition for corporate success. Good product design facilitates consumers' product adoption. But it is in almost all cases the firm's manufacturing and marketing strengths that make a wide consumer adoption possible. Given the design ability intertwined deeply with the other sources of competitive advantage, it could rarely be fully exploited independently. A case of Philips-designed digital compact cassettes illustrates the point. Philips' innovation has to bank on Matsushita's global manufacturing and marketing competences.

Thus we have come full circle. A primary source of competitive advantage has shifted from the raw muscle power of technology to the sweat and tears of manufacturing and marketing competences and then to design ability. This strategic shift represents firms' continued effort to cope with the shortened technological life cycle. Strategic alliances of a complementary nature may initially help alleviate the partners' respective weaknesses; however, in the long run, partners with strong manufacturing and marketing competences will likely come out to be dominant competitors in the industry.

REFERENCES

Buckley, Peter J. and Mark Casson (1988). "A Theory of Cooperation in International Business." In *Cooperative Strategies in International Business,* Farok J. Contractor and Peter Lorange, eds. Lexington, MA: Lexington Books, 31–53.

Chandler, Alfred D. (1990). "The Enduring Logic of Industrial Success." *Harvard Business Review,* 68 (March–April), 130–40.

Doz, Yves, C.K. Prahalad, and Gary Hamel (1990). "Control, Change, and Flexibility: The Dilemma of Transnational Collaboration." In *Managing the Global Firm,* Yves Doz and Gunnar Hedlund, eds. New York: Routledge, 117–143.

Hamel, Gary, Yves L. Doz, and C. K. Prahalad (1989). "Collaborate with Your Competitors and Win." *Harvard Business Review,* 67 (January–February), 133–139.

Harrigan, Kathryn R. (1987). "Strategic Alliances: Their Role in Global Competition." *Columbia Journal of World Business,* 22 (Summer), 67–69.

Jain, Subhash C. (1987). "Perspectives on International Strategic Alliances." In *Advances in International Marketing,* vol. 2., S. Tamer Cavusgil, ed. Greenwich, CT: JAI Press, 103–120.

Kotler, Philip and G. Alexander Rath (1984). "Design: A Powerful but Neglected Strategic Tool." *Journal of Business Strategy,* 5 (Fall), 16–21.

Kumpe, Ted and Piet T. Bolwijn (1988). "Manufacturing: The New Case for Vertical Integration." *Harvard Business Review,* 66 (March–April), 75–81.

Lei, David and John W. Slocum, Jr. (1991). "Global Strategic Alliances: Payoffs and Pitfalls." *Organizational Dynamics,* 19 (Winter), 44–62.

Levin, Richard C., Alvin K. Klevorick, Richard R. Nelson, and Sidney G. Winter (1987). "Appropriating the Returns from Industrial Research and Development." *Brookings Papers on Economic Activity,* Issue 3, 783–831.

Lorenz, Christopher (1986). *The Design Dimension: The New Competitive Weapon for Business.* New York: Basil Blackwell.

Ohmae, Kenichi (1990). *The Borderless World: Power and Strategy in the Interlinked Economy.* New York: HarperBusiness.

Prahalad, C.K. and Gary Hamel (1990). "The Core Competence of the Corporation." *Harvard Business Review,* 68 (May–June), 79–91.

Reich, Robert B. and Eric D. Mankin (1986). "Joint Ventures with Japan Gives Away Our Future." *Harvard Business Review,* 64 (March–April), 78–86.

Rosenbloom, Richard S. and Michael A. Cusumano (1987). "Technological Pioneering and Competitive Advantage: The Birth of VCR Industry." *California Management Review,* 29 (Summer), 51–76.

Rumelt, Richard P. (1986). *Strategy, Structure, and Economic Performance,* rev. ed. Boston, MA: Harvard Business School Press.

Schneider, Eric (1989). "Unchaining the Value of Design." *European Management Journal,* 7 (3), 320–31.

Teece, David J. (1986). "Firm Boundaries, Technological Innovation, and Strategic Management." In *The Economics of Strategic Planning,* Lacy G. Thomas, III, ed. Lexington, MA: Lexington Books, 187–99.

—— (1987). "Capturing Value from Technological Innovation: Integration, Strategic Partnering, and Licensing Decisions." In *Technology and Global Industry: Companies and Nations in the World Economy,* Bruce R. Guile and Harvey Brooks, eds. Washington, DC: National Academy Press, 65–95.

—— (1988). "Capturing Value from Technological Innovation: Integration, Strategic Partnering, and Licensing Decisions." *Interfaces,* 18 (May–June), 46–61.

Wall Street Journal (1991). "Matsushita, Pitting Itself Against Sony, Agrees to Back Philips's Digital Cassettes." July 8, p. B3.

Bibliography

BOOKS

Aaker, David (1988). *Developing Business Strategies,* 2nd ed. New York: John Wiley.

Abegglen, James C. and George Stalk, Jr. (1985). *Kaisha: The Japanese Corporation.* New York: Basic Books.

Abell, Derek F. and John S. Hammond (1979). *Strategic Market Planning.* Englewood Cliffs, NJ: Prentice-Hall.

Bartlett, Christopher A. and Sumantra Ghoshal (1989). *Managing Across Borders: The Transnational Solution.* Boston: Harvard Business School Press.

Barnet, Richard J. and R. E. Muller (1974). *Global Reach: The Power of the Multinational Corporations.* New York: Simon and Schuster.

Belsley, David A., Edwin Kuh, and Roy E. Welsch (1980). *Regression Diagnostics: Identifying Influential Data and Sources of Collinearity.* New York: John Wiley.

Bergsten, C. Fred and William R. Cline (1985). *The United States-Japan Economics Problem.* Washington, DC: Institute for International Economics, (October).

Blades, Derek, and Wendy Simpson (1985). *The OECD Compatible Trade and Production Data Base.* Paris: OECD Economics and Statistics Department Working Papers, No. 18, (January).

Booz, Allen & Hamilton (1982). *New Products Management for the 1980s.* New York: Booz, Allen & Hamilton.

Buckley, Peter J. and Mark Casson (1976). *The Future of the Multinational Enterprise.* London: Macmillan.

Bureau of Economic Analysis (1981). *U.S. Direct Investment Abroad: 1977 Benchmark Survey Data.* Washington, D.C: U.S. Department of Commerce.

—— (1985). *U.S. Direct Investment Abroad: 1982 Benchmark Survey Data.* Washington, DC: U.S. Department of Commerce.

———— (1986). *United States Trade Performance in 1985 and Outlook*. Washington, DC: International Trade Administration (October).

———— (1987). *U.S. Direct Investment Abroad: Preliminary 1985 Estimates*. Washington, DC: Bureau of Economic Analysis (June).

Business International (1982). *The Effects of U.S. Corporate Foreign Investment 1970–1980*. New York: Business International Corporation, May.

Buzzell, Robert D. and Bradley T. Gale (1987). *The PIMS Principles*. New York: The Free Press.

Casson, Mark (1979). *Alternatives to Multinational Enterprise*. New York: Holmes & Meier.

Central Intelligence Agency (1985). *Handbook of Economic Statistics 1985*. Washington, DC.

Channon, Derek and Michael Jalland (1978). *Multinational Strategic Planning*. New York: AMACOM.

Christopher, Robert C. (1983). *The Japanese Mind*. New York: Linden Press.

Clark, Rodney (1979). *The Japanese Company*. New Haven, CT: Yale University Press.

Davidson, William H. (1980). *Experience Effects in International Investment and Technology Transfer*. Ann Arbor, MI: UMI Research Press.

———— (1982). *Global Strategic Management*. New York: John Wiley.

———— (1983). *The Amazing Race: Winning the Technorivalry with Japan*. New York: John Wiley.

DeMente, Boye (1981). *The Japanese Way of Doing Business*. Englewood Cliffs, NJ: Prentice-Hall.

Doz, Yves, C. K. Prahalad, and Gary Hamel (1990). "Control, Change, and Flexibility: The Dilemma of Transnational Collaboration." in *Managing the Global Firm,* Yves Doz and Gunnar Hedlund, eds. New York: Routledge.

Drucker, Peter F. (1985). *Innovation and Entrepreneurship: Practice and Principles*. New York: Harper & Row.

Dunning, John H., and R. D. Pearse (1981). *The World's Largest Industrial Enterprises*. New York: St. Martin's Press.

———— (1985). *The World's Largest Industrial Enterprises 1962–1983*. New York: St. Martin's Press.

Edwards, Anthony (1984). *How to Make Offshore Manufacturing Pay*. Special Report no. 171. London: The Economist Publications.

Edwards, Keith L. and Theodore J. Gordon (1984). *Characterization of Innovations Introduced on the U.S. Market in 1982: A Final Report*. The Futures Group, Inc., U.S. Small Business Administration, Contract No. SBA-6050–0A-82.

Faith, Nicholas (1972). *The Infiltrators: The European Business Invasion of America*. London: Hamilton.

Fayerweather, John (1969). *International Business Management: A Conceptual Framework*. New York: McGraw-Hill.

Franko, Lawrence (1976). *The European Multinationals*. Stamford, CT: Greylock Press.

Furstenberg, F. (1974). *Why the Japanese Have Been So Successful in Business*. London: Leviathan House.

Gibney, Frank (1975). *Japan: The Fragile Superpower*. Rutland, VT: Charles E. Tuttle.

Graham, Edward M. and Paul R. Krugman (1989). *Foreign Direct Investment in the United States*. Washington, DC: Institute for International Economics.

Grant, Robert M. and Charles B. Fuller (1988). *The Richardson Sheffield Story: A British Winner*. London: London Business School.

Grunwald, Joseph, and Kenneth Flamm (1985). *The Global Factory: Foreign Assembly in International Trade*. Washington, DC: The Brookings Institution.

Hadley, Eleanor M. (1970). *Antitrust in Japan*. Princeton, NJ: Princeton University Press.

Hayes, Robert H. and Steven C. Wheelwright (1984). *Restoring Our Competitive Edge: Competing through Manufacturing*. New York: John Wiley.

Helleiner, Gerald K. (1981). *Intra-Firm Trade and the Developing Countries*. New York: St. Martin's Press.

Imai, Masaaki (1986). *Kaizen*. New York: Random House Business Division.

International Monetary Fund (IMF) (1978). *International Financial Statistics*. (February). Washington, DC.

—— (1983). *International Financial Statistics*. (February). Washington, DC.

—— (1987). *International Financial Statistics*. 40 (February). Washington, DC.

International Directory of Corporate Affiliations 1985/1986 (1985). Wilmette, IL: National Register Publishing.

Japan Science and Technology Agency (1981). *White Paper on Science and Technology*. Tokyo.

Kahn, Herman and Thomas Pepper (1980). *The Japanese Challenge: The Success and Failure of Economic Success*. New York: William Morrow.

Kaplan, Daniel P. (1988). *Using Federal R&D to Promote Commercial Innovation*. Washington, DC: Congress of the United States, Congressional Budget Office, (April).

Keegan, Warren J. (1989). *Global Marketing Management*. 4th ed. Englewood Cliffs, NJ: Prentice-Hall.

Kerlinger, Fred N. and Elazar J. Pedhazur (1973). *Multiple Regression in Behavioral Research*. New York: Holt, Rinehart and Winston.

Knickerbocker, Frederick T. (1973). *Oligopolistic Reaction and Multinational Enterprise*. Boston: Harvard Business School.

Kojima, Kiyoshi and Terutomo Ozawa (1984). *Japan's General Trading Companies: Merchants of Economic Development*. Paris: OECD.

Kotler, Philip and Gary Armstrong (1989). *Principles of Marketing*. 4th ed. Englewood Cliffs, NJ: Prentice-Hall.

Kotler, Philip, Liam Fahey, and Somkid Jatusripitak (1985). *The New Competition*. Englewood Cliffs, NJ: Prentice-Hall.

Leroy, Georges (1976). *Multinational Product Strategy: A Taxonomy for Analysis of Worldwide Product Innovation and Diffusion*. New York: Praeger.

Linder, Staffan B. (1961). *An Essay on Trade and Transformation*. New York: John Wiley.

Livingstone, James M (1975). *The International Enterprise*. New York: Halsted Press.

Lorenz, Christopher (1986). *The Design Dimension: The New Competitive Weapon for Business*. New York: Basil Blackwell.

Mitroff, Ian I. (1987). *Business Not As Usual: Rethinking Our Individual, Corporate, and Industrial Strategies for Global Competition*. San Francicso: Jossey-Bass.

Moxon, Richard W. (1974). *Offshore Production in the Less Developed Countries—A Case Study of Multinationality in the Electronics Industry*. Bulletin No. 98–99. New York: New York University Institute of Finance.

Nakane, Chie (1970). *Japanese Society*. Berkeley: University of California Press.

NEC Corporation (1990). *This is NEC 1990,* Tokyo: NEC.

Negandhi, Anant R. and B. R. Baliga (1981). *Tables Are Turning: German and Japanese Multinational Companies in the United States*. Cambridge, MA: Oelgeschlager, Gunn, and Hain.

Negandhi, Anant R. and Martin Welge (1984). *Beyond Theory Z*. London: JAI Press.

Neter, John, William Wasserman, and Michael H. Kutner (1985). *Applied Linear Statistical Models*. 2nd ed. Homewood, IL: Richard D. Irwin.

Ohmae, Kenichi (1982). *The Mind of the Strategist: The Art of Japanese Business*. New York: McGraw-Hill.

—— (1985). *Triad Power*. New York: The Free Press.

—— (1990). *The Borderless World: Power and Strategy in the Interlinked Economy*. New York: HarperBusiness.

Organization for Economic Cooperation and Development (OECD) (1985). *OECD Environmental Data: Compendium 1985*. Paris.

—— (1985). *Quarterly National Accounts*. no. 4. Paris, p. 11.

Ouchi, William (1981). *Theory Z: How American Business Can Meet the Japanese Challenge*. Boston: Addison-Wesley.

Pascale, Richard T. and Anthony G. Athos (1981). *The Art of Japanese Management*. New York: Simon & Schuster.

Porter, Michael E. (1980). *Competitive Strategy*. New York: The Free Press.

—— (1986). *Competition in Global Industries*. Boston: Harvard Business School Press.

Prahalad, C. K. and Yves L. Doz (1987). *The Multinational Mission*. New York: The Free Press.

Prestowitz, Clyde V., Jr. (1988). *Trading Places: How We Allowed Japan to Take the Lead*. New York: Basic Books.

Reich, Robert (1983). *The Next American Frontier*. New York: Times Books.

Robinson, Richard D., ed. (1987). *Direct Foreign Investment: Costs and Benefits*. New York: Praeger.

Root, Franklin R. (1987). *Entry Strategies for International Markets*. Lexington, MA: Lexington Books.

Rumelt, Richard P. (1986). *Strategy, Structure, and Economic Performance*. rev. ed. Boston: Harvard Business School Press.

Saso, Mary and Stuart Kirby (1982). *Japanese Industrial Competition to 1990*. Cambridge, MA: Abt Books.

Schuller, Frank C. (1988). *Venturing Abroad: Innovation by U.S. Multinationals*. Westport, CT: Quorum Books.

Servan-Schreiber, J.-J. (1968). *The American Challenge*. New York: Atheneum.

Shaiken, Harley (1987). *Automation and Global Production: Automobile Engine Production in Mexico, the United States, and Canada.* San Diego: Center for U.S.-Mexican Studies, University of California, San Diego.

Snow, C. P. (1981). *The Physicists.* London: Macmillan.

Stopford, John M. and Louis T. Wells, Jr. (1972). *Managing the Multinational Enterprise.* New York: Basic Books.

Terpstra, Vern (1987). *International Marketing.* 4th ed. New York: The Dryden Press.

Thurow, Lester C. (1985). *The Management Challenge.* Cambridge, MA: MIT Press.

Toyne, Brian and Peter G. P. Walters (1989). *Global Marketing Management: A Strategic Perspective.* Boston: Allyn and Bacon.

Tsurumi, Yoshi (1984). *Multinational Management.* 2nd ed. Cambridge, MA: Ballinger.

United Nations (1983). *Yearbook of Industrial Statistics 1981.* vol. 1. New York.

—— (1985). *Industrial Statistics Yearbook 1982.* vol. 1.

United Nations Center on Transnational Corporations (1983). *Transnational Corporations in World Development, Third Survey.* New York: United Nations.

—— (1988). *Transnational Corporations in World Development: Trends and Perspectives.* New York: United Nations.

U.S. Bureau of the Census (1981). *1977 Census of Manufacturers.* vol. 1, Washington DC: U.S. Government Printing Office.

U.S. Department of Commerce (1982). *Survey of Current Business,* (April).

—— (1987). *Survey of Current Business,* 67 (March).

—— (1988). *Business America,* 109 (April 25).

U.S. Federal Trade Commission (1982). *Statistical Report: Annual Line of Business Report 1976.* Washington, DC: U.S. Government Printing Office, May.

U.S. International Trade Commission (1981). *Imports under Items 806.30 and 807.00 of the Tariff Schedules of the United States, 1977–80.* Washington, DC, July.

—— (1990). *Imports under Items 9802.00.60 and 9802.00.80 of the Tariff Schedules of the United States,* Washington, DC.

Vogel, Ezra F. (1979). *Japanese Number One: Lesson for America.* Cambridge, MA: Harvard University Press.

von Hippel, Eric (1988). *The Sources of Innovation.* Oxford: Oxford University Press.

World Bank (1984). *World Tables.* 3rd ed. vol. 1. "Series 3. Economic Data." Washington, DC, p. 8.

Yoshino, Michael Y. (1976). *Japan's Multinational Enterprises.* Cambridge, MA: Harvard University Press.

Zaltman, Gerald, Christian R.A. Pinson, and Reinhard Angelmar (1973). *Metatheory and Consumer Research.* New York: Holt, Rinehart, and Winston.

ARTICLES

Abernathy, William J. and Phillip L. Townsend (1975). "Technology, Productivity and Process Change." *Technological Forecasting and Social Change,* 7 (August), 379–396.

Abernathy, William J. and James M. Utterback (1978). "Patterns of Industrial Innovation." *Technology Review,* 80 (June-July), 40–47.

Abernathy, William J. and Kenneth Wayne (1974). "Limits of the Learning Curve." *Harvard Business Review,* 52 (September–October), 109–119.

Acs, Zoltan J. and David B. Audretsch (1988). "Innovation in Large and Small Firms: An Empirical Analysis." *American Economic Review,* 78 (September), 678–690.

Ajami, Riad and David Ricks (1981). "Motives of Non-American Firms Investing in the United States." *Journal of International Business Studies,* 12 (Winter), 25–34.

Armstrong, J. Scott and Terry S. Overton (1977). "Estimating Nonresponse Bias in Mail Surveys." *Journal of Marketing Research,* 14 (August), 396–402.

Ayal, Igal and Jehiel Zif (1979). "Market Expansion Strategies in Multinational Marketing." *Journal of Marketing,* 43 (Spring), 84–94.

Aylmer, R. J. (1970). "Who Makes Marketing Decisions in the Multinational Firm?" *Journal of Marketing,* 34 (October), 25–30.

Baldwin, Robert E. (1971). "Determinants of the Commodity Structure of U.S. Trade." *American Economic Review,* 61 (March), 126–146.

Banting, P. M. and R. E. Ross (1973). "The Marketing Mix: The Canadian Perspective." *Journal of the Academy of Marketing Science,* 1 (Spring), 1–11.

Bartels, Robert (1968). "Are Domestic and International Marketing Dissimilar?" *Journal of Marketing,* 32 (July), 56–61.

Boddewyn, Jean J., Robin Soehl, and Jacques Picard (1986). "Standardization in International Marketing: Is Ted Levitt In Fact Right?" *Business Horizons,* 29 (November–December), 69–75.

Boyer, Edward (1986). "Foreign Investors Still Love the U.S." *Fortune,* May 12, 93.

Brooks, Harvey (1983). "Japanese Technological Advances and Possible United States Responses Using Research Joint Ventures." Presented at House Subcommittee on Investigations and Oversight and the Subcommittee on Science, Research, and Technology of the Committee on Science and Technology, 98th Congress, 1st session, June 29–30.

Brownstein, Vivien (1990). "A Weaker Dollar Will Help Keep the Deficit Shrinking." *Fortune,* April 23, 23ff.

Buckley, Peter J. (1979). "The Foreign Investment Decision." *Management Bibliographies and Reviews,* 5.

Buckley, Peter J. and Alexander E. Bogardy (1960). "When Should a Company Manufacture Abroad?" *California Management Review,* 2 (Winter), 16–27.

Buckley, Peter J. and Mark Casson (1988). "A Theory of Cooperation in International Business." In *Cooperative Strategies in International Business,* Farok J. Contractor and Peter Lorange, eds. Lexington, MA: Lexington Books, 31–53.

Buffa, Elwood S. (1984). "Making American Manufacturing Competitive." *California Management Review,* 26 (Spring), 29–46.

Burke, Marian C. (1984). "Strategic Choice and Marketing Managers: An Examination of Business-Level Marketing Objectives." *Journal of Marketing Research,* 21 (November), 345–359.

Business America (1990). "Statement of President Bush, Secretary Mosbacher on Super 301 Decisions." *Business America,* March 7, 6.

Business Week (1986). "Special Report: The Hollow Corporation." March 3, 56–85.

——— (1987). "Television Makers Are Dreaming of a Wide Crispness." December 21, 108–109.

——— (1988). "The Television of the Future," April 4, 62–63.

——— (1988). "The Global 1000—The Leaders," July 18.

——— (1988). "How Companies Stack Up Globally," July 18.

Buzzell, Robert D. (1968). "Can You Standardize Multinational Marketing?" *Harvard Business Review,* 46 (November–December), 102–113.

———, Bradley T. Gale, and Ralph G.M. Sultan (1975). "Market Share—A Key to Profitability." *Harvard Business Review,* January–February.

Caddick, J. R. and B. G. Dale (1986). "Sourcing from Less Developed Countries: A Case Study." *Journal of Purchasing and Materials Management,* 22 (Fall), 17–23.

Capon, Noel and Rashi Glazer (1987). "Marketing and Technology: A Strategic Coalignment." *Journal of Marketing,* 51 (July), 1–14.

Casson, Mark C. (1982). "Transaction Costs and the Theory of the Multinational Enterprise." In *New Theories of the Multinational Enterprise,* Alan M. Rugman, ed. London: Croom Helm, 24–54.

Caves, Richard E. (1971). "International Corporations: The Industrial Economics of Foreign Investment." *Economica,* 38 (February), 1–27.

——— (1974). "Multinational Firms, Competition, and Productivity in Host Country Markets." *Economica,* 41, 176–193.

Chandler, Alfred D. (1990). "The Enduring Logic of Industrial Success." *Harvard Business Review,* 68 (March–April), 130–40.

Cohen, Stephen S. and John Zysman (1987). "Why Manufacturing Matters: The Myth of the Post-Industrial Economy." *California Management Review,* 29 (Spring), 9–26.

Connolly, Robert A., Barry T. Hirsch, and Mark Hirschey (1986). "Union Rent Seeking, Intangible Capital, and the Market Value of the Firm." *Review of Economics and Statistics,* 68 (November), 567–577.

Coughlan, Anne T. and Lisa K. Scheer (1987). "Keiretsu Strength in Japanese Industrial Organization: Empirical Evidence on the Decision Participation Framework." A Working Paper, Northwestern University.

Craig, C. Samuel, Susan P. Douglas, and Srinivas K. Reddy (1987). "Market Structure, Performance and Strategy: A Comparison of U.S. and European Markets." In *Advances in International Marketing,* vol. 2, Tamer Cavusgil, ed. Greenwich, CT: JAI Press, 1–21.

Czinkota, Michael R. and Masaaki Kotabe (1990). "Product Development the Japanese Way." *Journal of Business Strategy,* 11, (November/December), 31–36.

Daniels, John (1970). "Recent Foreign Direct Manufacturing Investment in the United States." *Journal of International Business Studies,* 1 (Spring), 125–132.

Davidson, William H. and Richard Harrigan (1977). "Key Decisions in International Marketing: Introducing New Products Abroad." *Columbia Journal of World Business,* 12 (Winter), 15–23.

Day, George S. and David B. Montgomery (1983). "Diagnosing the Experience Curve." *Journal of Marketing,* 47 (Spring), 44–58.

Dell'Osso, Fillipo (1990). "Defending a Dominant Position in a Technology Led Environment." *Business Strategy Review,* Summer, 77–86.

Douglas, Susan P. and C. Samuel Craig (1983). "Examining Performance of U.S. Multinationals in Foreign Markets." *Journal of International Business Studies,* 14 (Winter), 51–62.

Douglas, Susan P. and Yoram Wind (1987). "The Myth of Globalization." *Columbia Journal of World Business,* 22 (Winter), 19–30.

Doyle, P., J. Saunders, and V. Wong (1986). "Japanese Marketing Strategies in the U.K.: A Comparative Study." *Journal of International Business Studies,* 17 (Spring), 27–46.

Doz, Yves, C.K. Prahalad, and Gary Hamel (1990). "Control, Change, and Flexibility: The Dilemma of Transnational Collaboration." *Managing the Global Firm,* Yves Doz and Gunnar Hedlund, eds. New York: Routledge, 117–143.

Drucker, Peter F. (1979). "Production Sharing, Concepts and Definitions." *Journal of the Flagstaff Institute,* 3 (January), 2–9.

——— (1989). "The 10 Rules of Effective Research." *Wall Street Journal,* May 30, A18.

Dunning, John H. (1977). "Trade, Location of Economic Activity and the MNE: A Search for an Eclectic Approach." In *The International Allocation of Economic Activity,* Bertil Ohlin, Per-Ove Hesselborn, and Per Magnus Wijkman, eds. New York: Holmes and Meier, 395–418.

——— (1988). "The Eclectic Paradigm of International Production: A Restatement and Some Possible Extensions." *Journal of International Business Studies,* 19 (Spring), 1–31.

Economist (1991). "Less is More." May 25, 75–76.

Einhorn, Hillel J. and Robin M. Hogarth (1981). "Behavioral Decision Theory: Processes of Judgment and Choice." *Annual Review of Psychology,* 32, 53–88.

England, George (1983). "Japanese and American Management: Theory Z and Beyond." *Journal of International Business Studies,* 14 (Fall), 131–142.

Fefer, Mark D., Rick Tetzeli, Tricia Welsh, and Wilton Woods (1990). "Why Toyota Keeps Getting Better and Better and Better." *Fortune,* November 19, 66–79.

Ferdows, Kasra and Richard S. Rosenbloom (1981). "Technology Policy and Economic Development: Perspectives for Asia in the 1980s." *Columbia Journal of World Business,* 16 (Summer), 36–46.

Flowers, Edward (1975). "Oligopolistic Reaction in European Direct Investment in the United States." Ph. D. Dissertation, Georgia State University.

Fortune (1986). "The International 500 and the World Economy." August 4, 180–205.

——— (1986). "Are Japanese Managers Biased Against Americans?" September 1, 72–75.

———— (1986). "Where the U.S. Stands." October 13, 28–40.

———— (1990). "Are the Japanese Buying Too Much?" Pacific Rim 1990 Special Issue, 98–101.

Franko, Lawrence G. (1978). "Multinationals: The End of U.S. Dominance." *Harvard Business Review*, 56 (November–December), 93–101.

Freeman, Richard B. and James L. Medoff (1979). "New Estimates of Private Sector Unionism in the United States." *Industrial and Labor Relations Review*, 32 (January), 143–174.

Gale, Bradley T. and Richard Klavans (1985). "Formulating a Quality Improvement Strategy." *Journal of Business Strategy*, 5 (Winter), 21–32.

Giddy, Ian H. (1978). "The Demise of the Product Cycle Model in International Business Theory." *Columbia Journal of World Business*, 13 (Spring), 90–97.

Graham, Edward M. (1974). "Oligopolistic Imitation and European Direct Investment in the United States." Ph. D. Dissertation, Harvard University.

Grosse, Robert (1981). "The Theory of Foreign Direct Investment." *Essays in International Business*. University of South Carolina, No. 3 (December).

———— (1985). "An Imperfect Competition Theory of the MNE." *Journal of International Business Studies*, 16 (Spring), 57–80.

Gruber W., D. Mehta, and R. Vernon (1967). "The R & D Factor in International Trade and International Investment of United States Industries." *Journal of Political Economy*, 75 (February), 20–37.

Hahn, Chan K., Kyoo H. Kim, and Jong S. Kim (1986). "Costs of Competition: Implications for Purchasing Strategy." *Journal of Purchasing and Materials Management*, 22 (Fall), 2–7.

Hamel, Gary, Yves L. Doz, and C. K. Prahalad (1989). "Collaborate with Your Competitors and Win." *Harvard Business Review*, 67 (January–February), 133–139.

Harrell, Gilbert D. and Richard D. Keifer (1981). "Multinational Strategic Market Portfolio." *MSU Business Topics*, 29 (Winter), 5–15.

Harrigan, Kathryn R. (1987). "Strategic Alliances: Their Role in Global Competition." *Columbia Journal of World Business*, 22 (Summer), 67–69.

Hayes, Robert H. (1985). "Strategic Planning—Forward in Reverse?" *Harvard Business Review*, 63 (November–December), 111–119.

Hayes, Robert H. and William J. Abernathy (1980), "Managing Our Way to Economic Decline." *Harvard Business Review*, 58 (July–August), 67–77.

Hayes, Robert H. and Steven C. Wheelwright (1979). "Link Manufacturing Process and Product Life Cycles." *Harvard Business Review*, 57 (January–February), 133–140.

————, eds. (1984). "The New Competitive Challenge for Manufacturing." In *Restoring Our Competitive Edge: Competing Through Manufacturing*, Robert H. Hayes and Steven C. Wheelwright, eds. New York: John Wiley.

Hedley, Barry (1976). "A Fundamental Approach to Strategy Development." *Long Range Planning*, 9 (December), 2–11.

Hefler, Daniel F. (1981). "Global Sourcing: Offshore Investment Strategy for the 1980s." *Journal of Business Strategy*, 2 (Summer), 7–12.

Herr, Ellen (1988). "U.S. Business Enterprises in 1987." *Survey of Current Business*, May, 50–59.

Hirschey, Robert C. and Richard E. Caves (1981). "Research and Transfer of Technology by Multinational Enterprises." *Oxford Bulletin of Economics and Statistics*, 43 (May), 115–130.

Houston, Franklin S. (1986). "The Marketing Concept: What It Is and What It Is Not." *Journal of Marketing*, 50 (April), 81–87.

Hufbauer, G. C. (1970). "The Impact of National Characteristics and Technology on the Commodity Composition of Trade in Manufactured Goods." In *The Technology Factor in International Trade*, Raymond Vernon, ed. New York: Columbia University Press, 145–231.

Jain, Subhash C. (1987). "Perspectives on International Strategic Alliances." In *Advances in International Marketing*, vol. 2., S. Tamer Cavusgil, ed. Greenwich, CT: JAI Press. 103–120.

——— (1989). "Standardization of International Marketing Strategy: Some Research Hypotheses." *Journal of Marketing*, 53 (January), 70–79.

Johanson, J. and J. E. Vahlne (1977). "The Process of the Firm—A Model of Knowledge and Increasing Foreign Market Commitments." *Journal of International Business Studies*, 8 (Spring/Summer), 22–32.

Johansson, Johny K. and Ikujiro Nonaka (1983). "Japanese Export Marketing: Structures, Strategies, Counterstrategies," *International Marketing Review*, 1 (Winter), 12–24.

——— (1987). "Marketing Research the Japanese Way." *Harvard Business Review*, 65 (May–June), 16–22.

Johnson, Keith N. (1987). "The Growing Foreign Role in U.S. Policy: America Can No Longer Shape Its Economic Destiny without Paying Heed to Investors from Overseas." *Fortune*, July 6, 36.

Johnson, Omotunde E.G. (1987). "Currency Depreciation and Export Expansion." *Finance and Development*, 24 (March), 23–26.

Kamien, Morton I. and Nancy L. Schwartz (1975). "Market Structure and Innovation: A Survey." *Journal of Economic Literature*, 13 (March), 1–37.

Keegan, Warren J. (1969). "Multinational Product Planning: Strategic Alternatives." *Journal of Marketing*, 33 (January), 58–62.

Kim, W. Chan (1986). "Global Production Sharing: An Empirical Investigation of the Pacific Electronics Industry." *Management International Review*, 26 (2), 62–70.

Kim, Wi Saeng and Esmeralda O. Lyn (1987). "Foreign Direct Investment Theories, Entry Barriers and Reverse Investments in U.S. Industries." *Journal of International Business Studies*, 18 (Summer), 53–66.

Kogut, Bruce (1985). "Designing Global Strategies: Comparative and Competitive Value-Added Chains." *Sloan Management Review*, 26 (Summer), 15–28.

Kotabe, Masaaki (1984). "Changing Roles of the Sogo Shoshas, the Manufacturing Firms, and the MITI in the Context of the Japanese 'Trade or Die' Mentality." *Columbia Journal of World Business*, 19 (Fall), 33–42.

——— (1985). "The Roles of Japanese Industrial Policy for Export Success: A Theoretical Perspective." *Columbia Journal of World Business*, 20 (Fall), 59–64.

——— (1989). "Assessing the Shift in Global Market Share of U.S. Multinationals." *International Marketing Review*, 6(5), 20–35.

——— (1989). " 'Hollowing-out' of U.S. Multinationals and Their Global Competitiveness: An Intrafirm Perspective." *Journal of Business Research*, 19 (August), 1–15.

———— (1990). "Corporate Product Policy and Innovative Behavior of European and Japanese Multinationals: An Empirical Investigation." *Journal of Marketing*, 54 (April), 19–33.

———— (1990). "The Relationship between Offshore Sourcing and Innovativeness of U.S. Multinational Firms: An Empirical Investigation." *Journal of International Business Studies*, 21 (Fourth Quarter), 623–638.

Kotabe, Masaaki and Janet Y. Murray (1990). "Linking Product and Process Innovations and Modes of International Sourcing in Global Competition: A Case of Foreign Multinational Firms." *Journal of International Business Studies*, 21 (Third Quarter), 383–408.

Kotabe, Masaaki and Sam C. Okoroafo (1990). "A Comparative Study of European and Japanese Multinational Firms' Marketing Strategies and Performance in the United States." *Management International Review*, 30 (Fourth Quarter), 353–370.

Kotabe, Masaaki and Glenn S. Omura (1989). "Sourcing Strategies of European and Japanese Multinationals: A Comparison." *Journal of International Business Studies*, 20 (Spring), 113–130.

Kotler, Philip and S. J. Levy (1973). "Buying is Marketing, Too." *Journal of Marketing*, 37 (January), 54–59.

Kotler, Philip and G. Alexander Rath (1984). "Design: A Powerful but Neglected Strategic Tool." *Journal of Business Strategy*, 5 (Fall), 16–21.

Kumpe, Ted and Piet T. Bolwijn (1988). "Manufacturing: The New Case for Vertical Integration." *Harvard Business Review*, 66 (March–April), 75–81.

Lawrence, Robert Z. (1987). "Imports in Japan: Closed Markets or Minds?" *Brookings Papers on Economic Activity*, 21, 517–548.

Lehnerd, Alvin P. (1987). "Revitalizing the Manufacture and Design of Mature Global Products." In *Technology and Global Industry: Companies and Nations in the World Economy*, Bruce R. Guile and Harvey Brooks, eds. Washington, DC: National Academy Press, 49–64.

Lei, David and John W. Slocum, Jr. (1991). "Global Strategic Alliances: Payoffs and Pitfalls." *Organizational Dynamics*, 19 (Winter), 44–62.

Leontief, Wassily (1956). "Factor Proportions and the Structure of American Trade: Further Theoretical and Empirical Analysis." *Review of Economics and Statistics*, 38 (November), 386–407.

Levin, Richard C., Alvin K. Klevorick, Richard R. Nelson, and Sidney G. Winter (1987). "Appropriating the Returns from Industrial Research and Development." *Brookings Papers on Economic Activity*, Issue 3, 783–831.

Levitt, Theodore (1983). "The Globalization of Markets." *Harvard Business Review*, 61 (May–June), 92–102.

Lipsey, Robert E. and Irvin Kravis (1985). "The Competitive Position of U.S. Manufacturing Firms." *Banca Nazionale de Lavoro Quarterly Review*, 153 (June), 127–154.

Lupo, Leonard A. (1973). "Worldwide Sales by U.S. Multinational Companies." *Survey of Current Business*, January, 33–39.

Mallen, Bruce (1973). "Functional Spin-Off: A Key to Anticipating Change in Distribution Structure." *Journal of Marketing*, 37 (July), 18–25.

Mansfield, Edwin (1981). "Composition of R&D Expenditures: Relationship to Size of Firm, Concentration, and Innovative Output." *Review of Economics and Statistics,* 63 (November), 610–615.

———— (1988). "Industrial R&D in Japan and the United States: A Comparative Study." *American Economic Review,* 78 (May), 223–228.

———— and Anthony Romeo (1984). " 'Reverse' Transfers of Technology from Overseas Subsidiaries to American Firms." *IEEE Transactions on Engineering Management,* EM–31(3) (August), 122–127.

March, J. G. (1978). "Bounded Rationality, Ambiguity, and the Engineering of Choice." *Bell Journal of Economics and Management Science,* 9 (Autumn), 587–608.

Markides, Constantinos and Norman Berg (1988). "Manufacturing Offshore Is Bad Business." *Harvard Business Review,* 66 (September–October), 113–120.

Mascarenhas, Briance (1984). "The Coordination of Manufacturing Interdependence in Multinational Companies." *Journal of International Business Studies,* 15 (Winter), 91–106.

Miles, Raymond E. and Charles C. Snow (1986). "Organizations: New Concepts for New Forms." *California Management Review,* 28 (Spring), 62–73.

Miller, Danny (1978). "The Role of Multivariate Q-Techniques in the Study of Organizations." *Academy of Management Review,* 9 (July), 515–531.

Monczka, Robert M. and Larry C. Giunipero (1984). "International Purchasing: Characteristics and Implementation." *Journal of Purchasing and Materials Management,* 20 (Fall), 2–9.

Moxon, Richard W. (1975). "The Motivation for Investment in Offshore Plants: The Case of the U.S. Electronics Industry." *Journal of International Business Studies,* 6 (Fall), 51–66.

Mullor-Sebastian, Alicia (1983). "The Product Life Cycle Theory: Empirical Evidence." *Journal of International Business Studies,* 14 (Winter), 95–105.

Nakatani, Iwao (1984). "The Economic Role of Financial Corporate Grouping." In *The Economic Analysis of the Japanese Firm,* M. Aoki, ed. Amsterdam: Elsevier Science Publishers, 227–258.

Nishikawa, Toru (1989). "New Product Planning at Hitachi." *Long Range Planning,* 22 (4), 20–24.

Norton, Robert E. (1989). "Unfair Traders: A Passing Storm." *Fortune,* June 19, 16.

Onkvisit, Sak and John J. Shaw (1988). "Marketing Barriers in International Trade." *Business Horizons,* 31 (May–June), 64–72.

Ouchi, William (1980). "Markets, Bureaucracies, and Clans." *Administrative Science Quarterly,* 25 (March), 129–141.

Pakes, Ariel and Zvi Griliches (1980). "Patents and R&D at the Firm Level: A First Report." *Economic Indicators,* 5, 377–381.

Perreault, William D., Jr., Douglas N. Behrman, and Gary M. Armstrong (1979). "Alternative Approaches for Interpretation of Multiple Discriminant Analysis in Marketing Research." *Journal of Business Research,* 7, 151–173.

Phillips, Lynn W., Dae Chang, and Robert D. Buzzell (1983). "Product Quality, Cost Position, and Business Performance: A Test of Some Key Hypotheses." *Journal of Marketing,* 47 (Spring), 26–43.

Port, Otis (1989). "Back to Basics." *Business Week,* Special 1989 Bonus Issue, 14–18.

Prahalad, C. K. and Gary Hamel (1990). "The Core Competence of the Corporation." *Harvard Business Review,* 68 (May–June), 79–91.

Rapp, William V. (1973). "Strategy Formulation and International Competition." *Columbia Journal of World Business,* 8 (Summer), 98–112.

Reich, Robert B. and Eric D. Mankin (1986). "Joint Ventures with Japan Gives Away Our Future." *Harvard Business Review,* 64 (March–April), 78–86.

Rhodes, Joe (1990). "Suds for All Seasons." *American Way,* October 1, 36–39.

Rose, Frank (1991). "Now Quality Means Service Too." *Fortune,* April 22, 97ff.

Rosenbloom, Richard S. and Michael A. Cusumano (1987). "Technological Pioneering and Competitive Advantage: The Birth of VCR Industry." *California Management Review,* 29 (Summer), 51–76.

Rugman, Alan M. (1982). "Internalization and Non-Equity Forms of International Involvement." In *New Theories of the Multinational Enterprise,* Alan M. Rugman, ed. London: Croom Helm.

Samiee, S. (1982). "Elements of Marketing Strategy: A Comparative Study of U.S. and Non-U.S. Based Companies." *Journal of International Marketing,* 1, 119–126.

Schlender, Brenton R. (1990). "Who's Ahead in the Computer Wars." *Fortune,* February 12, 59–66.

Schneider, Eric (1989). "Unchaining the Value of Design." *European Management Journal,* 7 (3), 320–31.

Schoenberger, Erica (1987). "Technological & Organizational Change in Automobile Production: Spatial Implications." *Regional Studies,* 21, 199–214.

Shapiro, Amran R. (1989). "A Rush to the Patent Office." *Across the Board,* 26 (June), 7–9.

Shepherd, William G. and Dexter Hutchins (1988). "There's No Trade Deficit, Sam!" *Financial World,* February 23, 28–32.

Sims, J. Taylor (1986). "Japanese Market Entry Strategy at Work: Komatsu vs. Caterpillar." *International Marketing Review,* 3 (Autumn), 21–32.

Skinner, Wickham (1969). "Manufacturing—Missing Link in Corporate Strategy." *Harvard Business Review,* 47 (May–June), 136–145.

Skrzycki, Cindy (1987). "America on the Auction Block: The Cheap Dollar Makes U.S. Assets Bargains for Foreigners but Our National Security May Be at Stake." *US News and World Report,* March 30, 56.

Sleuwaegen, Leo (1985). "Monopolistic Advantages and the International Operations of Firms: Disaggregated Evidence from U.S.-Based Multinationals." *Journal of International Business Studies,* 16 (Fall), 125–133.

Slovic, P., B. Fischhoff, and Sarah Lichtenstein (1977). "Behavioral Decision Theory." *Annual Review of Psychology,* 28, 1–39.

Sorenson, Ralph Z. and Ulrich E. Wiechmann (1975). "How Multinationals View Marketing Standardization." *Harvard Business Review,* 53 (May–June) 38–56.

Starr, Martin K. (1973). "Productivity is the USA's Problem." *California Management Review,* 15 (Winter), 32–36.

——— (1984). "Global Production and Operations Strategy." *Columbia Journal of World Business,* 19 (Winter), 17–22.

———— and John E. Ullman (1988). "The Myth of Industrial Supremacy." In *Global Competitiveness,* Martin K. Starr, ed. New York: W. W. Norton.

Stobaugh, Robert and Piero Telesio (1983). "Match Manufacturing Policies and Product Strategy." *Harvard Business Review,* 61 (March–April), 113–120.

Stout, Hilary (1990). "In a Major Turnaround, U.S. Is Posting Surplus in Trade with Europe." *Wall Street Journal,* July 10, pp. A1, A4.

Takeuchi, Hirotaka and Michael E. Porter (1986). "Three Roles of International Marketing in Global Strategy." In *Competition in Global Industries,* Michael E. Porter, ed. Boston: Harvard Business School Press, 111–146.

Takitani, Kenji (1973). "A Prototype for Japanese Investment in the United States?" *Columbia Journal of World Business,* 8 (Summer), 31–33.

Teece, David J. (1986). "Firm Boundaries, Technological Innovation, and Strategic Management." In *The Economics of Strategic Planning,* Lacy G. Thomas, III, ed. Lexington, MA: Lexington Books, 187–99.

———— (1987). "Capturing Value from Technological Innovation: Integration, Strategic Partnering, and Licensing Decisions." In *Technology and Global Industry: Companies and Nations in the World Economy,* Bruce R. Guile and Harvey Brooks, eds. Washington, DC: National Academy Press, 65–95.

———— (1988). "Capturing Value from Technological Innovation: Integration, Strategic Partnering, and Licensing Decisions." *Interfaces,* 18 (May–June), 46–61.

Utterback, James M. (1987). "Innovation and Industrial Evolution in Manufacturing Industries." In *Technology and Global Industry,* Bruce R. Guile and Harvey Brooks, ed. Washington, DC: National Academy Press, 16–48.

Vernon, Raymond (1966). "International Investment and International Trade in the Product Cycle." *Quarterly Journal of Economics,* 80 (May), 190–207.

———— (1974). "The Location of Economic Activity." In *Economic Analysis and the Multinational Enterprise,* John H. Dunning, ed. London: George Allen and Unwin, 89–114.

———— (1979). "The Product Cycle Hypothesis in a New International Environment." *Oxford Bulletin of Economics and Statistics,* 41 (November), 255–267.

———— (1986). "Can U.S. Manufacturing Come Back?" *Harvard Business Review,* 64 (July–August), 98–106.

Wall Street Journal (1991). "Matsushita, Pitting Itself Against Sony, Agrees to Back Philips's Digital Cassettes." July 8, p. B3.

Walters, Peter G. (1986). "International Marketing Policy: A Discussion of the Standardization Construct and its Relevance for Corporate Policy." *Journal of International Business Studies,* 17 (Summer), 55–69.

Ward, James J. (1973). "Product and Promotion Adaptation by European Firms in the U.S." *Journal of International Business Studies,* 4 (Spring), 79–85.

———— (1973). "How European Firms View Their U.S. Customers." *Columbia Journal of World Business,* 8 (Summer), 79–82.

Wells, Louis T., Jr. (1968). "Product Life Cycle for International Trade?" *Journal of Marketing,* 32 (July), 1–6.

Wheelwright, Steven C. (1985). "Restoring the Competitive Edge in U.S. Manufacturing." *California Management Review,* 27 (Spring), 26–42.

Whitelock, Jeryl M. (1987). "Global Marketing and the Case for International Product Standardization." *European Journal of Marketing,* 21, 32–44.

Williamson, Oliver E. (1979). "Transactions-Cost Economics: The Governance of Contractual Relations." *Journal of Law and Economics,* 22 (October), 233–261.

Wind, Yoram and Susan Douglas (1981). "International Portfolio Analysis and Strategy: The Challenge of the 80s." *Journal of International Business Studies,* 11 (Fall), 69–82.

Index

American dominance, 28
Amstrad (Alan Michael Sugar Trading), 27
Apple Computer, 208
Appropriability, 190, 192
Appropriability regime, 198, 205–6, 208
Assembly, internal versus external 27, 31–32, 38, 44–48

Balance-of-trade position, 170, 178
Benetton SpA, 58 n.3
Boeing, 138, 146–47
Braun, 143, 210

CAD/CAM (computer-aided design/ computer-aided manufacturing), 6, 187
Canon, 94, 137, 143
Capital, 11, 26; flow of, 7, 28; intensity, 192, 197; substitution of labor for, 97, 186
CAT scanner, 29–30
Caterpillar Tractor Company, 4, 155
Communications, 51, 65, 71, 159; digitalization of, 71; system, 53, 55
Comparative advantage, 5–6, 11, 14, 18–19, 63, 157, 170, 184, 194, 196

Competitive advantage, 2, 4–6, 12–14, 17, 18–19, 27, 49, 63, 65, 69–70, 74, 81, 85, 94–95, 104, 143, 176, 203; sources of, 19, 95, 100, 121, 139, 204–6, 211
Competitive environment, 28, 63, 96, 203, 207
Competitive position, 4, 11, 83–85, 95, 141, 171
Competitive strength, 3, 69, 135, 159; Japanese firms, 136–38; U.S. firms, 19, 172–78, 185, 194
Competitive urgency, 1–3
Competitive viability, 6, 19, 185, 188, 207
Complementary assets, 206–8
Components sourcing, 16, 46, 109–10, 135; developing countries, 49; internal versus external, 27, 32, 50, 73–74, 84; location, 42
Concentration ratio, 192
Configuration, 48; and coordination, 63–64, 187
Consolidated sales, 163–64, 172, 177–78
Continual improvement, 70–71, 84, 98, 107, 111, 122, 129, 138–42, 186, 195–96, 211

Coordination, 48, 64, 99–100, 121, 197
Copyright, 205, 207
Corporate performance, 6, 64, 192
Cost competitiveness, 66–67, 179, 188, 196
Culture-bound products, 49, 64, 85
Customer: delight, 144–45, 211; needs, 6, 17, 122–23, 127, 141, 148; relationship, 32; satisfaction, 121–22, 130, 144

Data concordance: between ESIC (Enterprise Standard Industrial Classification) and ISIC (International Standard Classification), 161–62; between SIC (Standard Industrial Classification) and TSUS (Tariff Schedules of the United States), 188–90, 198
Deindustrialization, 170
Digital Equipment, 27
Distribution, 3, 56–58, 92–93, 109, 120, 144, 146, 208
Dollar: appreciation of, 167–68; depreciation of, 136–37
Domestic employment, 18, 98, 153, 168–70, 184
Duty-free reentry, 9, 98–99, 184
Dynamic network, 66–67, 187

Eclectic approach, 14
Economies of scale, 11, 26, 29, 93–94, 108; production and marketing, 47, 52, 100, 108–9, 121; scope, 49, 203; specialization, 57, 96
Efficiency, 57; cost, 209; manufacturing, 6, 97, 203; marketing, 120
Electrolux, 94
EMI, 29–30
Ethnocentric approach, 92
Experience curve effect, 14, 95–96, 120, 122, 129, 135, 156
Export orientation, 44, 172, 176–77

Finance, 3, 98
First-mover advantage, 29

Follow-the-leader, 12
Ford Motor Company, 143–44, 210
Foreign direct investment, 7, 10–12, 27–29, 44, 95; benchmark survey of U.S. direct investment abroad, 16, 164; European and Japanese, 117–19, 137; U.S., 48, 161–63, 173, 176
Foreign employment, 169
Foreign exchange, 171
French Bull, 208
Functional mismatch, 3
Fuzzy logic, 142

General Electric, 30, 155
General Motors, 147, 206
Giant leap versus incrementalism, 138–42
Global competition, 1, 25, 63–64, 100–101; and hollowing-out, 170
Global competitiveness, 197, 199; Japan's 137–38; loss of, 68; technological capabilities for, 71; of U.S. firms, 160–63
Global integration versus local responsiveness, 2
Global marketing, 27, 93–94
Global market share, 171, 185; current competitiveness, 19, 157–58, 163–64; shift in U.S. firms', 171–79
Global product: definition of, 92–94; intermarket segmentation, 100–101; marketing standardization, 109
Global rationalization strategy, 35
Global sourcing strategy, 13, 26–27; complex nature of, 65; definition of, 6, 30; European versus Japanese, 40–41; taxonomy of, 33; types of, 30–33, 39–44; value chain, 4–5
Globalization versus localization, 2
Government: restrictions on imports of finished products, 158; subsidy, 4
GTE Sylvania, 205

Harmonized Tariff Schedule, 98–99, 9802.00.60 and 9802,00.80 (806/807) imports, 98
HDTV (high definition television) technology, 111, 140–41, 155, 206

High-tech versus high-touch
  dimension, 144, 211
Hitachi, 46, 137, 142, 145
Hollow corporation, 4, 98, 154
Hollowing-out, 4, 9, 70, 74, 84–85,
  154–57, 170. *See also*
  Deindustrialization
Honda, 94, 100, 139, 146
Honeywell, 4, 155, 208

IBM, 27, 55, 143, 208, 210
Imperfections in the marketplace, 46,
  157
Incremental improvement, 17, 30;
  giant leap versus, 138–42; product
  and product design, 94, 146–47
Industrial design, 19, 143–44, 210–11
Industrial development, 69–70, 170
Innovation: European and Japanese
  difference, 101; imitation versus,
  96; lead time, 13–14, 69, 155;
  product and process, 63–64, 69–70,
  76–77, 81–85, 95–101
Innovation-sourcing linkage, 16, 18,
  64; taxonomy of, 73–74
Intel, 46
Interface management, 4–6, 159
Intermarket segmentation, 92, 100
Internalization theory, 14, 46, 56
International Investment Survey Act
  of 1976, 16, 161
International product cycle model,
  10–13, 65–66, 178, 186; and
  innovative behavior, 95–97;
  limitations of, 13–15, 29
International trade, 7–9, 98, 163;
  intra-firm, 7–9, 28–29, 33–35
Intra-firm sourcing, 28, 156–58, 170,
  184, 197–98; contractual sourcing,
  67–68, 73, 86, 155–56, 171;
  definition of, 32
Inventory, 4, 65, 98, 146, 197
Investment position, 117–19, 137; and
  multinationality, 173, 176
Item 806/807 imports, 9, 98–99, 183–
  84, 188. *See also* Harmonized Tariff
  Schedule

JIT (just-in-time) manufacturing, 206,
  208
Joint venture, 12, 32, 65–67, 187, 207–
  8

Keihakutansho, 144
Keiretsu, 50–58; enterprise versus
  financial, 53–57; internal
  transaction, 56–57; origin of, 51–53
Kodak, 155

Licensing, 27, 32, 48, 66, 101, 187,
  206–7
L. M. Ericsson, 208
Logistical management, 2, 6, 26–27,
  65

Magnavox, 205
Make or buy decisions. *See* Infra-firm
  sourcing
Malcolm Baldrige Award, 147
Management contract, 32
Managerial flexibility, 183
Manufacturing ability, 6; lack of
  emphasis on, 111–12 n.1; loss of, 3–
  4, 98–99, 109–10; strategic weapon,
  69–70, 138, 154–55, 186–87, 206–9.
  See also Innovation
Market growth, 97–98, 127–29
Market performance, 15–18, 48–49,
  84–85, 129–31, 157–59, 162, 170
Market research, context-specific,
  145–47
Market share. *See* Global market
  share
Marketing: proactive, 92–93, 100;
  standardization of, 91–93; strategy,
  70, 99–101, 117–19
Matsushita Electric, 93, 142, 205,
  208–10
McDonnell-Douglas, 147
Merger and acquisition craze, 3, 56–
  57
Mitsubishi Electric, 142
Motorola, 46

NEC, 46, 71, 208
Network system, 66–67, 187

New product, 45; development of, 17
Newly industrialized countries, 4, 7,
    18, 77, 98, 158, 197
Nissan Motors, 142, 208
Northern Telecom, 208

OECD nations, 163–64, 167–68
OEM (original equipment
    manufacture), 111, 209
Offshore manufacturing, 33, 67, 168,
    195
Offshore sourcing, 9, 19, 184–88, 196–
    98
Off-the-shelf components, 27
Olivetti, 143, 210
Outsourceability, 103–4, 109–11
Outsourcing, 4, 98–99, 103–4, 109,
    156, 209
Ownership, 55, 65; control, 46

Paper entrepreneurship, 3. *See also*
    Merger and acquisition craze
Parker Pen Company, 93–94
Patents, 77, 137, 190, 205–7, 210. *See*
    also Appropriability regime
Philips, 30, 93, 141, 206, 209–11
Polycentric approach, 1, 10, 25, 93–
    94, 99; geocentric approach, 94
Price competition, 186–87
Proactive approach, 14, 30, 47;
    market segmentation, 92, 100;
    product development, 17–18, 109
Procter & Gamble, 210
Product adaptation, 16, 47, 99–100,
    108, 158; standardization versus,
    120–21
Product design, 3, 6, 18–19, 70–73, 94,
    98, 210–12; dominant, 205–9;
    family, 94; maintainability, 6, 210;
    manufacturability, 209–10;
    production, 67, 69, 97–98, 141–44,
    146–47, 155–56, 179; standardization
    of, 17, 94
Product development, 16–17, 138–47
Product differentiation, 12–13, 25;
    design, 210; positioning, 17
Product policy, 17, 36, 91–97, 99–101,

104, 107–9; global, 94–95;
    innovative ability, 100–101
Product proliferation, 25–26, 70
Product quality, 69, 96;
    manufacturing, 101, 121–22, 139
Product standardization, 6, 10, 17–18,
    48, 100, 109, 135
Production sharing, 66, 153
Productivity, 4, 66, 139; improvement
    of, 96–97
Project team, 143, 146, 211

R&D (Research and development), 2–
    6, 100–101, 130; continual
    improvement in, 186–87;
    employment, 18, 168–69; intra-firm
    trade, 158–59, 166–67;
    multinationality, 176–79; product
    policy, 108–9; role of parent firm
    and subsidiaries, 159, 167
RCA, 205
Research, pure versus applied, 139
Reverse engineering, 156, 187–88,
    198, 205, 211
Richardson Sheffield, 71, 73
Ricoh, 143

Sanyo, 205, 208
Sharp, 143, 205, 210
Siemens, 30
Skilled labor, 11, 158
Sony, 29, 93, 130, 140, 142–43, 147,
    205–10
Sourcing strategy. *See* Global
    sourcing strategy
Specialized competence, 66–67, 187
Standard component, 77
Standardization: adaptation, 2; core
    components, 25, 49, 94; marketing;
    91–93, 109; product design, 17, 94;
    product versus production, 100
Strategic alliance, 19, 51, 204–5, 207–
    11
Strategic readiness, 19, 168–70, 196–
    97
Subcontracting, 27, 67–68, 86 n.1, 98

Technological change, 97
Technological trajectory, 110–11
Technology, 68–69; diffusion, 29–30, 66; long-term vision, 71–73. *See also* Innovation
Texas Instruments, 46, 208
Toshiba, 30, 46, 137, 205
Toyota, 146, 207–8
Trade deficit, 7, 136–37, 173
Trade secret, 77, 156, 205, 207
Triad regions (the United States, European Community, and Japan), 3, 7, 108–9; marketing in, 99

Unification versus fragmentation, 2

Value chain, 1–5, 55–57, 187–88, 197
Volkswagen, 208

White Consolidated, 94

Xerox, 143, 210

Yankee ingenuity, 101, 110, 138

About the Author

MASAAKI KOTABE is a Professor of Marketing and International Business at the University of Texas at Austin. He has published widely on the interfaces of R&D, manufacturing, and marketing in major academic journals including the *Journal of Marketing*, the *Journal of International Business Studies*, the *Columbia Journal of World Business*, and the *International Marketing Review*.